The Dollar

and the

International

Monetary

System

Economics Handbook Series

Seymour E. Harris, Editor

Burns · SOCIAL SECURITY AND PUBLIC POLICY
Carlson · ECONOMIC SECURITY IN THE UNITED STATES
Coppock · INTERNATIONAL ECONOMIC INSTABILITY
Duesenberry · BUSINESS CYCLES AND ECONOMIC GROWTH
Hansen · THE AMERICAN ECONOMY
Hansen · THE DOLLAR AND THE INTERNATIONAL MONETARY SYSTEM
Hansen · ECONOMIC ISSUES OF THE 1960s
Hansen · A GUIDE TO KEYNES
Hansen · MONETARY THEORY AND FISCAL POLICY
Harris · INTERNATIONAL AND INTERREGIONAL ECONOMICS
Harrod · THE BRITISH ECONOMY
Henderson and Quandt · MICROECONOMIC THEORY
Hoover · THE LOCATION OF ECONOMIC ACTIVITY
Johnston · STATISTICAL COST ANALYSIS
Kindleberger · ECONOMIC DEVELOPMENT
Lebergott · MANPOWER IN ECONOMIC GROWTH
Lerner · ECONOMICS OF EMPLOYMENT
Taylor · A HISTORY OF ECONOMIC THOUGHT
Tinbergen and Bos · MATHEMATICAL MODELS OF ECONOMIC GROWTH
Valavanis · ECONOMETRICS

THE DOLLAR AND THE INTERNATIONAL MONETARY SYSTEM

ALVIN H. HANSEN

Lucius N. Littauer Professor of Political Economy
Emeritus, Harvard University

McGRAW-HILL BOOK COMPANY

New York • St. Louis • San Francisco • Toronto

London • Sydney

The Dollar and the
International Monetary System

Library of Congress Catalog Card Number 64-8728

26042

TO THE THREE DEVOTED WOMEN IN MY LIFE

MY WIFE

Mabel Lewis Hansen

AND MY TWO DAUGHTERS

Mrs. Leroy S. Merrifield

AND

Mrs. George Furiya

CONTENTS

FOREWORD

There is a major division of the countries of the non-Communist world into the great majority which are underdeveloped and very poor and the few which are highly developed and rich. The group of countries between these two classes is relatively so small that when countries are placed in a rank-order of relative development and affluence, there is not much of a continuum between the upper and the lower groups. Though diplomacy has inspired most authors and secretariats of intergovernmental organizations to call the poor countries the "developing" ones, the blunt truth is, of course, that the development and income gap between the two classes is continually widening. This process has been going on for a century at least, and is now going on more rapidly, so that the demarcation line is becoming ever sharper and more meaningful.

One implication of these well-known facts, important to the

economist, is that the problems of economic policy in the two classes of countries are very different in nature—much more so than has been generally recognized. This is true not least of the problems which concern international economic relations. Thus, while freer trade, and ultimately free trade, is a reasonable goal for the rich countries, this is clearly not the case for underdeveloped countries intent upon speeding up their development. One condition for averting the internationally intolerable situation toward which present trends are pointing is, indeed, the recognition of a "double standard of morality" in regard to commercial policy, leaving the underdeveloped countries freedom to regulate their foreign trade, while demanding that the rich countries increasingly liberate their trade with each other and, particularly, with the underdeveloped countries. For once, we would then be developing a double standard in the interest of the weak and not, as is usually the case, of the strong. But the underdeveloped need more commercial-policy help from the rich countries than free entrance to their markets. We should not deceive ourselves by believing that the underdeveloped countries' trading problem would be appreciably solved by a successful movement toward freer trade in the rich countries. There is also need for discriminatory treatment in favor of the underdeveloped countries. Such "aid through trade" raises an entirely different complex of problems from that of liberalizing the rich countries' trade in line with the main challenge posited by the Trade Expansion Act of 1962. However, if and when the rich countries get firmly set on the way toward such liberalizing of their own trade—which is by far the bigger part of international trade—this will free their hands to take up for serious treatment the problem of aiding the underdeveloped countries by trade discrimination in their favor.

In the field of international finance it is even more important to recognize the existence of two different types of problem. One complex of problems concerns the rich countries' need to stabilize the financial relations among themselves and, in this connection, to organize institutionally the preservation of international liquidity as more means of payment become required by the increasing commerce in the world. This is a complex of problems which the rich countries can solve among themselves. The underdeveloped countries' exchange problems are of an entirely different type. They are a reflection of their long-term (and, for practical purposes, permanent) need of importing more than they can pay for by their exports. This need of a net capital inflow becomes the more acute the more they press on with their development efforts. They will, therefore, quite normally have foreign exchange difficulties if they do not accept stagnation, and they will not always escape them even then. The rich countries, on the other hand, as they come to combine the solving of their financial problems among themselves with the adoption of reasonably sound internal economic policies, should never need to have foreign exchange problems. For the rich countries to succeed in reaching this situation is indeed strongly in the interest also of the underdeveloped countries. It would help to create the conditions necessary for the rich countries to go forward successfully in liberalizing their trade, which as already pointed out would make it more possible to consider commercial policies discriminating in favor of the underdeveloped countries. And it would mean that the rich countries would no longer have in their exchange situations an excuse, often in fact a compelling reason, for not increasing the flow of capital to underdeveloped countries in the form of grants and loans.

Recognizing the difference between these two complexes of problems is important for intellectual clarity. It is also in the interest of reaching practical political results in the discussion now taking place of improving the mechanism of international financial relations. The exchange difficulties of the underdeveloped countries must be recognized for what they are: a quasi-permanent feature of their situation. They are in need of grants and loans on a bigger scale. That the rich countries' willingness to provide more capital could be stimulated by including greater generosity on their part in a package scheme for solving their own totally different financial problems is an illusion, as pointed out in the present volume. It is a merit of the book, therefore, that it is frankly focused on the financial problems of the rich countries—and, more specifically, those of the United States. That this does not reflect any hardheartedness on the part of Alvin Hansen toward the underdeveloped countries' need of help is evidenced by the position he has consistently taken for decades—which in the Appendix of this book, where he leaves the main theme, he spells out again. But the financial problems of the rich countries have priority, and their solution would enable all of us who want the rich countries to do more for the underdeveloped countries in both finance and trade to fight for our opinion with more hope of success.

In this book Alvin Hansen again shows that remarkable combination of radicalism and conservative common sense that has made him more than a great scholar: a remarkable teacher and opinion molder. He is radical in the literal meaning of the word; that is, he is prepared to face the facts squarely and draw the rational inferences from the facts and from his value premises, wherever this may take him. At the same time, he is wise about the world. He knows that the problems he is discussing will not be solved by any speculative gadgetry. The practical political approach must be to look for means as simple as possible of gradually perfecting the institutional arrangements we already have. This type of approach, combining fearless freethinking with pragmatism, is what, in the decades of his diligent work, we have become accustomed to expect from the Grand Old Man of our profession.

In writing this preface, I feel humble and a little out of place. Alvin Hansen's book does not need my endorsement. I have a role to play in this connection only because he did us in Stockholm the honor, and gave us the stimulation and pleasure, of serving as visiting research professor at our institute in the academic year 1963–1964. His book is the first publication of the new institute. We feel that we could not have had a better beginning.

GUNNAR MYRDAL

The Institute for International Economic Studies
University of Stockholm

PREFACE

We do not worry about the balance of payments between the fifty states of the American Union. But sovereign nations are deeply concerned about this problem year in and year out. Clearly there is something seriously wrong with our international monetary mechanism. Compare our advances in technology with our backwardness in monetary arrangements and institutions.

In the first two chapters of Part One I endeavor to get at the root causes of the dollar crisis as seen from both sides of the Atlantic. This is followed by two chapters in which I attempt to disclose some of the idiosyncrasies of the gold standard as it currently operates. Next comes a survey of the evolutionary changes that are already going on in the international monetary system together with a critical examination of new proposals. In Part Two, standard objections from the right and the left are examined, involving the camp that fears the loss of discipline as well as the opposite camp that demands complete freedom and flexibility of exchange rates. The three chapters that follow endeavor to gain some insight into possible future developments derived from an examination of past and current trends. The whole current development is then viewed against the background of history. Part Two is essentially a collection of essays which are woven together by a central strand of thinking about current international monetary problems. Finally, there is an Appendix dealing with a highly important but ancillary matter, the financial problems of the developing countries.

One conclusion emerges. There are all sorts of things that can be done to strengthen the gold-exchange standard. There is no one exclusive or imperative reform. Many of the proposals supplement each other and some can stand quite well alone on their own feet. But they are not equally efficacious. A thoroughgoing reform requires considerable overhauling. But it may well be that the flow of events will give us piecemeal innovations, some minor, some major, and scattered over time. A scuttling of what we have and the substitution of a completely new model is not in the cards.

The gold-exchange standard is based on the assumption that free and unlimited convertibility of foreign exchange holdings into gold would provide a solid and dependable medium of international exchange. It has not worked out that way. Conversion of exchange holdings into gold, instead of serving to bolster confidence in the fiduciary component of international reserves, has been employed as a means of escaping the risk of devaluation. For many industrial countries the gold-exchange standard has become largely a euphemism.

The defect in the gold-exchange standard is, basically, that the fiduciary component is suspect because it is not insured against the risk of devaluation.

There is much talk about the need for more liquidity. But this, in fact, is not the vital problem that worries us. The crucial problem, though it is often covered up under the liquidity veil, is the breakdown of the gold-exchange standard.

An exchange guarantee would increase the acceptability of the fiduciary component—in short, it would help to make the gold-exchange standard a reality, not the limping one-legged standard it in fact is today.

If this were achieved, the fear of gold drains would cease and we would need less liquidity. The greater the gold drains, caused by the risk of devaluation losses, the greater the need for liquidity.

And so the two reform measures—exchange guarantee and increased liquidity—constitute, in a manner, alternative proposals. Yet they also supplement each other. We are, in fact, currently in the process of improving the gold-exchange standard partly by applying here and there the principle of exchange guarantee and partly by increasing, by various devices, international liquidity.

There are some strange blind spots in much of the current literature on international monetary problems. The dollar crisis is discussed as though it were the typical textbook imbalance caused by an inflationary overheating of the economy. Often there is little, and indeed sometimes no recognition of the unique character of the current crisis with its roots deep in a gigantic *money* transfer, and the difficulty of translating the money transfer into a *real* transfer.

The discussion often appears to assume that the whole adjustment must necessarily be made in the *trade* balance, overlooking altogether the possibilities that a part of the adjustment can be made in the capital account, especially if the exchange risk were removed by a gold-value guarantee.

An international bank whose credit creation power would be based on investment in the government securities of the member countries is often regarded as encroaching on dangerous territory. So, also, in its infancy domestic bank credit was thought to be dangerous. Domestic credit can be misused and international credit can be misused. But progress demands that we learn to use them wisely without causing either inflation or deflation. Many of the arguments now raised against an International Reserve System are more or less identical to the objections raised against the establishment of the Federal Reserve System and the International Monetary Fund.

Without trying to forecast what may come out of all the current discussions and proposals, we can perhaps detect strands of thinking and policies in process of development which, in a general way, indicate where we are and where we are going. At the risk of being proved completely wrong I venture the following observations.

1. For one thing it seems to me that both official and expert nonofficial thinking is hardening more and more against devaluations, and perhaps to a somewhat less degree also against currency appreciation. I do not, of course, refer here to the underdeveloped countries, which present a special case. But with respect to the leading industrial countries, especially the large gold holders—the United States, the United Kingdom, Switzerland, and the Common Market countries—I believe the above statement stands.
2. More and more, the leading countries are prepared to commit large sums in defense of each other's currency. Witness the extensive exchange operations to check the speculative movements against the German mark in March, 1961, the Swiss franc in July, 1961, the Dutch guilder and Italian lira in early 1962, the Canadian dollar in June, 1962, the pound sterling in 1961–1962 including the $900 million Basle arrangement and the massive drawing of $1.5 billion of nine different currencies from the IMF, the $1 billion credits granted to Italy by the U.S. Treasury and European central banks in March, 1964. And finally the massive $3 billion support to sterling in November, 1964, by the Group of Ten countries.
3. It can be expected that the United States will acquire and hold more and more foreign currencies, partly in the form of swap arrangements, and partly in the form of outright acquisitions through purchase and borrowing.

4. The United States can be expected to place more and more medium-term bonds (the so-called Roosa bonds denominated in foreign currencies) in foreign central banks and treasuries. This amounts to giving, bit by bit, an exchange guarantee to at least a part of the official holdings of dollars. In this connection it is conceivable that some adaptation of Mr. Lolli's gold certificate plan might become acceptable, for example, an offer by the United States to give gold certificates to official holders of dollars up to a certain per cent of the holdings by each country on the day when the offer was made public. Such gold certificates might carry a limited (say 2 per cent) interest rate.
5. The "general arrangements to borrow" device involving the Group of Ten leading industrial countries might be expanded beyond the massive $6 billion already provided. The currencies thus committed, once they were drawn upon, would come under the gold-value guarantee provided in the Bretton Woods Charter—a further extension of exchange guarantee.
6. It should not be entirely improbable that the IMF might be authorized to accept deposits of reserve currencies held by its members. This could bring a considerable part, perhaps most, of the current dollar holdings under the gold-value guarantee.
7. Finally, as a postscript, I make bold to think that it should not be utterly impossible to obtain an international agreement through the IMF to outlaw the private hoarding of gold.

All these things, or at least most of them, are in the cards, and along some of these lines I believe we can expect firm progress. In the meantime, continued discussion together with the accumulation of further experience may well within a decade turn up still bolder programs.

This book was written while I was serving as Visiting Research Professor in the Institute for International Economic Studies,

University of Stockholm. I came to Stockholm at the invitation of Prof. Gunnar Myrdal, Director of the Institute, who suggested that after writing extensively over many years on the domestic problems of the American economy, I should return to an area with which I had formerly been concerned and which had now become one of the burning questions of the day. This suggestion was very much welcomed by me since I had already been thinking of doing just that. Twenty years ago I wrote *America's Role in the World Economy*, in which I discussed in some detail the Bretton Woods Agreements. This volume had an extensive sale both in the United States and abroad, appearing in various language editions, and was also published in paperback form.

I wish to express my deep obligation to Professor Myrdal and the Institute for providing research facilities and complete freedom to work quietly without any distracting duties. I am grateful for the numerous discussions with Professor Myrdal and his associates, and also for the high-level seminars (composed of Stockholm's foremost banking and monetary experts) which Professor Myrdal organized to discuss my manuscript. I must also express my hearty appreciation of the expert services rendered by the Institute's secretarial staff.

Finally, I am indebted to the distinguished economists listed below (most of whom were my former students). In a particularly busy season in the academic year they generously took time to read part or all of my manuscript and made helpful criticisms. These comments uncovered a good many errors and often forced me to clarify my thinking. Of course, the critics did not always agree among themselves, and at times I felt unable to change my position. It is therefore especially important to say that I alone am responsible for any errors of statement or logic which the book may contain. The list referred to includes the following: Alice Bourneuf, Emile Despres, Charles Kindleberger, Gerald M. Meier, Lloyd Metzler, Richard Musgrave, Joseph Pechman, Walter Salant, William Salant, Paul Samuelson, James Tobin, and my colleague John H. Williams. And above all, I wish once again to express my appreciation of the care with which Prof. Seymour Harris read my manuscript and made detailed suggestions.

Also I wish to thank Dr. E. M. Bernstein, Signor Ettore Lolli of the Banca Nazionale del Lavoro of Italy, Prof. S. Posthuma of the Netherlands Bank, and Governor Xenophon Zolotas of the Bank of Greece for answering inquiries and sending me reprints and other materials.

ALVIN H. HANSEN

INTRODUCTION

Almost a generation ago Professor Hansen, in an article in the *Review of Economics and Statistics,* presented a novel theory of international disequilibrium. The most widely accepted definition of disequilibrium had been an adverse balance of payments as evident in substantial losses of reserves or a decline in the external value of the currency, or both. At that time, Hansen introduced a new interpretation: even without these symptoms, disequilibrium may prevail. The new condition is that, because of the external pressures, the authority precludes losses of reserves and/or a depreciation through restrictive monetary and/or fiscal policies at home, which in turn contributes to reduced output and rising unemployment.

In the current volume Professor Hansen deals with the problem of dollar saturation, its relation to economic policies and events abroad, and its effects on the American economy. He is concerned that our \$600+ billion economy should not be jeopardized by restrictive or inadequate expansionist policies because of the deficit in the U.S. balance of payments and the accompanying loss of reserves. There can be little doubt but that the expansionist policies of the United States in the years 1961 to 1964 suffered as a result of the dollar problem. Moreover, those who generally tend to favor restrictive monetary and fiscal policies find in the dollar saturation an excuse for supporting policies that are less expansionist than they ought to be in the current situation.

In order to avoid restrictive policies, or inadequately expansionist policies, Hansen considers intensively the numerous programs for increasing international reserves, the application of which would give the domestic economy greater freedom to operate without restraints imposed by the balance of payments. But this is just one facet of Hansen's treatment. He also considers, among other things, the impact of European policies on the dollar, the failure of Western Europe to carry its fair share of international aid, the unwisdom of dollar devaluation in present circumstances, and the state of the competitive position of the United States. He sees no evidence of serious deterioration; rather he finds that the burden of aid and capital movement largely account for the loss of reserves.

As usual, when Hansen tackles a subject, he throws a new, penetrating light. The reader will find some interesting observations on how to measure the balance of payments and deficits, on the need to guarantee the dollar against a devaluation as others are induced to hold increasing supplies of dollars, on the analysis and conclusions of the important Brookings Report on the Balance of Payments, and on the 1964 Tokyo Reports.

As Editor of the Handbook Series, I once more welcome Hansen's latest volume.

SEYMOUR E. HARRIS

• *part one* •

THE HEART OF THE PROBLEM

chapter one

THE U.S. BALANCE OF PAYMENTS

DOLLAR SHORTAGE

The United States is today the storm center around which international monetary problems revolve. This is nothing new, but the wind now blows in a different direction. Prior to 1950 the great world monetary problem was "dollar scarcity." The United States was always exporting too much and importing too little. Foreign countries did not earn enough dollars selling goods and services to the United

States (or to other countries in command of dollars) to pay for the goods and services purchased from the United States. There was a gap in the trade balance.

A trading country that buys less goods and services than it sells may even the score by buying assets—direct investments or foreign securities and real estate. The United States did this on a big scale in the twenties. In the decade 1924–1934 the overall accounts were sufficiently balanced so that the U.S. gold stock in January, 1934, stood at around $4 billion, the same level as in 1924 (both in terms of the old price of gold), although there were violent fluctuations up and down in the intervening period.

In the succeeding decade, 1934–1944, gold inflows into the United States (in terms of the new price of gold) amounted to $14 billion. Of this vast amount about one-third represented an offset to an export surplus, and two-thirds an offset to a capital flight from Europe induced first by the threatening international situation and finally by the outbreak of war.

Thus it was that the United States held 27 per cent of the world's monetary gold stock in 1913, 44 per cent in 1924, and 60 per cent in 1944. At the 1948 peak the aggregate gold holdings amounted to about $25 billion. The United States was accumulating "cash." It was mopping up the world's stock of gold.

In the twenties and thirties the United States was, in the eyes of the world, the *bête noire*. The American tariff, boosted still higher in the Smoot-Hawley Tariff Act, and the American Depression were the chief irritants. Books were being written about the twentieth-century Midas. Europeans were directing homilies at the United States demanding that it "put its house in order." The United States was not playing the game fair. It wanted to sell but not to buy. The task of remedying the inbalance in world trade devolved upon the United States.

The deficit countries could indeed have acted to balance up their accounts (and were in fact often forced to do so) by restricting their purchases of U.S. goods. One restriction led to another. In the final analysis, however, both economics and international "political morality" pointed the finger at the surplus country—the United States.

DOLLAR GLUT

Since 1950 the tables have been turned. The dollar scarcity problem is gone. But so firmly was the idea planted in the minds of everyone concerned with international trade that monetary authorities continued to talk about "dollar scarcity" long after it had been metamorphosed into the "dollar glut." Thus the Annual Reports of the International Monetary Fund were still deeply concerned about dollar scarcity as late as *1953*. Finally in 1954, the Annual Report cautiously stated that the world had begun to move toward the elimination of the dollar gap. As late as January, 1958, *Lloyds Bank Review* ran charts under the banner "The Dollar Gap" which purported to show that this was still the serious international problem. The U.S. gold reserves did indeed increase from 1955 to 1957, and the Suez crisis did bring a temporary U.S. payment surplus. These short-run developments were, however, swamped by basic trends beginning in 1950 which brought a cumulation of deficits aggregating $10.7 billion in 1950 to 1956 inclusive. Nevertheless, appended to the charts (p. 46) was a concluding note which worried about U.S. exports outstripping U.S. imports and about the falling reserves of countries outside of the dollar area.

Beginning with 1950 the United States has been paying out more dollars to foreign countries than they pay for the goods, services, and assets which they wish to purchase from the United States. The United States has become a deficit country. Its payments exceed its receipts, and so it is losing cash—gold—or increasing its short-term liabilities.

The Western European countries, notably the Common Market countries and Switzerland, are now the surplus countries. It is they who are now absorbing more and more of the world's international reserves.

The U.S. overall deficits (or surpluses) for the period 1948 to 1962 are given in Table 1-1, together with U.S. gold stocks for certain years. It will be noted that foreigners did not demand full payment in gold, especially in the earlier years. They counted, as part payment, liquid dollar holdings —deposits in New York banks or U.S. Treasury bills or other short-term U.S. government securities. But official holdings *could* all be converted on demand into gold. And the Continental monetary authorities did demand gold.[1]

Why were the experts so slow about recognizing that the United States had switched over from being a surplus country to a deficit country in terms of international payments? The answer is very simple: There has been in fact no switch in the "trading balance."[2] The United States continues, as of yore, to export far more goods and services than it imports. The United States still has, as we shall see, a huge surplus in its trade account. In these terms we are still confronted with "dollar shortage."

Do the recent losses of gold indicate that the United States is losing out in its competitive position in world trade? What criteria should be used to judge? In what follows, we attempt to evaluate various criteria of competitiveness.

[1] Beginning with July, 1963, gold outflows declined. Indeed the U.S. gold stocks stood in April, 1964, at a level slightly above that of July, 1963.

[2] For short I use the term "trading balance" to include goods and services, excluding military expenditures abroad from the "services" category. For "goods" alone I use the conventional phrase "merchandise trade."

Table 1-1. *U.S. Payments Deficits or Surpluses,* 1948–1963*
(*in billions of dollars*) *and Gold Stocks,* 1948, 1956, *and* 1963 (*in round numbers*)

Year	*Deficits (−) or surpluses (+)*	*Gold stocks, billions*
1948	+$1.0	$25
1949	+ 0.2	
1950	− 3.6	
1951	− 0.3	
1952	− 1.0	
1953	− 2.2	
1954	− 1.6	
1955	− 1.1	
1956	− 0.9	22
1957	+ 0.5	
1958	− 3.5	
1959	− 3.7	
1960	− 3.9	
1961	− 2.4	
1962	− 2.2	
1963	− 3.1†	15.5

* Note should be taken of the fact that the U.S. official figures of balance of payments overstate the deficits. This is due to the fact that the United States, unlike most other countries, does not set out the short-term claims of U.S. commercial banks on foreigners against their short-term liabilities to foreigners. The statistics include the *gross* short-term liabilities instead of the *net* figures because *all* the short-term liabilities can readily be converted into gold since private holdings can easily be shifted over to the central banks. Still the *net* figures would tell a more accurate story.

Also it should be noted that our net international assets, long-term and short-term, have been growing all through the period of balance-of-payments deficits.

† The deficit was much lower in the second half of 1963 due largely to the proposed interest equalization tax. The low annual rate of $1.5 billion in the first 5 months of 1964 (which may have been temporary) was due to such factors as (1) the tax on new foreign issues, (2) higher interest rates, (3) reduced overseas government spending, and (4) an increase in U.S. exports induced by rising European incomes. The deficit in the last half of 1963 was less than one-half that of the first half of that year.

THE EXCHANGE-MARKET ANALYSIS

Walter Gardner, in his brilliant seminar paper at Harvard University, December 5, 1960, introduced an "exchange-market" analysis of the U.S. balance of payments.[3] This, I think, is a highly useful concept, but he did not, I feel, carry the analysis quite far enough. He included in his exchange-market balance the noncommercial transactions which, as he himself put it, "have nothing to do with markets and profit opportunities." The big items in his noncommercial category are, of course, military expenditures abroad and foreign aid.[4] No classification of these items can be entirely satisfactory. The competitiveness of a country in its trading and financial relations with other countries cannot be judged in terms of governmental transactions politically determined. It relates to a country's capacity to face its competitors in the marketplace where goods and services are exchanged and in the financial markets where securities and assets are traded. Competitiveness has to do with market forces and profit opportunities—"market-oriented" factors.

It is of course true that government expenditures abroad become forces in the exchange market and so, in due course, influence the trading balance. But this does not happen overnight. And the structure of trade may prove to be highly resistant. The money transfers will not automatically or easily become real transfers. This will be discussed later, in more detail.

[3] Walter Gardner, "An Exchange-market Analysis: The U.S. Balance of Payments," *IMF Staff Papers*, vol. 8, pp. 195–211, 1960–1961.

[4] Some government transfers affect trade directly, for example tied loans. Yet even here it is by no means certain that tied loans will increase exports. Countries having earned "free dollars" from exports to the United States can shift these free dollars from purchases of U.S. products to purchases from third countries.

MERCHANDISE NET EXPORTS

The United States has steadily been running a merchandise net export surplus of considerable magnitude. There was, of course, a decline from the early postwar years when the United States was the only important supplier. Europe rapidly recovered in the early fifties, and the period 1951 to 1956 can perhaps be regarded as approaching more normal competitive conditions.[5] By 1958 to 1963—the years of serious deficits in the U.S. balance of payments—the merchandise surplus had risen substantially above the figure for the recovery period of 1951 to 1956.

True, the U.S. *share* of world markets has declined. This decline may in part be due to a relatively unfavorable development of U.S. export prices compared with European export prices. The U.S. export prices rose from an index of 94 in 1955 to 103 in 1962, while the more stable export prices of Western Europe rose only slightly from 97 to 100.[6] With respect to *manufactured* goods, moreover, the unit values rose by 2.4 per cent a year in the United States and by only 0.3 per cent a year in Western Europe.[7] There is, however, general agreement among price experts that all currently available export prices are tricky and may well be misleading.[8] The unit value indexes of exports "cover only a

[5] I believe, however, that it would generally be agreed that the U.S. competitive position was still abnormally strong in 1951 to 1956, and that so strong a position could not be expected to continue.

[6] *International Financial Statistics*, August, 1963, p. 30.

[7] See The Brookings Report, p. 39. According to K. O. Faxén (*Ekonomisk Tidskrift*, 1963) the export prices for industrial products for the leading industrial countries rose from 100 to 104 from 1958 to 1962 while U.S. prices rose from 100 to 108.

[8] European export prices in 1963 were only about 2 per cent higher than in 1960, while GNP prices had risen 12 per cent and cost of living also 12 per cent. This divergence could be due in part at least to contrived policies such as the practice of European exporters to

small and not necessarily representative part of trade in manufactured goods."[9] Other factors also played a role. The Brookings Report makes note of the fact that a substantial part of the decline (1951 to 1963) in the U.S. *share* of world markets is due not to competitiveness but to the fact that two geographical areas for which we are major suppliers—Canada and Latin America—have suffered in recent years from stagnation and were therefore unable to import as much as normally from the United States.

TRADE IN MANUFACTURES

When merchandise trade is broken up into its component parts, it is found that certain sectors suffered more than others. Merchandise trade includes manufactured goods, industrial raw materials, agricultural products and foodstuffs, and some may contend that the real test of competitiveness can best be found in the balance of trade in *manufactured* goods. This view is clearly too restricted since the United States is a major supplier of agricultural products and foodstuffs and industrial raw materials,[10] and these must all be taken account of in an appraisal of the U.S. overall role in world trade. Admittedly a sector that represents 40 per cent of the aggre-

---

charge lower prices for exports than for domestic deliveries and governmental support to export prices by such devices as exemptions and rebates of taxes. See *International Financial Statistics*, August, 1963, p. 30, and *Materials Submitted to the Joint Economic Committee*, 88th Cong., 1st Sess., 1963, pp. 7, 11.

[9] See Hal B. Lary, *The United States as World Trader and Banker*, National Bureau of Economic Research, Princeton, N.J., 1963, p. 57. He concludes that the "rise after 1953 in the general level of prices does not appear to have been markedly greater, if at all, in the United States than in most leading industrial countries."

[10] In 1961 the U.S. exports of merchandise, by categories, was as follows: agricultural products and foodstuffs, $4.9 billion; industrial materials, $6.0 billion; manufactured goods, $8.1 billion.

gate merchandise exports can tell a large part of the story. And the U.S. share of world exports of manufactures has not done as well as the share of merchandise exports as a whole. While the share of merchandise exports remained constant from 1953 to 1962, the share of exports of manufactures declined from 26 per cent in 1953 to 21 per cent in 1959 and to 20 per cent in 1962.[11] The United States has however substantially held its own since 1959.

MOTOR VEHICLES, METALS, AND MACHINERY

In considering the U.S. position in world competition attention has perhaps most frequently been called to one important group of manufactures, namely, motor vehicles, iron and steel, and industrial machinery. These items constitute a large fraction of total industrial manufactures. They deserve, therefore, particular attention, since they account for a loss of over $1 billion in U.S. exports from 1954 to 1961.[12] In the case of automobiles, however, vigorous competition (compact cars) quickly met the foreign inroads on our market. In general, however, it is in the area of steel products that the competitive position of the United States is threatened.

This relates especially to the price development in the investment boom of 1955–1957. From 1954 to 1957 the prices of producers, equipment rose 22 per cent, metals and metal products 18 per cent, and machinery and motor products 17 per cent. Contrasted with this price rise ranging from 19 to 22 per cent, wholesale prices in the economy as a whole (excluding the capital goods sector) rose only 3 per cent. Hourly

[11] See Brookings Report, p. 65, and *Compilation of Studies Prepared for the Sub-Committee on International Exchange and Payments*, 87th Cong., 2d Sess., p. 376.

[12] See Brookings Report, p. 68. Data from the International Trade Analysis Division, Department of Commerce.

earnings in metals and metal products, machinery, and automobiles rose by about 15 per cent, not including, however, the large fringe benefits which constituted no small part of the package. Cause and effect price-wage relationships are of course not easy to disentangle. The boom demand created a climate in which wage demands were strongly pressed. Increasing productivity and rapidly rising profits made it possible to grant wage demands which in a rising market could easily be offset by price increases. These price increases disrupted the U.S. internal price structure, affecting the internal balance.[13]

More serious still was the impact on the international front. Steel prices and the prices of steel products, once the boom phase had been shaken out,[14] rose out of line with world prices. This basic sector in the U.S. economy deserves the special scrutiny of our policy makers. It is the weakest spot in our competitive position. Still, important as this is, it would be a mistake to judge the overall competitive situation of the United States from one segment of the economy. Rarely can one find a time when the general picture is not blurred by dislocations in special sectors.[15]

SERVICES

Merchandise trade alone fails, however, to provide an adequate index of U.S. competitiveness. "Services" constitute

[13] See my *Economic Issues of the 1960's*, pp. 15–17.

[14] While prices of steel products also rose in Europe during the 1955 to 1957 investment boom, they declined sharply later while the U.S. prices remained high.

[15] One further qualifying comment about the merchandise trade balance. A part of the good showing in the merchandise trade balance is related to tied loans, and this has nothing whatever to do with competitiveness. As noted above, however, tied loans may not be fully effective.

an important part of the international exchange economy. Consider, for example, tourism as an import or export item. In this area the United States is a weak competitor for she lacks the famous historical monuments of the past. But here we may perhaps be on the upgrade. The rapid rise in the income of large masses of the European population, the convenience of air travel, and awakened worldwide interest in American life and institutions all make tourism an item of growing importance as an American export. On the other side American tourist expenditures abroad may be leveling out somewhat.

Taking account of market services of all kinds, the U.S. record is favorable. Excluding, as logic requires,[16] military expenditures abroad and concentrating wholly on market forces, we find that the "service balance" increased from $1.6 billion per year in 1947–1949 to $2.0 billion in 1951–1956, and to $2.6 billion in 1958–1962.

Investment income is an important service item and it has been rapidly increasing. This helps to present a favorable balance-of-payments prospect. Should investment income (interest and dividends on American-owned foreign investments) be included in the category of items by which we attempt to judge the competitive position of the United States? Investment income is a product of *past* investment. A growing surplus in the goods and services account, determined heavily by a large and growing investment income, may not indicate a strongly competitive economy today. Clearly we shall not be able to maintain our place in the world market if we rest our oars on past accomplishments. We must

[16] I exclude U.S. military expenditures abroad from my services category. Indeed this is already implicit in the phrase market-exchange goods and services. Military expenditures abroad do not fit into the category of a market exchange of goods and services. They belong properly in the category of governmental transactions including grants, loans, and military aid.

continue to lead in the development of new products and new techniques.

CAPITAL FLOWS

A more difficult question relates not to investment income but to long-term capital inflows and outflows. A vigorously expanding economy with profitable investment opportunities is able to attract capital. Is this not indicative of competitiveness?

Stagnation and slow growth are likely to produce a low level of imports and this contributes to a surplus in the goods and services account. As an index of competitiveness this seems to lead to the absurd conclusion that the more stagnant an economy the more competitive it is! Yet this was formerly the orthodox way to achieve a balance.

THE IMPACT OF FULL EMPLOYMENT

In contradistinction to this viewpoint, the fact that high employment and a rapidly growing economy tend to pull capital inward and thus to produce a payments surplus suggests that *growth* may be a significant index of competitiveness.[17]

[17] The difficulty of disentangling cause and effect relationship is evident in the undoubted fact that both imports and exports have in a measure a feedback effect on each other. If imports decline, foreign countries' sales decline and so they can buy less. This affects the first country's exports. If exports are low a country's buying power is reduced and this affects imports.

It may here be noted that U.S. exports increased at exactly the same percentage rate as the GNP, namely, 38 per cent, from the period 1951–1956 to 1958–1962. A higher rate of growth would undoubtedly have produced a higher rate of both exports and imports. Through the feedback effect each would have stimulated the other. A higher rate of growth might therefore have produced a larger U.S. share in aggregate world trade including both imports and exports.

Had we pursued full employment policies, the U.S. GNP could have increased rapidly in the decade 1953–1963. The United States is less dependent upon world trade than our European competitors because of our vast internal market. If they had depended on their smaller internal markets, European countries could not have enjoyed as great a rise in per capita income as they did achieve by a very great expansion of exports. The difference is that per capita increases in output in Europe needed larger sales volume than the small domestic markets could offer. Higher growth rates in the United States, however, were within our reach based primarily upon an expanding *internal* market. This might have helped our payments balance because of the impact of growth upon the net inflow of capital. On the other hand, higher growth rates might mean larger imports.

A high and growing per capita real income depends on increased factor efficiency. But this may or may not involve any growth or even the maintenance of a country's *share* in world trade. That depends on many things,[18] among them, in what sectors of the economy increased productivity may be occurring. If the growth in efficiency is found in the import-competing industries this could mean in a full employment economy a transfer of productive factors out of export industries into the growing and more efficient domestic industries. This would indeed cause a decline in the ratio of exports to GNP but not necessarily any decline in the ratio of exports to imports, or any worsening of the country's balance-of-payments position.

[18] In the materials submitted to the Joint Economic Committee (88th Cong., 1st Sess.) 1963, it was pointed out by Robert Aliber, staff economist, Committee for Economic Development that the fall in export earnings of the primary producing countries during the last decade affected U.S. exports to these countries very seriously. This tended to reduce our *share* of world exports since these markets are relatively more important for us than for Europe. See "Materials," p. 11. See also the Brookings Report, p. 60.

ORTHODOX VERSUS MODERN VIEW

Orthodox economics was prepared to accept a decline in income as a means of curing a payments deficit. This is no longer regarded as tolerable. Orthodox opinion held not only that a decline in income was acceptable, but also that this was the only certain means of achieving cost reduction, and thus a stronger competitive position. This also is no longer accepted doctrine. In the nineteenth century, depressions brought a cut in money wage rates and therefore low costs relative to foreign competitors. Today money wage cuts are not tolerated, and so depression means low-capacity output and therefore high unit costs.

There remains the slower process of cost reduction through research and technology together with wage and price restraints. Given the level of technique, lowest unit cost can be achieved at high-capacity utilization, but only if appropriate wage and price policies are pursued.

High employment levels promote capital movements that tend in the short run to improve the overall payments position. On the other hand high employment and growth stimulate imports and this operates unfavorably on the payments balance.

THE INCOME AND PRICE EFFECTS

To sum up this part of the discussion, let us endeavor to bring together the various full employment effects, separating out (1) the income effect and (2) the price effect on the balance of payments. The modern view is that the income effect is unfavorable with respect to the net import of goods and services but favorable with respect to net capital inflow. The modern view denies that low unit costs can be achieved at low-capacity output. On balance, therefore, where does this leave us? Can we improve our balance-of-payments position by pursuing full employment and high growth rate policies? The orthodox answer was "No," based both on the income effect and the price effect. Modern theory comes out with a more agnostic view. There are forces working both ways.[19a]

Walther Lederer has made an analysis of U.S. exports to Western Europe from 1952 to 1963 in which he shows that U.S.–European relative price changes appear in fact to have had little influence on U.S. exports. The big factor in raising U.S. exports was changes in the real income of European countries. Lederer is careful to point out, however, that the data do not tell us how large the price differentials would have to be, or for how long they would have to be effective, to produce large results.[19b] But within the ranges actually experienced, the price effect was minor.

PRICE COMPETITION

Prices obviously play a somewhat smaller role in the competitive struggle now than formerly.[20] To be sure, an exporter

[19a] Professor Seymour Harris has pointed out that direct investment abroad, in addition to having an unfavorable direct effect on the balance of payments, also has unfavorable indirect effects: When the branch factories begin to operate they will displace exports from the United States not only in European markets but also in third countries and may even invade the American domestic market. See *The U.S. Balance of Payments, Materials Submitted to the Joint Economic Committee*, 88th Cong., 1st Sess., 1963.

On the other hand, it may be noted that U.S. plants abroad often buy supplies from the parent U.S. plant so that direct investment abroad may to a degree stimulate exports from the United States.

[19b] See Walther Lederer, *The U.S. Balance of Payments, Hearings before the Joint Economic Committee,* July 29 and 30, 1963, part 2, pp. 281–288.

[20] For a stimulating discussion of the rather modest impact of tariffs and relative prices compared with the decisive role of product differentiation as the central dynamic element in the development of world

must be able to offer his product at a price that falls within a certain range. But this range for many products may be fairly wide. No doubt sharp price competition continues to prevail in a large sector of foreign trade. Yet everywhere growing importance must be attached to marketing, salesmanship, advertising, contacts, and ability to please the customer in terms of style, novelty, etc. Moreover, it must be remembered that the manufacturer's price may be less (often far less) than half the retail price after taking account of tariffs, transportation, and handling costs.[21]

Living in Stockholm one is impressed with the wide variety of imports that are available (canned foodstuffs, furniture, household appliances, clothing) from all parts of the world—

---

trade, see Tord Ekström, Gunnar Myrdal, and Roland Pålsson, *Vi och Västeuropa*, pp. 90, 92–94. See also in this connection, Gunnar Myrdal, *The Challenge to Affluence*, Pantheon, New York, 1963, p. 155.

Commenting on the question whether prices are in the modern economy a significant indication of competitive power, and thus of the export potential, Thomas Balogh, Balliol College, Oxford University, says: "They are not. Machines and durable consumer goods in particular have become an increasingly large part of foreign trade. In this context, comparisons of prices paid even if some sense could be attributed to the index number, mean less and less. The American imports of small European cars were not due mainly to price but to convenience and taste. The impact of the Volkswagen, now almost irreversible, need never have happened had American compact cars been available. Competition with America in machine tools in third markets depends on the general attractiveness of foreign machine tools and not merely on price. Availability, knowledge, delivery periods, credit, servicing, and above all, quality, the embodiment of new technical knowledge, therefore, and not merely price, are the determinants of competitive supremacy." See *Statements on the Brookings Institution Study, The United States Balance of Payments in 1968,* Joint Economic Committee, 88th Cong., 1st Sess.; 1963, p. 45.

[21] In a recent survey by *France Actuelle* of American exports to France price is scarcely mentioned as a factor. Novelty, style, new kinds of products, scientific and instructive toys, etc.,—these play the dominant role.

Scotland, Italy, United States, Germany, England, Poland, Denmark, Japan, France. The Swedish market is a high-income, high-quality market.

There is, of course, in all developed countries a low-income, price-conscious market in which cutthroat price competition from the low-wage countries plays an important role. The United States in particular offers to world traders both a large high-income market for high-priced quality goods and also a large low-income market for low-priced goods. Japanese competition is the familiar case. But these cut-price imports are blocked by tariffs, import quotas or so-called "voluntary" restrictions, so that the price effect is not allowed to exercise its full play.

All in all in the modern world, price competition is relatively less important than "marketing competition."[22] And if marketing is to be effective, income must be high. Hence growth of exports depends very heavily on high and rising incomes in the importing countries. The income elasticity of demand for imports may be more significant than price elasticities.[23]

Those economists who place great faith in relatively small shifts in the exchange rates probably exaggerate the role of price elasticity. They exaggerate the feasibility of correcting

[22] Dexter M. Keezer, in his *New Forces in American Business* (McGraw-Hill, New York, 1959), calls attention to the fact that the concept of competition has changed to that of "rivalry for customers." Competition has become a "titanic struggle to beat each other in the market" by means of intensive and persuasive selling techniques.

[23] Robert J. Aliber, staff economist, CED, points out that changes in the trade structure, due to the increased availability of European export supplies and to changes in American tastes, may be wrongly attributed to relative price differentials. For this reason Mr. Aliber believes that even the price elasticity figure of 2.5 used in the *Brookings Report* is too high. See *The U.S. Balance of Payments, Materials Submitted to the Joint Economic Committee on the Brookings Institution Study*, 88th Cong., 1st Sess., 1963, pp. 13–14.

a payments imbalance via price differentials and their impact upon the exchange of goods and services. This is not to say that price differentials can be disregarded. The exchange-market economy remains, of course, a price economy. A balanced judgment of the role of price is called for, and it is clear that its role in the modern economy is changing.[24] Technological research plays a major role. Today's prices become obsolete tomorrow because products and production processes have changed.[25]

THE TRADE BALANCE AND THE CAPITAL BALANCE

More or less, the payments deficit country will be affected by the relation of its price structure to that of other countries and by relative growth rates.[26] As far as we can tell from historical experience (which in the nature of the case must be very inconclusive) the net effect of growth may go either way depending upon the relative weight of the conflicting factors under different structures of world trade and finance. With respect to the relative importance of the price factor and the growth factor, no conclusive answer can be given. But it is at least possible (perhaps even probable) that the

[24] For a comprehensive statement on relative prices and competition see Hal B. Lary, *The United States as World Trader and Banker*, pp. 56–68.

[25] See *The Economic Review*, National Institute of Economic and Social Research, London, May, 1962, pp. 21–37; and *Summary Report of the Engineering Research Committee*, Engineers Joint Council, May 25, 1962.

[26] The Brookings Group Report (pp. 18–23) contains an illuminating discussion of the relative roles of demand-oriented growth versus supply-led growth. If the domestic demand increases faster than the supply capabilities of an economy, imports will tend to grow more than exports. If, however, the productive potential increases more than the domestic demand, then exports will tend to increase more than imports.

growth factor is more important and that a favorable growth rate will more effectively promote adjustments over time.

Jeffrey G. Williamson of the University of Wisconsin has made historical analysis of the relation of the long-run upswings and downswings—rapid growth rates and sluggish growth rates—upon the balance of payments in the United States from 1890 to 1914. He finds that periods of retardation and relative stagnation tended to produce *trade* balance surpluses while periods of upswing produced trade balance deficits. But the trade surpluses and deficits were swamped by the capital inflow in upswing periods and capital outflows in downswing periods, so that high employment and rapid growth periods produced *overall* balance-of-payment surpluses while retardation and temporary stagnation produced balance-of-payments deficits. The same relationship has held in the recent postwar period of semistagnation—large capital outflows and balance-of-payments deficits. The dominant factor, he finds, was the relative profit opportunities at home and abroad. Short-term capital movements may intermittently reinforce the long-term capital outflow, but these, except in short periods of real crisis, are over the long run relatively small compared to the bulk of capital going abroad in search of higher rates of return.

Adjustments tending to eliminate a payments deficit can of course be made over time both in the trade balance and in the capital account balance. It is a question how far one or the other predominates. Keynes put it this way 35 years ago: "My own view is that at a given time the economic structure of a country, in relation to the economic structures of its neighbors, permits a certain 'natural' level of exports, and that artificially to effect a material alteration of this level by deliberate devices is extremely difficult."[27] History tends to support this view. As one illustration, the European share of

[27] *Economic Journal*, March, 1929, p. 6.

world exports was 45 per cent in 1938 and approximately the same (47 per cent) in 1962.[28] The economic structure of a country is primarily determined by the skills and resourcefulness of its citizens and by its natural resources. These basically determine the structure of its trade with other countries (similarly determined by human and natural resources) and this is not likely to be changed substantially by moderate price changes.

THE OVERALL PICTURE

From what has been said above it is evident that a clean-cut measure of competitiveness is not easily available.[29] We

[28] See Robert Z. Aliber, *The U.S. Balance of Payments,* Joint Economic Committee, 88th Cong., 1st Sess., pp. 12–13.

An amazing example of the stability of trade structures is the record of German exports in 1913 and 1929. All this despite the war and inflation upheaval, the loss of home territory, her colonial empire, railroad equipment, merchant marine, and $7 billion of foreign investments. For a full account see my *Economic Stabilization in an Unbalanced World,* pp. 8–13, including a discussion of similar proofs of stability of trade structures in the United Kingdom and France. Below are given a few examples from the German experience.

A. German Export: Commodities

	Percentage of total value 1913	Percentage of total value 1929
Iron and steel	13.2	14.2
Chemicals	9.5	10.2
Coal, coke, briquets	7.2	6.4
Paper & paper mfgs.	2.7	3.7
Silk & Rayon	2.5	3.0
Copper, brass, & bronze	2.7	3.0

B. German Exports: Continent

	Percentage of total value 1913	Percentage of total value 1928
Europe	76.1	74.8
America	15.3	14.6
Asia	5.5	7.7
Africa	2.1	2.3
Australia	1.0	0.6

[29] On the difficulties of measuring competitiveness see P. R. Narvekar, "The Role of Competitiveness in Japan's Export Perform-

can, however, gain some impression of the shifts in competitiveness from a quick, overall statistical survey of the changes in the U.S. balance of payments during the last dozen years.[30] With this in view I present below summary tables of the various component parts, beginning with merchandise trade and finally an overall picture of the exchange-market balance and the transfer balance.

---

ance, 1954–1958," *Staff Papers,* International Monetary Fund, vol. 8, pp. 86–87, November, 1960.

[30] Mr. Thomas Balogh, Oxford University, England, points out the folly of judging the U.S. competitive position largely in terms of its payments deficits. Against the surrender of gold and low-interest-bearing liabilities incident to these deficits, he places the increases in American investments abroad—investments that, according to the Department of Commerce, earn well over 15 per cent. He cites President Kennedy's estimate of $35 billion (book value) of American investments abroad and argues that this was a gross understatement of market value. Balogh warned lest the "unwarranted inferiority complex which has beset American decision-making" may prevent that "efflorescence of American technological ingenuity and superiority through innovation which has been the basis of the vast exports of manufactures, especially capital goods." Balogh deprecated the tendency of balance-of-payments statistics to "reflect an ebbing of the American gold reserve week by week, instead of emphasizing the immense increase day by day in American wealth and productive power at home and abroad." *Materials Submitted to the Joint Economic Committee*, 88th Cong. 1st Sess., 1963, pp. 40–41.

A. R. Conan, author of *Capital Imports into Sterling Countries*, and one of the authorities invited by the Joint Committee to appraise the Brookings Report, (see the *U.S. Balance of Payments, Materials Submitted to the Joint Economic Committee*, 88th Cong. 1st Sess., 1963, p. 101), says that the recent decline in the U.S. share of world trade in manufactures "does not reflect any general decline in the competitive position of the United States but was occasioned by special factors of a transient nature. Moreover no adequate support is found for the view that the trend of U.S. export prices, at least during the past few years, has seriously impaired competitiveness."

See also Sir Donald MacDougall, *The Dollar Problem: A Reappraisal,* International Finance Section, Princeton, N.J., no. 35, November, 1960. On balance, MacDougall takes an optimistic view of the competitive position of the United States.

U.S. merchandise exports soared to $16 billion in 1947 while imports fell to $6 billion. But from 1947 on, Europe rapidly recovered. For the pre-Korean period, 1947–1949, merchandise exports averaged $13.8 billion, while imports averaged $6.8 billion. Thus merchandise exports exceeded merchandise imports by $7 billion. But this reflected the low postwar productivity of European countries. The Marshall aid program and the boom after the Korean Conflict hastened their rehabilitation. The share of the United States in world trade was settling down to more normal proportions. But the

*Table 1-2. U.S. Merchandise Trade**
(in billions of dollars; average per year)

Years	*Merchandise exports*	*Merchandise imports*	*Merchandise export surplus*
1947–1949	+$13.8	−$ 6.8	$7.0
1951–1956	+ 14.0	− 11.3	2.7
1958–1962	+ 18.5	− 14.7	3.8

* The minuses contribute to an overall deficit; the pluses to a surplus. Data from: *Survey of Current Business*.

value was more than maintained, merchandise exports rising to $18.5 billion per year in 1958–1962.[31] Indeed the net export surplus rose to $3.8 billion per year compared with $2.8 billion in 1951–1956. These data are summarized in Table 1-2.

Meanwhile services netted $1.6 billion per year in 1947–1949; $2.0 billion per year in 1951–1958; and $2.7 billion per year in 1958–1962. Combining services and merchandise we get a net excess of exports of goods and services of $8.6

[31] World trade data were profoundly distorted in the year 1950 by the September, 1949, currency devaluations and by the Korean Conflict and in the year 1957 by the Suez crisis. I have therefore excluded these years from my data. See the *U.S. Balance of Payments of 1968*, The Brookings Institution, Appendix, Table 1.

billion in 1947–1949; $4.7 billion in 1951–1956; and $6.4 billion in 1958–1962. These data are summarized in Table 1-3.

Table 1-3. *The "Trading Balance:" Goods and Services (in billions of dollars; average per year)*

Years	*Merchandise export surplus*	*Services export surplus*	*Net trading balance surplus: goods and services*
1947–1949	+$7.0	+$1.6	+$8.6
1951–1956	+ 2.7	+ 2.0	+ 4.7
1958–1962	+ 3.8	+ 2.7	+ 6.5

The spectacular goods and services surplus of $8.6 billion in 1947–1949 could not of course be maintained once Europe had recovered her competitive position. But after the shakedown the United States still retained a strong surplus position which has been substantially increased in 1958–1962.

Table 1-4. *Net Private Capital Flows (in billions of dollars; average per year)*

Years	*Net flow of private long-term capital*	*Net short-term capital outflows*	*Net private remittances**	*Total*
1947–1949	−$0.8	+$0.9	−$0.6	−$0.5
1951–1956	− 0.9	+ 0.3	− 0.5	− 1.1
1958–1962	− 2.2	+ 0.5	− 0.5	− 3.2

* Admittedly this item is rather difficult to classify. But since it is a relatively small and highly stable item, its inclusion here creates no disturbing problem. More disturbing is the fact that "errors and omissions" are dropped into the "short-term capital" basket.

In terms of goods and services the dollar shortage is far from being over. This statement, to be sure, oversimplifies the complex interrelationship of all the factors involved in the overall balance-of-payments picture. Still in the tangle of casual relationships (about which more later) it is important not to lose sight of the fact that as a world trader in goods and services, the United States has a large and growing surplus.

In addition to the goods and services balance there is the private capital account (long-term and short-term) and net private remittances. These data are summarized in Table 1-4.

PRIVATE LONG-TERM CAPITAL OUTFLOWS

The one item that stands out conspicuously is the extraordinary increase in the gross outflow of private long-term capital from the United States once world recovery got firmly under way. Prior to 1955 the great bulk of funds flowing abroad consisted of government grants and loans. After 1955 private capital outflow leaped forward. Two factors play a role here: a worldwide climate buoyant with profitable expectations; and the easing of exchange restrictions and the eventual return to convertibility (1958) of most European currencies. The impact of these two factors can be seen in the steady growth of long-term capital outflow from the United States as shown in Table 1-5. The shift from a mere $550 million in 1953 to $2.6 billion in 1958 goes a long way to account for the $2 billion increase in the U.S. overall deficit from 1953 to 1958. U.S. long-term capital was moving abroad to share in the high profits of the worldwide postwar recovery. Some part of the capital outflow may well have been delayed repatriation of funds which had sought refuge in the United States from war-threatened Europe in the late thirties.

Professor James W. Angell has said that the two main causes of the U.S. deficits are "the very heavy net exports of capital, on both private and governmental account." Sir Roy Harrod of Oxford University in hearings before the Joint Economic Committee stated that there is no doubt that the cause of the recent deterioration in the U.S. balance of payments was "the greatly enlarged outflow of private U.S. capital overseas which started in 1956."[32]

Table 1-5. *U.S. Private Direct and Long-term Portfolio Capital Outflow**

	Billions
1953	$ 550
1954	987
1955	1,064
1956	2,554
1957	3,301
1958	2,595
1959	2,298
1960	2,544
1961	2,609
1962	2,766
1963	3,576

* *Economic Report of the President*, 1964, p. 298.

Here we encounter two seemingly contradictory aspects of the competitive strength of the United States as far as capital flow is concerned. On the one hand direct and portfolio investment abroad, especially in the case of U.S. investments in Western Europe, indicate a weakness on the part of the United States in its capacity to attract investment funds. Investment opportunities appear to have been better elsewhere. On the other hand the United States has a vastly superior capital market where ample funds are available at comparatively low rates of interest. The United States has

[32] See *Materials Submitted to the Joint Economic Committee*, 88th Cong., 1st Sess., 1963, pp. 32, 196.

been weak in terms of profitable investment outlets but strong as a supplier of capital. Both factors, however, have contributed to the recent U.S. persistent deficits.

GOVERNMENT TRANSFERS

So far we have been attempting to evaluate the *market* forces, both in the trade and capital accounts, that determine a country's balance-of-payments position. But, especially in our post war world, there are also nonmarket, noncommercial factors at work, namely, governmental transactions.[33] Here there is little or no question of relative prices, relative rates of growth, or other factors that influence a country's competitive position in the exchange of goods, services, and assets across international boundaries. Governmental transactions—grants, loans, military expeditions abroad—present us with a transfer problem based largely upon political considerations. And what impact this transfer problem may have upon the balance of payments depends upon the extent to which the money transfer can be translated into a real transfer—one that will show up either in the trade account or the capital account. If adjustments are not quickly induced in either the trade or capital accounts, deficits will appear in the balance of payments. The point to stress here is that such imbalances are not incurred in the first instance by lack of competitiveness. They are caused by nonmarket forces. But a flexible and highly responsive (i.e., competitive) society can sooner or later adjust to imbalances created by governmental transactions based upon political considerations.

Over against the private account including both trade and

[33] In addition to governmental transfers there are also other political factors that influence commercial transactions such as export subsidies, credit guarantees, and compensating taxes on imports in lieu of turnover or sales taxes.

capital items, (i.e., the exchange-market balance) stands the government account, the government transfer balance. This includes: (1) grants and loans to foreign countries (economic and military aid) and (2) military expenditures abroad.

Grants and loans were exceptionally large in 1947–1949 and declined substantially by 1958–1962. Offsetting this was the large increase in military expenditures abroad. Altogether, aggregate government transfers declined a bit in 1951–1956, but rose again in 1958–1962. The data for government transfers are summarized in Table 1-6.

Table 1-6. Government Transfers
(in billions of dollars; average per year)

Years	*Government grants and loans*	*U.S. military expenditures abroad*	*Total government transfers*
1947–1949	−$5.6	−$0.6	−$6.2
1951–1956	− 2.4	− 2.4	− 4.8
1958–1962	− 3.2	− 3.1	− 6.3

Table 1-7 sets out the exchange-market accounts against the government transfer account. The former are determined by market and profit opportunity factors. The latter is determined purely by political considerations. Once the decisions are made and executed, however, they become market forces that influence the private sector. The increase of $1.5 billion in government transfers from 1951–1956 to 1958–1962 exerted to a degree a feedback effect on the trade balance. But there were other factors at work such as the increased outflow of private long-term capital. The feedback effect on the trade balance, while substantial, was not sufficient to offset both the increase of $1.5 billion in government transfers and the increase of $1.3 billion in private long-term capital outflow.

The explanation can be found in Keynes's "sticky mass."[34] For every new dollar paid out, a part did indeed come back to buy American goods. The rest was taken out in cash. In part the cash was gold; in part it was dollars held as deposits in New York banks or in highly liquid U.S. government securities. The net export surplus did indeed rise but it failed

Table 1-7 Exchange-market Balance versus Government Transfer Balance (in billions of dollars; average per year)

	Exchange-market balance			*Overall payments*
Years	*Goods and services*	*Private (net) capital transfers*	*Government transfer balance*	*surplus (+) or deficits (−)*
1947–1949	+$8.6	−$0.5	−$6.2	+$1.9
1951–1956	+ 4.7	− 1.1	− 4.8	− 1.2
1958–1962	+ 6.5	− 3.2	− 6.3	− 3.1

to keep pace with the growing outflow of private and public funds.

The notable thing about Table 1-7 is the fact that the goods and services surplus of $6.5 billion amply covers the government transfers. If the private capital account could be brought into balance, the overall U.S. payments account would be in balance. This to be sure is an oversimplification. For example, loans to Canada, Japan, and Israel quickly show up in the trade balance.

The data in Table 1-7 tend to support the view that the persistent deficits of 1958 to 1962 can not be attributed pri-

[34] See the discussion of the transfer problem later in this chapter.

marily to any deterioration in the U.S. competitive position in the world markets. "Our balance-of-payments deficit does not arise because of any general inability to compete in international markets."[35] The U.S. position has, moreover, recently improved owing to wage and price inflationary pressures in Western Europe.

Walter Lederer puts it admirably in the following statement: "In a world where international transactions consist not only of commercial transactions but also of politically induced movements of money, competitiveness of a country with political net payments has to be stronger than it would if international transactions were governed exclusively by commercial consideration."[36] And the point is reinforced by Richard N. Cooper as follows: "It is therefore possible for a country to have a competitive position which is very strong, but not 'strong enough' to cover its foreign commitments."[37]

In other words, the dollar would have to be considerably *undervalued* in order to achieve an equilibrium in its balance of payments.

A conventional way (widely used by nearly all advanced countries though undesirable in terms of the best allocation of the world's productive resources) to ensure, or to attempt to ensure, that governmental monetary transfers will be speedily translated into a real transfer is to make it a tied loan or grant.[38] An untied loan or grant could, to be sure, start a circle of transactions which could eventually emerge as an export from the lending country. But this may not happen. The loan transfer may not wind up in a real transfer. Instead

[35] The Fowler Report, on *Promoting Increased Foreign Investment in U.S. Corporate Securities,* Apr. 27, 1964, p. 1.

[36] See Walther Lederer in Seymour Harris (ed.), *The Dollar in Crisis,* Harcourt, Brace & World, New York, 1962, p. 133.

[37] See Richard N. Cooper in *ibid.,* p. 139.

[38] True the tied loan, as explained earlier, may not work since free dollars may be transferred to purchases from third countries.

it may show up as a deficit in the balance of payments of the lending country.

In a smoothly functioning system of multilateral trade we assume no lag, no breaks in the circuit of trade. If the third countries choose to spend the dollars to purchase U.S. goods, all is well. The United States would not experience deficits if the triangular circuit were complete. The U.S. deficits are partly due to the fact that the untied dollars handed out to foreign countries in military and economic aid have come to rest largely in the hands of the banks of the European suppliers. The dollars are hoarded. West Germany's official holdings of gold and foreign exchange increased from an average of $2.4 billion in 1953–1955 to $6.1 billion in 1958–1963. And the same holds true, in greater or less degree, for many of the European countries. Continental Europe's official holdings of gold and foreign exchange increased from $11.6 billion average in 1953–1955 to $21.8 billion average in 1958–1962.

THE TRANSFER PROBLEM

Thirty-five years ago this problem was debated in the columns of the *Economic Journal* by Keynes and Bertil Ohlin. They were discussing the German reparation payments problem. Could the transfer of funds induce a corresponding increase in German exports, so that the money transfer would be fully reflected in the trade balance?

Keynes argued that the money transfer would not easily produce a real transfer of goods and services. He assumed that if German exports were to increase it would be necessary to cut German export costs and prices. This would mean a sharp reduction in German wages relative to efficiency wages in other countries. In terms of practical politics this would be very difficult. Even so a drastic cut in German export prices would not help much unless the price elasticity of demand for German exports was considerably greater than one.

Ohlin objected that Keynes failed to see the income effect (increased aggregate demand) on trade. The money transfer, he argued, would shift the aggregate demand curve upward. Thus the demand for German exports *at the same price* would rise. The argument on both sides might have been greatly clarified had the parties to the dispute employed a little geometry. Ohlin stressed the income effect, Keynes the price effect. In his reply, Keynes professed inability to understand his opponent fully. Still he saw the plan of attack clearly enough to rearrange his own battalions a bit, the net effect of which was to yield ground. On balance, economic opinion voted the victor's palm to Ohlin.

But it was a Pyrrhic victory. The facts of life were (and are) against Ohlin. The money transfer does not automatically or easily produce a real transfer. Trade does not follow hard upon finance. Ohlin allowed insufficient room for lags—lags which may involve years. And in the meantime fresh impulses may widen the gap still more between trade (lagging behind) and finance. The record of U.S. deficits in its recent balance of payments tells the story. The outflow of funds has not been offset by an equivalent increase in the net export surplus of goods and services. Keynes was right when he said: "In the case of German Reparations we are trying to fix the volume of foreign remittance and compel the balance of trade to adjust itself thereto. Those who see no difficulty in this are applying the theory of liquids to what is, if not a solid, at least a sticky mass with strong internal resistances."

The money transfer does not in the short run show up in the trade balance. Keyne's intuitive judgment was correct. We are not dealing with a liquid. There is some response, as the statistics show, but it is not instantaneous or adequate to fill the gap. Ohlin's income effect does indeed operate. But the trade balance lags behind. There is "many a slip twixt the cup and the lip." The international price structure is not sufficiently competitive and flexible to produce an adequate offset to the outflow of money transfers.

The gap is instead more likely to be closed by equilibrating offsets in the capital account. Thus the German reparation payments in the twenties were paid only so long as offsetting American loans to German local governments etc. were forthcoming. In his *Gold and the Dollar Crisis* (p. 26) Triffin refers to the emphasis placed by Professor Taussig and his students on the cushioning effect of capital movements as offsets to current account disequilibria. This was a corrective to the one-sided emphasis that the classicals placed upon adjustments in the trade balance. In this connection note the statement by John H. Williams: "The historical answer to unbalanced trade and productivity has been international investment."[39] Note also Gunnar Myrdal's *An International Economy*, in which he says: "Another of the heavy odds against the restoration of a reliable international payments system is the decline of the international capital market, and the small chance of its effective resuscitation" (p. 79). And again: "I cannot help feeling that the end of private international finance as we once knew it is somewhat of a loss for our civilization. It represented a wealth of established mores, trained talents, experience, and worldwide relations. Redirected to comply with present needs, it could still play an important role" (p. 111).

In recent years the U.S. payments deficits have in large part been covered by the short-term lending to the United States implicit in the accumulating dollar holdings by foreigners. The primary equilibrating factor was credit, not cash.

[39] John H. Williams, *Economic Stability in a Changing World: Essays in Economic Theory and Policy*, Oxford University Press, New York, 1953, p. 163.

When we pay in dollars we *create* international money. When we pay in gold we merely *transfer* international money.[40]

THE BASIC CAUSES OF THE U.S. DEFICITS

In this chapter I have stressed the difference between the *trading* balance (including both goods and services) and the *transfer* balance and also the difference between the exchange-market balance and the government transfer balance. These distinctions are of the greatest importance. Are the U.S. deficits of the last six years due to basic shifts in trade or are they due to shifts in the transfer of funds? If the deficit were due to a drastic falling off of exports, primary attention should be directed to our export situation. The trouble might lie in our own export industries, or the trouble might be found in restrictive import policies on the part of foreign countries. If the deficit were due to a drastic increase in U.S. imports the cause might conceivably be located in inefficiency in those American industries that compete with imports. If it is a trade-oriented deficit that is one thing. But if it is a transfer-oriented deficit, that is quite a different matter. True, in the long run, the trade will respond to established transfer flows. But in the short run transfer shifts cannot be offset by corresponding trade shifts without serious disruption in international trade relations. Transfer shifts can however be met without causing dislocations by deliberately offsetting capital flows implemented by adequate institutional arrangements. But in the contemporary world economy it may require international monetary machinery to facilitate the flow of funds across international borders.

Thus the U.S. balance-of-payments deficits emerge basically from two situations, neither of which have to do with the

[40] See James Tobin's statement in *Hearings before the Joint Economic Committee,* Nov. 12–15, 1963, p. 552.

short-run, cyclical or episodic types of imbalances for which the International Monetary Fund was set up or that central bankers contend with when they make short-term loans to tide a country over a temporary crisis. The two persistent sources of the U.S. balance-of-payments problem are (1) the U.S. program of military and economic foreign aid and (2) the New York capital market which, on top of the government aid programs, supplies capital to foreign countries. The current U.S. balance-of-payments problem is perhaps unique in all history. Yet many economists and bankers discuss the problem as though it were just the familiar short-run, cyclical, or episodic case.

What I am saying does not mean that adjustments can not be made over time which could end the overall U.S. deficits even though the New York market continues its role as major supplier of funds abroad and the United States continues its aid programs. The progressive rise of investment income alone will automatically play an increasing role as a balancing factor. And the feedback effects will gradually show up in the trade balance and perhaps also in the capital account. If however a more equitable distribution of foreign aid cannot be achieved, and if European capital markets cannot be substantially improved, it is highly improbable that the goods and services account can fully make the needed adjustments barring policies (tariff increases, exchange control, etc.) that are injurious to a prospering and growing world trade.

Professor Zolotas, governor of the Bank of Greece, has summed up the matter admirably as follows:

> As a matter of fact, in the last two years the annual outflow of long-term capital alone accounts for more than the corresponding overall deficit in the U.S. balance of payments. The still existing restrictions on capital exports in several industrial countries, and, more significantly, the organizational and institutional shortcomings of capital markets outside the U.S., impose on her, in addition to the responsibilities of a reserve center, the task of

satisfying capital requirements in the rest of the world, including the highly developed countries. This situation is incompatible with the smooth functioning of the gold exchange standard, which requires some measure of correspondence in the availability and freedom of movement of capital among major trading countries. The resulting strains from this lopsided operation of the international financial mechanism are being accentuated by the movement of short-term funds, partly in reference to interest rate differentials. Under these conditions one can hardly deny the necessity for the industrial countries of Europe to liberalize and develop their capital markets in accordance with the overall potential of their economies. This, however, is likely to be a gradually evolving process, leaving the main burden of the task at present to the United States. The resistence of the latter to the easy solution of direct capital controls should be generally appreciated.[41]

[41] *Summary Proceedings*, Annual Meeting, IMF, 1963, p. 93.

chapter two

THE OTHER SIDE OF THE COIN

In Chapter 1 we looked at the balance-of-payments problem from the side of the United States. In this chapter we turn the coin around. How does it look from the foreign side?

THREE ILLUSTRATIVE CASES

The next few paragraphs contain elementary illustrative materials which some readers may wish to skip. We shall try in this section to see how the "sticky mass" reacts to monetary transfers—how the gap between the outflow of funds and the trade balance develops. We shall consider three specific cases: (1) American foreign aid to underdeveloped countries, (2) military expenditures abroad, and (3) floating of foreign securities in the New York market. Why does the money transfer fail to produce an offsetting effect on the trade balance?

Foreign Aid Loans The United States makes an untied development loan, let us say to India. India uses the dollars to buy equipment for a new steel plant from a German manufacturing firm in Düsseldorf. The income of the Düsseldorf manufacturer, together with that of his work force and suppliers, will increase and this will tend to lead to some increase in imports, a part of which may come from the United States.

The German firm deposits the dollar draft received in payment in its Düsseldorf bank and receives German marks in exchange. The Düsseldorf bank may now do one of two things. It may already have an account in a New York bank on which it draws whenever it is called upon to sell dollar exchange to German importers. World trade is increasing, and so the Düsseldorf bank may conclude that it should increase its balance with the New York bank. The dollar holdings of the Düsseldorf bank are increased.

Alternatively the Düsseldorf bank may conclude that its dollar holdings are quite adequate. In this case it will sell its dollars for marks in the foreign exchange market. The German Central Bank, the Bundesbank, will buy these dollars if it finds it necessary to intervene in the market in order to check an appreciation of the German mark. On the basis of these increased reserves the banking system can now expand its loans and investments. Later we shall consider the monetary implications of this.

The Bundesbank now forwards the dollar draft to a New York bank for collection, and invests the balance in some highly liquid form—an interest-earning deposit account or a U.S. Treasury bill or other U.S. government security. The Bundesbank will not want to invest the dollars in long-term securities (and indeed is regulated in this matter by law) because it wants to be able to draw upon it in any emergency that might arise. There could develop an increased demand for dollar exchange from German importers or German speculators. Or the Bundesbank may fear that the dollar might possibly be devalued, and it wants to be able to turn its dollar holdings, if necessary, into gold. Indeed it may decide at once to convert into gold.

Here we encounter a fundamental problem of monetary management, namely, the effect of growing central bank holdings of international reserves upon monetary expansion and inflationary developments. Central bank credit expands *pari passu* with central bank holdings, of which gold and foreign exchange form a part. And an expansion of central bank credit provides commercial banks, as noted above, with fuel for expanding their loans and investments. Thus the accumulation of gold and foreign exchange assets by the central bank automatically sets in motion monetary expansionist forces. This is one reason why a money transfer does *tend* to affect the trade balance. Aggregate demand is increased. Employment rises. This is the *real income* effect on imports. The expansion may go so far as to produce inflationary pressure. German prices will rise in relation to the U.S. prices. This is the Keynes[1] cost-price differential effect.

All this is true. But if the economy is already at full employment, as was the case in recent years in West Germany, the

[1] I am of course referring here to the 1929 Keynes, not the 1936 Keynes, who in the *General Theory* raised the income effect to a high place in economic analysis.

central bank will wish to counteract the expansionist affect of the growing volume of foreign exchange holdings on commercial bank credit. It can do so by selling securities in the open market as an offset to the growing gold and foreign exchange holdings. Central bank credit may then fall back to where it was before. Gold and foreign exchange holdings will have gone up, but security holdings of the central bank will have gone down.

Military Expenditures Abroad A similar sequence of events could evolve in the case of U.S. military expenditures on American forces stationed in Germany. The Army buys all manner of things from German merchants and services from German railroads, public utilities, etc., to supply the needs of its troops and their families. To be sure, a part is supplied directly by shipments from the United States, but the bulk is in the form of German goods and services. German firms therefore come into possession of the dollars pumped out to pay for these military operations. They deposit these dollars in their various commercial banks. These banks will in turn add them to their New York dollar holdings, or they will cash them at the German Central Bank. German official holdings of dollars are thus increased, and some part of them may quickly be converted into gold.

It is highly probable, especially in the case of the military expenditures, that the money transfer will not show up to any large extent in the trade balance. The direct effect will be small. Military expenditures are scattered far and wide throughout the entire country and are not pointed (as might possibly be the case with the Indian loan) toward American products.

"During the period 1954–1962, the United States spent $15 billion for military purposes in Western Europe. In the same period, the Western European countries in which these expenditures were made added $13 billion to their official gold and foreign exchange reserves."[2]

Private Capital Outflow Consider finally the case of private long-term capital outflow from the United States. This might involve direct investment in factories abroad, or it might involve American purchases of foreign long-term securities. The New York capital market has a breadth and depth unmatched anywhere in the world. The United States is a capital-rich country with an enormous flow of funds seeking an outlet in profitable financial investments. The gross savings in the United States amount to some $85 billion per year. Much of this finds a direct outlet in investment in plant, equipment, and residential building, but much is afloat seeking an outlet in mortgages, state and local bond issues, corporate securities, and foreign securities.

"One of the silliest aspects of the international financial scene at the moment," said the *London Financial Times* in its July, 1963, issue, "is that the continental countries with far larger external reserves than they know what to do with, are regularly going to the New York capital market for funds to finance their development activities."[3] The U.S. payments deficits are in part due to the fact that the European capital markets are by far less perfect than the New York capital market.

European states, cities, and corporations with good credit

[2] Walter S. Salant et al., *The United States Balance of Payments in 1968*, The Brookings Institution, Washington, 1963, p. 194. The Report adds the comment that "military expenditures" was of course only one of many factors. The Report recognizes that the figures only indicate a tendency.

[3] Secretary of the Treasury Douglas Dillon referred in his address to the International Monetary Fund Annual Meeting in 1962, to the "anomaly apparent today—with borrowers in some of the surplus countries seeking credit in a deficit country." *Summary Proceedings*, 1962, pp. 41–42.

ratings float bonds easily in New York at lower rates of interest than can be found in Europe but at higher rates than American investors can expect from correspondingly good American securities. These governments and corporations convert the dollars obtained from the security flotations into their domestic currencies at their respective central banks, as explained above. The central banks become loaded up with dollar holdings. They would be happy to sell these dollars to European importers of American goods, or to European investors in American securities. But throughout the period of large U.S. payments deficits—1958 to 1963—the American economy has been running at a semidepressed level. This means that there was an excess of savings in relation to domestic investment outlets. The U.S. excess savings in part absorbed European securities. On the investment side, Europeans' surplus funds found relatively unfavorable investment outlets in the United States owing to its relatively low growth rates.

European capitalists do indeed invest in American securities, confident of America's future, but the net capital flow has been heavily the other way. And in the last dozen years European suppliers have fully recovered their competitive position. Hence there has been neither any rush to buy American securities nor any powerful urge to increase their purchase of American products. The money transfer has not been translated fully into a *real* transfer.

WHAT SURPLUS COUNTRIES CAN DO

How does it happen that West Germany, to pursue our illustration further, chose not to spend her extra dollar holdings? Why did Germany not choose to import more? Germany could have raised wages (a process which is, indeed, now going on) and cut into her extraordinary high rate of postwar profits.[4] This would have increased her imports and thereby raised her consumption standards. She could have reduced her tariffs still more and removed other restraints on imports.[5] She could have undertaken a program of domestic expansion. She could have chosen to employ her hoarded "excess" gold and dollars in foreign investment or in foreign aid loans.

All this sounds easy enough on paper, but in practice there are seemingly insurmountable obstacles as all men of affairs in politics and business know. A policy of domestic expansion in an already full employment society might bring inflationary pressures. Exporters and businessmen would vigorously oppose rapidly rising wages and encroachment on profits. And international investment is confronted with serious national barriers. If we had a truly international capital market where investment funds flowed freely, as is the case between the various regions within the United States, there would be no balance-of-payments problems. Finally, there is the much-needed foreign aid outlet. But this involves international co-operation for the achievement of world goals. It is outside of the calculus of nationalistic or business interests.

Central bankers and government officials know full well,

[4] Income distribution shifted heavily in postwar Germany. "While in 1913 and again in 1938 the lower half of the population received 23 to 24 per cent of the total income, by 1950 it received only 16 per cent. In contrast the top 5 per cent received 27 per cent. . . . Tax policy, wage policy, employment policy have operated to increase the disparity of income between the rich and the poor in Germany." See my *The American Economy*, McGraw-Hill, New York, 1957, pp. 15–16, and also the citation to Henry C. Wallich's *Mainsprings of the German Revival*, Yale, New Haven, Conn., 1955, p. 147. All this of course helped to make possible rapid capital formation and promoted reconstruction. Thus, as so often happens in economics, we encounter a tangle of conflicting goals.

[5] Germany did make unilateral tariff reductions, for example, in 1957.

however, that we are all in the same boat. This induces a certain restraint in converting dollar balances into gold. At long last it is coming more and more to be recognized that in international monetary matters, national self-interest demands a considerable degree of international cooperation. International interdependence operates to restrain official holders from pulling the trap. Yet so long as the excess holdings are not funded or are not protected by an exchange guarantee, central bankers will continue to fear devaluation.

The hoarding of international reserves is not merely a matter involving the instinctive caution of central bankers. There lurks here also the deeper issue of international politics. A surplus country holds in its hands a trump card and can in some measure call the tune. The United States is trapped, so to speak, with its balance-of-payments deficits—deficits which have emerged primarily because it has been pouring out vast sums for foreign aid and for the security of the free world. Monetary explosives could threaten the unity of the free world. In the final analysis, however, the United States occupies a position of strength by reason of the unquestioned fact that without the continual maintenance of the dollar price of gold, the highly prized gold hoards would lose most of their value.

WHAT DEFICIT COUNTRIES CAN DO

Could the large U.S. deficits (and European surpluses) of the last several years have been prevented by vigorous action on the part of the United States?[6] Yes, of course they could

[6] Some may say we could have kept inflation down. Yet here our record with respect to the cost of living and the GNP deflator is better than that of Western Europe but not so good with respect to export prices. We could, it is said, have pushed exports harder. This is easier said than done. We have indeed stepped up our export promotion program. In consequence of the experience gained in the

if sufficiently drastic measures had been taken—measures that many countries do not hesitate to employ. But the question always arises: Would it be worth the price both to ourselves and to the world? The United States could, for example, have raised its tariffs, imposed import quotas, introduced exchange control, restricted tourist expenditures abroad, and limited the sales of foreign securities in the New York capital market. The United States could have managed quite well acting by itself, if prepared to sacrifice the goals of freedom of trade and free exchange. These policies would have hurt us, and they would have hurt foreign countries even more.

In fact the United States has instituted some relatively mild measures to protect its balance of payments. But drastic measures have been avoided. Instead it has let the gold flow out. This has been, I believe, the correct policy. Drastic measures by deficit countries can scarcely fail to disrupt the established structure of industry and trade. In the short run a serious disequilibrium cannot quickly be met on trade lines without causing grave dislocations in the world economy. In contrast efforts to remedy any international imbalance by surplus countries can often have a salutory effect. As we have seen, however, such action raises difficult domestic problems which make it hard to act. It follows from all this that international credit arrangements may need to be devised to take the shock and to give time for a gradual adjustment of the trade structure, or to create conditions favorable to an offsetting capital flow. Herein lies the heart of any international monetary reform.

So, looking at the other side of the coin the surplus coun-

---

postwar reconstruction Americans have greatly increased their knowledge of European countries and indeed of countries round the globe. Our exporters are not yet as expert or aggressive as the knowledgeable European exporter. Still, in terms of "export know-how," Americans have surely reduced somewhat the former gap. On the other side, the Europeans have gained in mass-production techniques.

tries allowed things to drift and the United States took no drastic action. As dollar outpourings increased, trade did indeed respond but not adequately. Trade lagged behind and deficits developed.

DOLLARS OR GOLD

This being the case, a choice had to be made. The surplus countries could take payment either in dollar holdings or in gold. Dollar holdings could be invested in short-term earning assets—deposits, U.S. Treasury bills and other U.S. government securities. Gold, on the other hand, is an unearning asset. But gold throughout history has been a safe bet. The price of gold in London has increased tenfold in the last 600 years. But this represents a very poor long-term investment, only about one-half of one per cent per year.

Narrow, nationalistic interests appear to have weighed heavily in favor of gold. But the more the surplus countries took payment in gold, the more the likelihood increased that massive speculation might force dollar devaluation. In the whole postwar period, however, the entire fabric of international trade and prosperity has been built up on the dollar. The short-run nationalistic interests of the surplus countries might vote for central bank gold hoarding. But the longer-run interests might advisedly cast the vote for dollar holdings even though this involved some pecuniary risk—a risk however which has to be weighed against the loss of interest earnings incurred when reserves are held in the form of gold.

I repeat that we must not overlook the undoubted fact that the postwar world has witnessed by far more responsible international cooperation than earlier periods in monetary history. A program of international monetary collaboration is in fact gradually being built up. But it is only a beginning.

Granting all these qualifications, and without wishing to

make invidious comparisons, it is of interest to note how the surplus countries have in fact weighed the relative risks involved. The answer can be found in a measure in the *changes* in the ratio of central bank gold holdings relative to their holdings of aggregate reserves.

Immediately, when attention is turned to the matter of gold ratios, it becomes evident that the countries of the free world fall into four classes: (1) the United States and the United Kingdom; (2) the Common Market countries plus Switzerland; (3) the Scandinavian countries, Canada, and Japan; and (4) all other countries of the free world, largely the underdeveloped countries. The gold ratios (per cent of reserves held in gold) for these four groups were as follows in 1963:[7]

	Per cent
The United States and United Kingdom	98
Common Market and Switzerland	70
Scandinavia, Canada, and Japan	21
All other countries	32

From 1953 to 1963, the Common Market countries plus Switzerland increased their gold holdings more than threefold, the United States lost gold, while the rest of the free

[7] Sweden with a 25 per cent gold ratio, Norway with 9 per cent, and Denmark with around 27 per cent are especially interesting cases. They are all comparatively rich countries that could well afford to hold large gold reserves if prudence so dictated. Sweden, Canada, and Japan are all members of the "Group of Ten" leading industrial countries, and of this group they alone show no interest in holding large gold reserves. In the meantime they are accumulating year by year substantial "profits" from the interest earnings on their foreign exchange holdings. In contrast it would require a very large devaluation of the dollar to offset the "losses" which the Common Market countries and Switzerland have already sustained in the postwar period by reason of their large holdings of unearning gold reserves. At a 3 per cent interest rate it would require a 35 per cent devaluation of the dollar every ten years. Is there any prudent banker who would really regard this as a good bet?

world barely maintained their holdings. In 1963, the key-currency countries held $18.3 billion of gold, the Common Market and Switzerland held $14.4 billion, and all other countries together held only $6.5 billion.[8]

So the whole matter of gold drains revolves essentially around the six Continental high-gold-ratio countries.[9] These are the countries whose surpluses are the counterpart of the U.S. balance-of-payments deficits. We are therefore particularly concerned, at this point in our analysis, with the disposition which these countries have made of their surpluses. What part has been taken out in gold, and what part in liquid dollar holdings?

From Table 2-1 a rating can be made of the six Continental large gold-holding countries, West Germany, France, Italy, Belgium, Holland, and Switzerland.

From this table one obtains a rough appraisal of the propensity of these central banks to hoard gold and to shift to gold holdings. In three countries the gold ratios were very high throughout the period, and in three countries (West Germany, Italy, Holland) the ratios were sharply increased. High and rising gold ratios indicate a tendency to emphasize short-run, nationalistic interests and suggest a certain lack of international cooperation. Using an unweighted average for all six countries together the gold ratio increased from 60 per cent to 75 per cent from 1953 to 1963. The aggregate gold holdings increased 243 per cent in this decade, while the foreign exchange holdings increased about 100 per cent. After 1958 foreign exchange holdings increased little or not at all except for France.

[8] Taking *all* foreign countries into account, holdings of gold and dollar exchange (including private holdings) increased by $26 billion from 1953 to 1962. Of this $5 billion came from new gold production, $7 billion from U.S. gold stocks, and $14 billion from increased dollar holdings. Sterling balances meanwhile remained substantially stable.

[9] Luxenbourg and Belgium are statistically regarded as one country.

Could these central banks have acted collectively there would no doubt have been a greater recognition of the danger of rocking the international monetary boat—a greater appreciation of the longer-run benefits that come from international cooperation. Instead, each central bank acted pretty much on its own and on these terms sought its own short-run self-interest. The index of central bank gold hoardings displayed

Table 2-1. *Official Gold and Foreign Exchange**
(end of period)

	Gold holdings (in billions of dollars)			*Foreign exchange (in billions of dollars)*		
	1953	*1958*	*1963*	*1953*	*1958*	*1963*
West Germany	$0.3	$2.6	$ 3.8	$1.4	$3.1	$3.3
France	0.6	0.8	3.2	0.2	0.3	1.3
Italy	0.3	1.1	2.3	0.4	1.0	0.7
Switzerland	1.5	1.9	2.8	0.3	0.1	0.2
Belgium	0.8	1.3	1.4	0.3	0.2	0.4
Holland	0.7	1.1	1.6	0.4	0.4	0.3
All six countries	$4.2	$8.8	$15.1	$3.0	$5.1	$6.2

* Compiled from *International Financial Statistics*, August, 1963, pp. 17–18. These six countries not only hold large gold ratios; they also hold large reserves relative to imports. For 1963 their ratio of reserves to imports was 49 per cent. In contrast the reserve holdings of the Scandinavian countries was only 22 per cent of their imports.

in Table 2-1 points convincingly to the need for an improved structure of international monetary collaboration.

The unexpected large dollar deficits beginning in 1958 left the United States dazed and bewildered. And this was no less true of the central banks of Western Europe. A serious storm appeared to be brewing, and the orthodox shelter was gold. Professor Bent Hansen, in his distinguished *Central Bank of*

Egypt Lectures (1962) said that we should not forget that it was precisely the European central banks which in 1960 hoarded gold acquired from the United States and thereby created the 1960 dollar crisis. This blunt statement is well supported by the facts. The Common Market countries[10] plus Switzerland added $1.9 billion to their gold holdings from the end of 1959 to the end of 1960, while the United States lost $1.7 billion. But they learned a lesson. Already in December, 1961, the "general arrangements to borrow" was concluded in Paris and finally ratified in October, 1962.

The various dollar crises of the last half-dozen years occurred against the background of the large U.S. payments deficits of 1958 to 1963. But the immediate impulse that produced the crisis in each case was the gold drains and the fears they gave rise to. International cooperation was indeed hastily engineered to help weather the storm. But such co-operation came after the event, not before, and for the most part the cooperation consisted of ad hoc arrangements. This is not the way to deal with so serious a problem as the stability of international monetary relations. To be sure we are far and away in advance of the chaotic interwar period. The International Monetary Fund, together with the subsidiary arrangements it has helped to engineer, place us on firmer ground than before. Still we need a structure which can not only effectively meet crises, if and when they arise, but more importantly can help to *prevent* crises.

[10] The main gold hoarders in the year 1960 were Italy, France, the Netherlands, and Switzerland which together added $1.5 billion gold to their reserves from the end of 1959 to the end of 1960. Italy in particular absorbed $454 million of gold and at the same time reduced her foreign exchange holdings by $328 million.

chapter three

GOLD HOARDING

PRIVATE HOLDINGS OF FOREIGN EXCHANGE

Dealings in foreign exchange are carried on by private banks and traders. Banks dealing in foreign exchange have on hand a till-box supply of foreign currencies for tourists etc. More important, however, are the working balances which they hold in foreign correspondent banks in the form of demand deposits, time deposits or short-term government securities. These liquid funds—currencies, deposits, and government securities—constitute the international medium of exchange which is turned over and over and passed from trader to trader and bank to bank in the settlement of transactions across international borders.

Purchases of goods, services, securities, and assets draw down these working balances. Sales abroad refill them. The aggregate volume of transactions in any one year is financed by an average quantity of working balances multiplied by the "transactions velocity." This is the international equation of exchange. If we denote the value of all international transactions at T,[1] the average quantity of working foreign exchange balances as M, and the transactions velocity as V, we get the familiar equation $M = T/V$ applied in this case to the international sphere.

This equation suggests that as trade grows there will be (within limits imposed by feasible variations in V) a growing need for private foreign exchange working balances. There is, indeed, no exact relation between our M and T. The old rigid quantity theory does not hold. But just as there is a relation (within limits) between the volume of domestic transactions and the need for domestic money, so is there one between the size of international trade and the need for international money. It has been suggested that as domestic or foreign trade increases all that is required is enlarged credit facilities in national currencies.[2] This would seem to imply that if there is enough domestic money, there will automatically be enough international money and, therefore, there can be no such thing as a shortage of international liquidity.

The market-exchange economy does indeed automatically produce, without deliberate creation of foreign exchange, working balances of foreign currencies. New gold is produced and sold in exchange for a domestic currency. The buyer has

[1] Note that T as used here means the *money* value of transactions.

[2] See *Monthly Review*, Federal Reserve Bank of New York, p. 115, August, 1963.

acquired new international money. A foreign trader may sell goods to a firm in the United States and receive payment in dollars. As soon as these dollars fall into the possession of the foreign trader they become international money. The change in ownership has transformed domestic money into foreign exchange. If these dollar holdings are spent on American goods, the foreign exchange is used up and disappears. If they are not spent, the United States will have a payments deficit. Thus the volume of foreign exchange can grow partly from gold production and partly from the payments deficits of key-currency countries.

It is often said that, apart from net additions to monetary gold, the only way in which international reserves can be increased is through U.S. or U.K. payments deficits.[3] But this statement is likely to be seriously misleading. In addition to the ordinary trading transactions (and quite apart from any increase in IMF quotas or new units created by a new international credit-creating bank), foreign exchange can deliberately be created by governmental borrowing in foreign capital markets or from foreign central banks for the specific purpose of acquiring foreign exchange.

International transactions, purchases, and sales across international borders, will more or less tend to balance out in each trading country. But there is little likelihood that a perfect balance will occur. There will almost always be deficits or surpluses. If a country wishes to maintain a fixed rate of exchange in terms of gold, and if it tends to run deficits, it may have to restrict private transactions in order to maintain a balance. It could impose import quotas, restrict tourist expenditures, ration the supply of foreign exchange available to importers, etc. But if the country wishes to maintain freedom in private dealings across international borders, it will have to authorize its central bank to accumulate a supply of *official*

[3] Or payments deficits of some other reserve currency country.

international monetary reserves which can be tapped by private dealers when they run out of foreign funds.

OFFICIAL RESERVES

The amounts of foreign exchange held by private dealers are, as noted above, "*working* balances," sufficient to meet day-to-day requirements. The official gold and foreign exchange holdings are properly speaking "*reserve* balances." They are available on call in the event that an overall deficit occurs in the buying and selling operations of private traders. If, on the other hand, a surplus develops in the private transactions, dealers in foreign exchange will find that they may hold an excess of foreign exchange—more than is required for working balances. These dealers may then wish to sell their foreign exchange to the central bank against their country's own currency. The central bank therefore becomes a sort of reservoir in which a reserve is stored that can be tapped when needed and in which gold and foreign exchange can be stored when surpluses develop.

So long as gold constituted the whole of international reserves the problem was simply a matter of the aggregate quantity of the world's monetary gold and how it was distributed. Was there enough to tide countries over temporary imbalances? These imbalances could be due to (1) seasonal, cyclical, or special episodic events or (2) structural changes in demand and supply conditions caused by the introduction of new products or new techniques of production. The former, being temporary, could fairly easily be taken care of; the latter might require considerable time to effect structural adjustments such as the development of new industries, etc. Such were the problems in the past.

But now two developments have profoundly changed the picture. First, the causes of imbalance are no longer related merely to demand and supply conditions arising in the private sector. Since 1914 vast funds have been transferred across international borders by governments—war loans, reparation payments, foreign aid grants and loans, military expenditures abroad, etc. These amounts have been so vast as to preclude the possibility of quick adjustments in the trade balance or in the private capital account balance. Second, as became evident after World War I, the world's gold supply has not been increasing rapidly enough. For one thing much of it was hoarded. Even allowing for hoarding, gold production has not kept pace with the growing needs of world trade and other international transactions. Several measures were taken to economize on gold. Gold coin was withdrawn from circulation. Gold was freed for international use by reducing the gold cover for domestic currencies. And finally, countries were encouraged (Genoa Conference of 1922) to keep a part of their international reserves in the form of foreign exchange, specifically in liquid dollar and sterling holdings.

The latter device could clearly cause trouble. The United States and United Kingdom would of course be compelled to stand ready to pay out gold or the whole structure of stable exchange rates would totter. Hence, assuming that gold production was inadequate, the system could function only if the *surplus* countries were prepared to take payment not in gold but in the form of liquid dollar and sterling holdings.[4] The more they did this, the greater the ratio of foreign exchange holdings to gold holdings. The greater the ratio, the more shaky the gold-exchange structure became. There seemed to be no escape except to end somehow the persistent dollar and sterling deficits. But if this were achieved, we should then have to shift back, in the absence of deliberate policy, to the bare bones, so to speak, of the gold standard

[4] Holdings of sterling balances have remained fixed at about 7 or 8 billion dollars during the last decade.

with its inadequate growth of international reserves. It is against the background of this dilemma that we shall consider the problem of gold hoarding.

As is well known, most of the leading countries of Western Europe have acquired in recent years an "excess" of dollar balances over and above the needed working balances. Yet it is exactly the countries that are supplying the growing volume of foreign exchange which are also the countries that are short of foreign exchange. The United States and the United Kingdom do not possess sufficient international reserves to offset comfortably the heavy intermittent raids on the dollar and the pound sterling. The dollar, in particular, has persistently been under pressure. The United States does not hold enough gold and foreign currencies to feel fully at ease. It is like a bank whose cash holdings are always a bit short of the potentially pressing demands of its depositors. Being short of cash, the United States has at times found it necessary to fall back upon ad hoc credit arrangements with foreign central banks. The United Kingdom is, though somewhat more sporadically, in a similar position. Yet, apart from gold, it is in these two currencies that most of the world's trade and financial transactions are carried on.

The underdeveloped countries are always short of international reserves. Here the real trouble is much more serious and deep-seated than merely to be short of cash. These countries are capital-poor. In contrast, the aggregate wealth of the United States government and its citizens is around $2,000 billion,[5] not including a large stock of financial assets invested in foreign countries. Underdeveloped countries are poor both in capital assets and in international monetary reserves. Being poor in capital, they cannot afford to hold large quantities of cash in the form of either gold or foreign exchange. Imports are always so desperately needed that any available funds are

[5] *U.S. Statistical Abstract.*

quickly used up. The basic need underlying their international payments difficulties is an adequate inflow of long-term capital from the rich countries of the Western world.

THE ROLE OF GOLD

International cash still consists very largely of gold. Gold was incorporated as an integral part of the international monetary mechanism devised at Bretton Woods. Formerly it was thought to be an indispensable instrument for the management of the domestic money supply no less than for international payments. That day is past. Gold no longer controls the domestic money supply of any leading industrial country. Everywhere deliberate monetary management has taken the place of the automatic gold standard.

In 1860 somewhat more than one-half of the money supply in the United States consisted of metallic money—gold and silver. Today $12 billion of gold satisfies the legally required 25 per cent ratio of gold to the note and deposit liabilities of the Federal Reserve Banks. Resting on this slim margin of gold holdings (i.e., the 25 per cent required gold reserve), is the vast superstructure of currency and demand deposits which constitutes the money supply—$30 billion of Federal Reserve notes and $210 billion of demand deposits. Thus the currently required gold backing amounts in fact to only about 8 per cent of the aggregate domestic money supply.

Actually that 25 per cent ratio is an anachronism—a hangover from the era of metallic money and the gold standard. The money supply in the United States is no longer controlled by this slender gold base. It is controlled by the managers of the Federal Reserve System.

Although gold is no longer of any significant importance to the domestic supply of money, this is far from being the case with respect to the international monetary reserves. Currently the international monetary reserves held by the central banks and governments of the non-Communist world consist of about $42 billion of gold and around $22 billion of foreign exchange holdings. The foreign exchange holdings of Continental Europe and the non-sterling underdeveloped countries consist primarily of U.S. dollars. The foreign exchange holdings of the sterling area (including parts of Asia and Africa) consist of sterling. These holdings are, as noted above, in the form of deposits in New York and London banks, short-term Treasury bills, certificates, notes, and longer-term U.S. and U.K. government securities. The aggregate foreign official holdings amounted to about 15 billion U.S. dollars in 1963 and around 7 to 8 billion dollars worth of U.K. pounds sterling.

Obviously we are still living close to the nineteenth century as far as international money is concerned. Gold constitutes today about two-thirds of the total international monetary reserves. In short, while we have achieved managed domestic currencies we have not yet achieved a truly managed international currency.

Moreover the figures given above minimize the real role of gold in the current international world. This is true because the whole system of international exchange revolves primarily around the leading industrial nations. Eight industrial countries (United States, United Kingdom, France, West Germany, Italy, Switzerland, Belgium, and the Netherlands) held nearly $35 billion[6] of the aggregate $42 billion of monetary gold (including IMF holdings) in 1963. Using a slightly different classification, Continental Europe, the United Kingdom, and the United States held in 1963 about $37 billion of the world's monetary gold stock.[7] Contrast this with the

[6] The gold holdings of the International Monetary Fund are here included. See International Financial Statistics, IMF.

[7] Of this total the United States held $15.8 billion, and the United Kingdom $2.5 billion.

relatively small amounts of official foreign exchange held by all these countries combined. More than 80 per cent of the international money supply held by the central banks and governments of the advanced industrialized Western world consists of gold.

Obviously gold still rules the roost in international exchange. It is therefore not to be wondered at that, whenever the problem of an adequate supply of international reserves comes up for consideration, one leading proposal is to raise the monetary price of gold. Sir Roy Harrod, the leading proponent of this policy, urges a doubling of the price of gold. If this were done, the free world's monetary gold stock would rise to $84 billion. Including the official foreign exchange holdings, the aggregate supply would have risen to $106 billion, this in a world in which aggregate import trade amounts to about $130 billion.

PRIVATE GOLD HOARDS

But not all the world's gold supply is in the monetary pot. A considerable amount is held in private hoards. From 1953 to 1963 the aggregate increase in the monetary gold stock was only $5.3 billion. But aggregate gold production in this decade amounted to $10.6 billion and reported Russian sales to $1.6 billion.[8] Thus more than half of the new gold went into hoards and to some small extent into industrial uses. Nobody knows, however, how much is held in private hoards, but some estimates place it at well above $15 billion.

It would therefore seem that those who wish to increase the world's monetary liquidity via the route of increasing the supply of monetary gold should be interested in ways and means of drawing the vast stocks of hoarded gold into the monetary gold pot.

[8] IMF Annual Report, 1963, p. 169.

However there is a far more important issue at stake here than that of merely increasing the monetary gold stock. The gold hoards do more than hold out of use a large stock of gold, harmful as this obviously is to the world economy so long as international liquidity depends heavily on gold. The impact of private gold hoarders upon short-term speculative capital movements—the problem of "hot money" is even more harmful. It is perhaps fair to say that the American people would not have been particularly worried about the U.S. deficits in its balance of payments during the last six years (1958 to 1963) were it not for the loss of a large part of our gold reserves, a part of which loss went into private hoards.

It is difficult to see how anyone can deny that private gold hoarding is, under existing international monetary conditions, a serious evil which should be eradicated if at all possible. The International Monetary Fund in its 1960 Report said unequivocally: "It is in the interest of the Fund members that gold should be available in official reserves rather than go into private hoards." The Fund Report commented in this connection on the fact that many countries have granted more freedom for the sale of gold in free markets, both within countries and between countries, and that this has facilitated the flow of gold into private hoards.

THE NEW DEAL GOLD POLICY

What could be done to end private gold hoarding? An obvious method would be for the IMF and all its members to agree to adopt precisely the policy which was put into effect by the United States thirty-years ago in the Administration of President Franklin Roosevelt and extended in January, 1961, by President Eisenhower. Early in the New Deal, Congress authorized the Secretary of the Treasury to require every person in the United States to relinquish, in exchange for dollar currency, all gold coins, gold bullion and gold certificates in his possession. Already by the end of March, 1933, the public, in response to this compulsory, enforced cashing-in of gold, had surrendered $200 million of gold, and another $30 million or so was relinquished during April. Thereafter small driblets came in. The whole operation was carried through quickly and expeditiously. The President declared that the title to all gold rested with the government. Gold was no longer coined and all gold was by law withdrawn from circulation. Gold could, however, be employed by the Federal Reserve System for international payment. The monetary authorities, under the provision of the Gold Reserve Act of 1934, were empowered to sell gold for industrial uses and for export at one-fourth of 1 per cent above the declared par value of $35 per oz, and to buy gold at one-fourth of 1 per cent below $35 per oz. Gold for export was to be delivered to foreign central banks.

On January 14, 1961, President Eisenhower issued an executive order which prohibited any U.S. private citizen or U.S. owned corporation from purchasing and holding gold *outside* the United States. The order moreover required U.S. citizens and corporations to sell any gold (or securities representing gold) held abroad by not later than June 1, 1961.

There is good reason to believe that private gold hoarding could be virtually eliminated if an agreement could be made through the IMF between all its members requisitioning all gold held within the borders of each country and prohibiting the purchase and sale of gold except between central banks and government treasuries, and for industrial uses.

Said Robert V. Roosa, the Under Secretary of the Treasury: "Perhaps in an ideal world the interrelated monetary systems would function even better if private individuals were not allowed to own gold in any country, and if no London gold market existed."[9]

It would be difficult to think of any control measure that is easier to enforce than a law prescribing hoarding and dealings in gold. A gold hoarder could of course keep his gold indefinitely and might never be found out. But he would have no legal sales outlet. He could presumably sell his gold secretly to an industrial user, but this market would be severely limited. There would be no place to go except to sell to the monetary authorities.[10] He could do this under the requisitioning law and obtain full par value for his gold if he relinquished his holdings within the proclaimed time limit. If he gave up his gold later than the date set by law, he would suffer a penalty loss. Under these conditions there can be little doubt that the gold hoards would quickly be recovered for monetary use, precisely as was the case in the American experience.

Some might object that in certain countries a large proportion of the population wish to speculate in gold. There are, however, plenty of interesting and legal ways to gamble. Gold hoarding is something more than a mere gambling device. It imposes a continual threat to international monetary stability. It would be ludicrous, were it not so serious, that powerful nations tremble in fear of petty gold speculators. That great nations continue to protect and even encourage this antisocal activity would be incredible were it not an obvious present fact.

[9] *Compilation of Studies Prepared for the Subcommittee on International Exchange and Payments*, Part 5, p. 349.

[10] See the excellent statement by Per Åsbrink (Riksbankschef and the Swedish representative in the IMF Board of Governors) in the *Proceedings* of the 1963 Annual Meeting, pp. 125–128. Among other things note the following: "It seems by no means self evident that private hoarders should indirectly have the privilege of getting that price (i.e., the $35 per oz.) whenever it pleases them to dispose of their hoards." The U.S. Treasury, he said, could reserve its purchase price "for gold that is newly mined."

Critics may say that the prohibition of private gold hoarding amounts to confiscation of private property. This is clearly not the case. In the United States all citizens who responded to the compulsory cashing-in of gold were fully compensated for the surrendered gold. And gold mining companies could continue to sell newly mined gold at the par value rate. No property rights were expropriated. In any event no government guarantees the price of any asset, not even gold. Any sovereign government is free to change, up or down, the price of gold, and governments have frequently done so.

THE MACHLUP PLAN

A second possible method of eliminating gold hoarding would be to adopt the Fritz Machlup plan. Machlup proposes that the official buying price of gold should be reduced in a series of steps as follows: "If the leading monetary authorities of the free world were to reduce, over a period of several years, the price of gold by, say, three-fourths of 1 per cent every three months, one could expect that several billion dollars' worth of gold would be de-hoarded and offered for sale to the monetary authorities."[11]

GOLD ON AN ESCALATOR

Another proposal, aimed among other things at drawing out hidden hoards, paradoxically operates in exactly the opposite direction. Machlup's plan aims to eliminate hoards by *lowering* systematically the buying price of gold. The Miyata-Wonnacott plan (independently arrived at) aims to eliminate gold speculation by systematically *raising* the price

[11] See *Factors Affecting the U.S. Balance of Payments,* Joint Economic Committee, 87th Cong., 2d Sess., Part 3, p. 226.

of gold by small gradations which would be announced beforehand so as to remove any uncertainty about the future price of gold.[12] The government would make a firm declaration setting forth a definite program of periodic small increases. The annual percentage increases would have to be less than the short-term interest rate, say one-half of 1 per cent each quarter, or 1 per cent every six months. Since gold would appreciate under this plan by less than the interest rate, gold speculators could make no profits from the periodic increases in the monetary price of gold.

The success of the plan rests on the assumption that a firm declaration announcing the policy and stating definitely the precise period in which it would be carried out, five years for example, would end speculative hopes of any large devaluation which could yield substantial profits for gold hoarders. If such hopes could be disposed of, all hoarding induced by rumors of a major devaluation would stop and de-hoarding would begin.

Such a policy could presumably be carried out unilaterally by any member of the IMF if the aggregate increase in the price of gold did not exceed the limit of 10 per cent imposed by the Bretton Woods Agreement. But it might have little significance unless done by the United States, and the United States as the main key-currency country has a special obligation to maintain the monetary price of gold. A slow, gradual, and pre-announced devaluation of the dollar might possibly be less disturbing to international stability than a single sharp increase in the dollar price of gold. Moreover, under a step-by-step plan, announced in advance, forward markets would tend to smooth out the price increase.

[12] *Ibid.*, p. 228. K. Miyata is a Japanese economist and P. Wonnacott is the author of *The Canadian Dollar, 1948–1958* (University of Toronto Press, Toronto, 1961) and associate Professor of Economics at the University of Maryland.

WIDENING THE GOLD POINTS

An alternative plan would be to increase the selling price of gold one-half of 1 per cent every six months and at the same time reduce the buying price of gold every six months by one-half of 1 per cent. This would put a double squeeze on the gold speculator—(1) the removal of any chance of making profit out of a large devaluation and (2) the systematic reduction in the buying price of gold. This plan would amount to a progressive widening of the U.S. gold buying and selling support prices. It would tend to increase uncertainty since the market ratio of gold to the dollar could move either up or down. This would increase the risks of speculation and reduce possible gains derived from gold hoarding.

THE PIQUET PLAN

Still another proposal[13] that would certainly put a damper on gold speculation and gold hoarding is the Piquet Plan which would involve a major overhauling of the Bretton Woods Agreement. Under this scheme the U.S. government would announce that while it will continue to adhere firmly to its commitment to sell gold at $35.0875 per oz in unlimited quantities, it will no longer guarantee to buy gold at $34.9125 an oz, though for the time being it might continue to do so. In short, the United States would no longer commit itself to uphold the value of gold. The mere announcement of this change in policy might frighten gold hoarders enough to bring out the gold hoards. Gold would become a drag on the market. The United States would sell gold, but it would not buy gold. The United States would be prepared to face

[13] Howard Piquet, Legislative Reference Service, The Library of Congress. *Factors Affecting the U.S. Balance of Payments,* Joint Economic Committee, 87th Cong., 2d Sess.

unflinchingly the possibility of losing most or indeed all of its gold stock.

THE LERNER PLAN[14]

Abba Lerner has proposed a similar plan. The U.S. government should announce, he says, that it will no longer buy any gold. If done unilaterally this would violate our current international commitments under the Bretton Woods Agreement and would be a breach of faith. Barring that, it would require a new international agreement designed to substitute an entirely new system for the current gold–dollar standard.

Lerner's plan could however be instituted gradually without any breach of faith. We could quite legally sell our gold to foreign central banks but not below the currently fixed price. Since foreign banks are apparently fairly eager to change their dollar holdings into gold, we could undoubtedly dispose of a large part of our $15 billion gold stock. Just how much is, however, problematical. Gold is an unearning asset, and it is by no means unlikely that after disposing of say $5 billion or so the "marginal utility" of an interest-earning dollar might rise above the marginal utility of an unearning gold dollar. But again, maybe not. Perhaps we could sell all our gold, though I think this is very doubtful. At all events Lerner would probably be satisfied if we just simply stop trying to check the outflow of gold. This might ultimately, he would hope, completely exhaust our gold supply.

Some would of course argue that once we let go, the gold stock would quickly flow out. Speculators would seize the reins and drive the dollar down in a mad race to get rid of dollars as fast as possible.

Let us suppose that the proposal to get rid of all our gold somehow works out. What then? If the United States acts

[14] Unpublished manuscript circulated by the author.

unilaterally and dumps all its gold on the market, it could perhaps be assumed that gold might lose most, if not all, of its monetary value. Should this happen international monetary reserves would have dropped to less than half their former volume leaving little more than the foreign exchange balances. A great shortage of international liquidity would ensue. With gold wholly or largely out of the picture a great scramble for some highly esteemed, eagerly sought for currency would develop. Lerner argues that the United States should and could put in a bid for the first place. It could achieve this by setting up a new U.S. dollar with fixed purchasing power in terms of goods and services as measured by a "specified index number." This highly stable dollar (if achieved) would eagerly be sought after by all countries. The net effect would be an appreciation of the dollar in terms of foreign currencies. This would cause U.S. exports to fall and U.S. imports to rise. The gigantic U.S. deficits that would develop would be large enough to satisfy the world's demand for liquidity. Thus Lerner's solution of the current U.S. payments deficits is to create still larger deficits—this time not primarily through grants, loans, and capital outflows, but through enlarged net imports. But with gold out, we would no longer worry about these deficits. And the U.S. deficit would supply the world with ample international liquidity. So runs the Lerner argument.[15]

[15] In the December 24, 1960 issue of the *London Economist* there appeared what might be termed a "Gold Fable," the gist of which was as follows: In March, 1961, so goes the fable, the U.S. gold stock fell below $16 billion. That no more than two-fifths of the world's gold should be buried under the United States naturally shook everyone's confidence. The dollar price of gold shot up to $49. Then came the thunderbolt. The Federal Reserve announced that its undertaking to buy and sell gold at $35 per oz had lapsed. Immediately the IMF undertook, up to Dec. 31, 1961, to buy gold at $35 per oz, from central bankers who received in return deposits with the Fund. Gold flowed into the Fund from all quarters. Visiting finance ministers were

Suppose now, however, that the U.S. loss of gold took a route so gradual that gold did not lose its monetary value. A violent redistribution of reserves would however have taken place. The United States would have lost nearly all its reserves, and foreign monetary authorities would have increased their gold holdings by about $15 billion. Presumably most or all of the gold would have gone to the gold-hungry Continental European central banks. What then would the United States do for reserves?

This alternative possibility is not considered by Lerner. Presumably the United States would have to try to float securities on European markets to obtain foreign currencies. Swap agreements with central banks would be of little value for this purpose since they would provide only short-term credits.

Lerner's "solid dollar" is based on his firm conviction that the United States can and should adopt a program of rigid price stability. He does not tell us whether this price index is to be the deflated GNP price index, the consumer price index, or the wholesale price index. This is a highly important and difficult problem and cannot just be assumed as easily agreed upon. And finally, many economists question the wisdom of a policy of rigid stability. They accept a policy of reasonable price stability but are prepared to play this tune by ear.

Moreover, as all the world knows, it is easy to plump for price stability but no easy matter to ensure its maintenance even within fairly wide limits. No country has ever succeeded

---

comforted to see the bars of gold stacked high in the Fund's vaults. Later, as an economy move, the gold was sold to dentists for $2.50 per oz. It was explained to the public that money is whatever the public chose to accept as such, and everybody was happy except a few central bankers who had to be sent to a Zurich nursing home. So endeth the fable!

in maintaining a rigidly fixed price index. Lerner recognizes this and would put his price–index dollar on an escalator. He would indemnify all foreign holders, every quarter, for any losses sustained if the price–index dollar had depreciated.

A GOLD–VALUE GUARANTEE

Finally, there is a completely different approach to the problem of official gold hoarding, namely, a gold-value guarantee. I suggest two possible plans: (1) a full-scale gold-value guarantee[16] and (2) a risk-sharing scheme.

With respect to the first plan, let the United States offer to all official holders of dollar balances a firm gold-exchange guarantee under which losses sustained by official holders in the event of a future devaluation of the dollar would be fully compensated.[17] To ensure complete confidence in this ex-

[16] See statement by Professor Gottfried Haberler, "The State and Prospects of the American Economy," *Lloyds Bank Review,* 1961, in which he supports an exchange guarantee.

[17] See my letter of December 21, 1960, to the *New York Times,* as follows:

To the Editor of the *New York Times:*

Two proposals with respect to the gold problem, recently put forward by two distinguished representatives of the financial community, deserve the most careful attention of the incoming Administration. To these I now wish to add still another suggestion.

The two proposals to which I refer are as follows:

1. That the 25% gold cover against the note and deposit liabilities of the Federal Reserve Banks be repealed. This suggestion was made by Mr. Roy Reiersen (*N.Y. Times*, Nov. 19, 1959) and more recently by Mr. Henry Alexander, Chairman of Morgan Guaranty Trust. Such action would free the $12 billion of gold now completely immobilized, thus making the entire gold stock of $18 billion available as international reserves.
2. That American citizens, who now are forbidden by law to hoard gold within the territory of the United States, should

change guarantee, let the U.S. government pledge that all the gold profits made by the U.S. Treasury from the devaluation would be applied to indemnify the losses suffered by foreign official holders of dollar balances.

Any losses in excess of the U.S. gold profits could further be guaranteed by the U.S. depositing with the IMF a U.S. gov-

---

also be prohibited from hoarding gold abroad. It is said on good authority that the recent speculation in gold abroad was primarily the work of American gold hoarders. A law prohibiting such action by American citizens has recently been proposed by Mr. Alexander. [In January, 1961, this was put into effect by an executive order issued by President Eisenhower.]

These two suggestions are of the utmost importance and should at once be adopted by the Congress. I wish now to add a third. There remains the danger that foreign central banks and Governments might, under certain circumstances, feel duty-bound (as agents responsible to their own countries) to convert their dollar balances into gold, even though, as members of the free-world international community, they would certainly be reluctant to do so. We could, however, completely avert this danger by making a firm exchange guarantee in terms of gold to all foreign governments and central bank holders of dollar balances. This would protect them against any possible loss arising from any future increase in the dollar price of gold.

A mere statement by the President or the Secretary of the Treasury that the United States will not devalue the dollar is not adequately convincing under all circumstances. We should not hesitate to back such a statement with a firm exchange guarantee. If we mean what we say, such a guarantee could not cost us anything. Such a guarantee would remove completely any alarmist fears which might lead to conversion of dollar balances into gold, and would thereby remove all danger of a forced devaluation.

There is good precedent for this. The European Monetary Agreement guarantees payment to all members in gold. This means that if the United Kingdom, for example, should devalue the pound vis-à-vis the dollar, all central bank members of the European Monetary Agreement holding sterling balances arising out of operations under the agreement would be guaranteed against losses arising from such devaluation.

A modified version of this proposal might possibly be considered.

ernment security adequate to cover all losses of official holders. Such a security would need to carry no interest, but it would be marketable at full face value at the moment of devaluation. And finally, in the highly doubtful event that any claim might still result despite all these precautions, the United States would agree in advance to submit such claims for adjudication by the International Court at The Hague.

The U.S. Government could offer a firm exchange guarantee to any foreign Government and central bank which would voluntarily, in consideration of such an exchange guarantee, make a premium contribution to an Exchange Insurance Fund established by the U.S. Government. Just as in the case of the Federal Housing Administration the guarantee of mortgages is protected by an insurance fund, so here an insurance fund would stand between the U.S. Government and the foreign beneficiaries of the exchange guarantee. Thus by making a small premium contribution, foreign Governments and central banks could convert part of their present idle and unearning gold reserves into earning dollar assets.

In the event that a fundamental disequilibrium should develop over the long-run in the United States balance of payments (despite the vigorous efforts which no doubt will be taken by the incoming Administration to promote American exports) the correct procedure, from the standpoint of financial stability of the free-world in general, would be not the devaluation of the dollar (the pivotal currency of the free world) but the appreciation of such foreign currencies as are out of line with the dollar. This applies at the present time to the German D. Mark. Germany could either appreciate her currency or else foster a rise in German wages. German costs are unduly low largely because wages in Germany have not been permitted to rise in line with productivity increases.

Having made a firm exchange guarantee against possible losses to holders of dollars balances, these balances could then be permitted to rise without causing any undue concern. Indeed the U.S. balance of payments would in these circumstances tend sooner or later to reach an equilibrium vis-à-vis the world international monetary requirements of growth since holders of excess dollar balances could certainly find profitable investment in an expanding and prosperous America. In this manner the vast and growing volume of U.S. foreign aid would find a correcting counterflow in long-term investment by foreigners in American industrial securities, American industry and American real estate.

Let us see what such an ironclad commitment might, even in an extreme case of devaluation, cost the U.S. government. As the following calculation will indicate, the cost would be minimal. Let us suppose a 20 per cent devaluation. In 1963 the United States held (in round numbers) $15 billion in gold. A 20 per cent devaluation of the dollar (a 25 per cent rise in the price of gold) would yield a gold profit for the U.S. government of about $3.75 billion. In 1963 the official dollar balances held by foreigners amounted to about $15 billion. Hence the gold profits would in this case have covered all the losses suffered by official holders of dollars.

But it is said that private holders of dollars, if the danger of devaluation were imminent, might wish to sell their holdings to their central banks. Private holdings could thus easily and quickly become official holdings. Let us imagine the worst. In 1963 private holdings of dollar exchange amounted to about $9 billion. If half of these had been converted into official holdings—an unlikely event—a 20 per cent devaluation would have entailed a net loss to the United States of $0.9 billion. Spread over many years a loss of less than $1 billion would be a small price to pay for a substantial gain in international monetary security.

Prudence might however dictate that the gold-value guarantee would apply only to official holders in the amounts actually held on the day the guarantee was announced. This limited guarantee should be politically feasible.[18]

An ironclad guarantee such as this could scarcely fail to end gold speculation in possible dollars devaluation, and it

[18] It is sometimes asserted that it would be politically difficult to offer a guarantee to foreigners while not doing so for American holders. It should be noted however that a U.S. devaluation would not affect American holders while it would cause a loss to foreign holders. Indeed the U.S. Supreme Court in the famous gold case of 1934 based its decision precisely on the point that U.S. citizens could claim no damages.

would very probably induce a considerable amount of de-hoarding.

Official holders of gold might well decide that under such an ironclad guarantee by the U.S. government it would make no sense to hold large amounts of gold—an unearning asset. They might well therefore sell most of their gold to the United States. This would be no cause for alarm as far as the gold-exchange guarantee is concerned. With larger gold holdings the United States would make extra gold profits from any devaluation equal to the extra losses which foreign official holders of dollars would suffer from holding all of their reserves in dollars and which the U.S. government would have to indemnify. Increased gold holdings by the United States would, however, entail the burden of holding an unduly large part of the world's gold.

On August 13, 1962, three distinguished Europeans, testifying before the Joint Economic Committee of the 87th Congress, 2d Session, supported a gold-exchange guarantee. They were Prof. Jurg Niehans of the University of Zurich, Prof. Alan C. L. Day, of the London School of Economics, and Signor Eltore Lolli, executive vice-president of the Banca Nazionale del Lavoro. Signor Lolli suggested that foreign holders of dollar balances be offered gold guarantee certificates which would bear no interest.[19]

If the disequilibrium were only short run or temporary, the gold-exchange guarantee would serve to get us over the hump. It would do so because, by eliminating speculative

[19] Obligations arising under the European Payments Union (now defunct) were protected by an exchange guarantee. The E. P. unit of account, consisting of 17 European currencies (and equal to one U.S. dollar), is still in active use. A Danish bond issue denominated in the European unit of account was marketed in April, 1964, by an underwriting syndicate of European and U.S. banks. Being redeemable in any one of 17 convertible currencies it is in effect protected by an exchange guarantee.

raids on gold, short-term capital movements would be less likely to be cumulative to a point which might force an unwarranted devaluation. Then the long-term adjustment process could continue without disturbing the structure of fixed exchange rates.

The second plan (i.e., the risk-sharing) is less ambitious and therefore would probably be more acceptable to the United States. It would be implemented in two ways—(1) the plan proposed by Signor Lolli and (2) a modification of his proposal. Both variants would be completely voluntary; official holders would be under no compulsion to cooperate.

Official holders under the first variant would be offered the privilege of escape from the risk of devaluation by accepting in lieu of their dollar holdings non-interest-bearing gold certificates which carry the gold-value guarantee. Acceptance of this therefore means that official holders lose completely the advantage of earning interest (usually around 3 or more per cent) on their reserve holdings. Offsetting this is the gain of escape from possible devaluation losses. Obviously it is a risk-sharing scheme.

The other variant is a compromise which would be more attractive to foreign holders of dollars, and something of this sort would probably be necessary to induce any wide acceptance of the plan. Let the United States offer gold certificates bearing 2 per cent interest. Official holders would lose some interest as compared with the continued holdings of dollars, but they would be compensated for this by escaping possible devaluation losses.

Foreign official holders would then have the free choice of holding their reserves in any one of three forms and in such proportions as they might wish: (1) gold, (2) low-interest-bearing gold certificates, and (3) dollars.

To make the plan still more palatable to the United States, the offer of gold certificates could be limited to the amount of dollars held by each official holder as of the date when the plan was publicly announced. Or the offer could apply to only a fraction, say one-half, of the actual dollar holdings.[20]

A PRACTICAL PROGRAM

A concluding note: There are some things that the United States can do unilaterally to reduce speculative raids on gold.

(1) We can repeal the law requiring a 25 per cent gold reserve against the note and deposit liabilities of the Federal Reserve Banks. This would strengthen confidence in our determination to use all our gold resources if need be to defend the dollar.

Actually this legal requirement is sufficiently flexible so that President Kennedy was able to pledge the entire U.S. gold stock in defense of the dollar in his message early in 1961. Chairman Martin has said that "the gold cover requirement does not pose any obstacle to the use of our gold reserves in defense of the dollar." He believes that a "full explanation of what the statute requires and the procedures for meeting its requirements" is all that is needed.[21]

(2) We can offer to all official holders of dollar balances a genuinely firm gold-value guarantee or else limited amounts of gold certificates with or without interest.

(3) We are free under the Articles of Agreement[22] of the

[20] This restricted and limited plan has however the disadvantage that central banks could shift in and out between guaranteed and unguaranteed dollars, and such shifts might give signals of nonconfidence which could be contagious to private speculators.

[21] See Hearings, *The U.S. Balance of Payments*, Joint Economic Committee, Part 3, p. 381, 88th Cong., 1st Sess., 1963.

[22] The Fund itself could widen the gold points as much as it chooses, under Article IV (2). See the analysis of the legal aspects made by Prof. Robert A. Mundell, of McGill University, in *Hearings before the Joint Economic Committee*, Nov. 12–15, 1963, p. 590.

IMF and the Bretton Woods Agreements Act passed by the Congress, to establish a spread between the Treasury's buying and selling price of gold up to 1 per cent below and above the par value of $35 per oz. This should be done. This widening of the gold points would introduce a certain element of uncertainty which could make at least some contribution toward the goal of reducing the role of gold speculators.

All these actions, undertaken unilaterally by the United States, are perfectly legal under our existing international commitments. They need not await prolonged international conferences and agreements. They are feasible and useful steps that could at once be taken by the U.S. government.

chapter four

GOLD RATIOS

This chapter should be regarded by the reader as essentially a pedagogical exercise. A more realistic discussion and appraisal of actual proposals relating to gold ratios, such as those by Prof. S. Posthuma and Dr. Bernstein, will be found in Chapter 6.

In one section of the preceding chapter we considered various possible ways of dealing with the problem of private gold hoards. Even more important is the problem of excessive gold hoarding by central banks. The central banks of eight leading industrial countries[1] held 83 per cent of the gold

[1] These countries are the United States, the United Kingdom, West Germany, France, Italy, Belgium, the Netherlands, and Switzerland.

holdings of all free world countries combined. These countries have been reluctant (or have found it unnecessary) to hold any large fraction of their international reserves in the form of foreign exchange.

THE KEY CURRENCIES[2]

Two of these countries—the United States and the United Kingdom—are key-currency countries whose international reserves consist almost exclusively of gold. Sterling balances are employed as foreign exchange primarily by the so-called sterling area countries. Dollar balances are widely held throughout the free world but especially in Western Europe, Canada, and Latin America. Understandably the two key-currency countries could be expected to hold large stocks of gold, but the huge holdings by the United States—largely a legacy from World War II—have clearly been excessive and still are when viewed in terms of a rational international monetary system.

SIX HIGH-GOLD-RATIO COUNTRIES

In 1963 the six large gold-holding countries of Continential Europe[3] held $15.1 billion of gold and only $6.2 billion of foreign exchange, mainly dollars. While this $6.2 billion is a relatively small portion of their aggregate reserves, it is absolutely large enough to present a serious threat in terms of further gold drains. Excluding these six countries and the key-

[2] The term "key-currency" was coined by Prof. John H. Williams and it quickly came into general use. Professor Williams stressed the key-currency approach during the debate on Bretton Woods. The emphasis which he placed on building an international monetary system on a few strong currencies deserves current recognition.

[3] The Common Market countries and Switzerland.

currency countries, the remaining countries of the free world held only $6.5 billion of gold and $15.6 billion of foreign exchange. These figures reveal very clearly what the so-called gold-exchange standard really means. For the leading industrial countries of Continental Europe it is primarily a gold standard; for the rest of the free world it is primarily a foreign-exchange standard.

The high gold ratios of Switzerland, Holland, Belgium, France, Italy, and West Germany indicate a lack of confidence in the gold-exchange standard. This is certainly not due to any lack of confidence in the financial stability of the key-currency countries as such or in the basic strength and wealth of their economies. Something is missing in our international financial mechanism. Confidence cannot flourish unless rooted in institutional arrangements that give it continuous nourishment and support.

The whole system of insurance, both public and private, which plays such an overwhelming role in modern life, rests upon the principle of the sharing of risks. There are, indeed, risks involved in the holding of any foreign currency. But these risks are unnecessarily intensified by the lack of mutual confidence. If all leading countries could unite in sharing the risks involved in the holding of each other's currencies, the risks themselves would in no small measure disappear. In the area of international monetary matters, the famous statement by President Franklin Roosevelt is particularly true: "We have nothing to fear except fear itself."

The French Finance Minister, M. d'Estaing said at the IMF meeting in 1963 that the wide difference in gold ratios certainly do not reflect "an equitable distribution of the burdens of international monetary cooperation." And the *Monthly Review* of the New York Federal Reserve Bank of November, 1963, commented that the "current system is not fully reciprocal in the sharing of currency risks between countries which hold uneven proportions of gold and foreign exchange."

A GOLD-RATIO FORMULA

Professor Posthuma, a director of the Netherlands Central Bank, has made an interesting proposal,[4] which with important modifications could make a major contribution toward a mutual sharing of risks, thereby removing in a very large measure the periodic fears of currency crises. Employing with modifications his approach, I submit, not as a proposal but rather as a device for illuminating the problem, a scheme under which the major industrial countries would undertake to hold not more than 60 per cent of their international reserves in the form of gold.

This suggestion appears at first glance to be a very modest one and possibly of no great significance. But the more I have thought about the matter, the more I come to the conclusion that its possible impact upon the international monetary machinery could be revolutionary. And it ramifies into areas that at first are scarcely visible.

[4] S. Posthuma, "The International Monetary System," Banco Nazionale del Lavoro *Quarterly Review*, no. 66, September, 1963, and "Changes in the International Monetary System, Institute of World Economics, Kiel University, July 19, 1963.

Under Professor Posthuma's proposal the major industrial countries would take payment in the case of future dollar deficits in the proportion of 60 per cent in gold and 40 per cent in dollars. As he puts it the "U.S. deficits should be covered in gold and dollars in the proportion of 60:40."

The proposal, of course, has no significance except for the six large gold holding countries of Western Europe–Belgium, the Netherlands, Switzerland, West Germany, France, and Italy. From 1953 to 1963 the three smaller countries took full payment in gold; indeed their dollar holdings declined by $213 million. All six drew $10,081 million in gold and $4,430 million in dollars, or 69.5 per cent in gold.

The gold ratios of the eight leading gold-holding countries in 1963 were as follows, listed in rank order:[5]

	Gold ratio, %
United States	99
Switzerland	93
United Kingdom	87
Netherlands	86
Belgium	78
Italy	69
France	66
West Germany	56

To achieve all at once the 60 per cent gold ratio would of course be impossible. On the one hand, if it involved unloading the excess gold holdings, who would buy them? On the other hand, to add sufficiently to the holdings of foreign exchange to bring the level up to 40 per cent of aggregate reserve holdings would be no easy matter for most of these countries, especially for the United States and the United Kingdom.

THE FORMULA APPLIED TO SIX COUNTRIES

The simplest and most feasible application of this proposal would be to limit it to the six gold-holding Continental countries—the only countries in the world (apart from the key-currency countries) that hold anything even approaching the 60 per cent gold ratio. To implement the plan, these countries would either have to sell large stocks of gold or else acquire in some way large amounts of foreign exchange. Gold sales

[5] Compiled from *International Financial Statistics,* August, 1963, pp. 17–18.

In contrast to the high gold ratios of the Common Market countries and Switzerland, the Scandinavian countries prefer interest yielding foreign exchange to gold. Sweden's gold ratio is 25 per cent, Norway's 9 per cent, Finland's 21 per cent and Denmark's 27 per cent.

would have to be made to the United States and the United Kingdom. There would be no other place for it to go. Unless these key-currency countries stood ready to buy gold, the bottom would drop out of the gold market. The price of gold would plummet.

To achieve a 60 per cent ratio the six large gold-holding countries would have to sell $2.25 billion of gold in exchange for dollars.

All this assumes that the formula is pushed to completion in one fell swoop. This, of course, is not necessary. The plan could be set up as a goal to work toward gradually. The only requirement would be that the six large gold-holding countries stop accumulating gold. With the expansion of world trade and continuing U.S. and U.K. deficits (hopefully moderate ones), the gold-holding countries would gradually approach the 60 per cent ratio. They could, moreover, hasten the day by deliberately purchasing dollars in exchange for gold.

When all is said and done, however, it is obvious that the net effect would scarcely be overwhelming. Still a sale of $2.25 billion of gold to the United States would give the United States a considerable boost and, as a long-run solution, would limit the gold drains. A far more revolutionary application of the suggested program is at least theoretically conceivable, though probably impractical (as we shall see) unless accompanied by a considerable overhauling of international monetary machinery.

THE FORMULA APPLIED TO ALL MAJOR COUNTRIES

Let us suppose that the plan is also made to apply to the key-currency countries. The U.S. monetary authorities are already struggling hard (as we shall see in later chapters) to accumulate large holdings of foreign currencies to be used in defense of the dollar when speculative movements cause heavy unloading of dollar balances by foreign holders. Similarly, the United Kingdom has in recent years acquired large balances of foreign currencies from time to time but only for short intervals to meet temporary drains.

The international reserves of the United States consist almost entirely of gold. Assuming no loss of its gold holdings of over $15 billion, the United States would have to acquire about $10 billion of foreign exchange to qualify under the plan. The United Kingdom would have to acquire $1,260 million. The United States and the United Kingdom would have to buy the required foreign exchange from countries with strong convertible currencies. This means that they would have to float new issues of government securities in the capital markets of leading European industrial countries. To the extent that this proved to be difficult, the central banks of these strong-currency countries would be under obligation to purchase any part of these issues that could not be absorbed by the capital markets, crediting the U.S. and U.K. balances with funds newly credited from central bank credit.

The United States and the United Kingdom would invest these balances in foreign bank deposits and highly liquid foreign government securities. This would absorb a certain amount of liquidity from the money and capital markets of the foreign countries in question and this might call for offsetting open market operations by their respective central banks.

Once the United States and the United Kingdom became supplied with foreign exchange equal to 40 per cent of their aggregate international monetary reserves, these key currencies would be equipped with a sufficient amount of ready cash other than gold to make them immune to speculative raids of any foreseeable magnitude.

Switzerland with a gold ratio of 93 per cent would have to acquire $1,510 million of foreign exchange to qualify under Posthuma's plan, assuming no gold sales. Holland comes next with an 86 per cent gold ratio, involving the purchase of $800 million of foreign exchange. For Belgium the required purchase would be $525 million; for Italy, $500 million; and for France, $435 million. West Germany already qualifies with a gold ratio of 56 per cent. It should be noted, however, that Germany's aggregate holdings of monetary reserves in relation to merchandise imports are exceptionally high—51 per cent against 45 per cent for the rest of Continental Europe. West Germany holds an abnormal amount of both gold and foreign exchange. Clearly the matter of equitable distribution is not wholly a matter of gold ratios.

All told the eight largest gold-holding countries would have to absorb over $15 million of newly created foreign exchange to qualify under the 60 per cent gold ratio, assuming (as would probably be the case) that the advanced countries would not unload their present gold holdings upon the rest of the world. If this could be achieved it would amount to a substantial increase in world liquidity. These data are summarized in Table 4-1.

Table 4-1. *Foreign Exchange Purchases Required under the Posthuma Plan*

	Millions
United States	$10,000
Switzerland	1,510
United Kingdom	1,260
Netherlands	800
Belgium	525
Italy	500
France	435
Germany	none
Total	$15,030

A $15 billion increase plus an increase of say $3 billion in monetary gold (which in turn would require another $2 billion of foreign exchange) would raise aggregate international reserves within five years from the current $62 billion to $82 billion. These figures correspond closely to the $82.6 billion projected by the Brookings Institution's study for 1968 on estimates of the need for larger international reserves.

The aggregate purchases required of the six Continental countries, all of whose foreign exchange holdings could be expected to consist primarily of dollars, amounts to about $4.25 billion. The plan could therefore involve a considerable increase in the demand for dollars. But this is only the beginning. The import trade of these countries increased in the decade 1953 to 1963 from $16.1 billion to $40.2 billion, an increase of 10 per cent per year. This rate of increase is greater than can reasonably be expected in future years. Still the need for increased international reserves implicit in a growing volume of international transactions will be substantial, and most of this under the plan would be in dollars.

The gold holdings of the six European countries increased from $4.2 billion in 1953 to $14.3 billion in 1963. In the United States and the United Kingdom gold holdings declined by $6 billion, while in the remaining countries of the free world gold holdings increased scarcely at all from $6.0 billion to $6.5 billion. It would be the aim of the plan to decrease the demand for gold in the gold-holding countries and to increase the demand for foreign exchange. In particular it would greatly increase the demand for dollars.

For the United States the plan would reduce the need for gold and increase the United States need for foreign exchange. From the standpoint of its foreign exchange liabilities, the current excess dollars held by foreigners would gradually melt away because the minimum 40 per cent foreign exchange requirement would progressively transform what is now excess dollars into required foreign exchange holdings.

A 60 per cent gold ratio could bring about an enormous increase in foreign exchange within, say a five-year period, provided countries, especially the United States and the United Kingdom, could successfully place their government securities in foreign capital markets or with foreign central banks and governments, and thereby acquire the needed foreign exchange. This might, however, not be feasible. The capital markets of Continental West Europe may not be prepared to absorb these vast flotations of United States and United Kingdom securities. And if not, would the central banks stand ready to buy them? Ah, there's the rub! It is just such considerations as these that would make it difficult (more likely impossible) to obtain acceptance of the plan. Unless new monetary machinery can be devised which would help to internationalize the free world's capital market, any such plan is likely to remain dead. In order to implement the plan, therefore, it may be necessary to establish a new international institution (representing a number of the strongest currency countries) which would be empowered, within appropriate limits, to fill the currently prevailing void caused by imperfections of the international capital market as now constituted. As a very minimum an exchange guarantee to protect official holders of foreign currencies would have to be instituted. But more about this in Chapter 6.

These innovations could lead gradually to a better distribution of gold and to a widespread holding of foreign exchange by all the leading industrial countries. The plan, if successful, would give a tremendous impetus to the development of international financial integration. The requirement that a minimum of 40 per cent of international reserve holdings be in foreign currencies could lead to a crisscross network of credit relationships across international borders.

chapter five

THE CHANGING MONEY MECHANISM

THE UNITED STATES AND THE IMF

Any discussion of the evolutionary changes which have occurred in the international monetary system must obviously begin with the International Monetary Fund. The activities of the IMF have very much influenced the general development of international monetary and trade conditions, and this in turn has been of great value to the United States. The IMF has also played a role in the development of supplementary arrangements outside of the IMF proper—arrangements in which the United States has been an active participant and often a leading promoter. Nonetheless, note should be made of the fact that the United States has made limited use of the IMF to help it over its payments difficulties.

In July, 1963, however, the United States entered into a $500 million standby agreement with the Fund. Fund dollar holdings had risen to 75 per cent of the U.S. quota, and under the Articles of Agreement once this point is reached the Fund cannot accept dollars from countries wishing to make repayments to the Fund in dollars. Under the standby agreement the United States can draw other currencies and sell these to countries needing them for repayment. On February 13, 1964, the first drawing of $125 million was made.

The United States has been, throughout the postwar period, the main financial support of the IMF. Although the Fund has available for lending a vast pool of currencies (weighted more or less according to the relative size of each economy), it has until recent years loaned out mainly U.S. dollars. In addition to the extensive grants and loan activities of the United States, extending over the whole postwar period, the United States has supplied most of the funds loaned out by the IMF.[1]

One might suspect that a rich dispenser of funds would certainly not itself be struggling with balance-of-payments deficits. Indeed, any generally well-informed citizen may be excused if he finds this difficult to understand. The very term "deficit" makes one think of a poor country, not one that can be expected to help others. It is therefore important to stress the point that a country in international payments difficulties may in fact be a very rich country.

[1] As a result of repayments in dollars of past drawings, the United States may however no longer be a *net* lender.

A payments deficit has nothing whatever to do with whether a country is rich or poor. Whenever the United States or the United Kingdom is having balance-of-payments difficulties, one often reads alarmist newspaper stories which imply that bankruptcy is staring these countries in the face. Nothing could be farther from the truth. In the midst of its payments deficits, the United States has continued to supply the free world with economic and military aid. Beginning with the Marshall aid program in 1947, the United States has made grants and loans aggregating about $90 billion. In the meantime her per capita wealth has been increasing, though in recent years at an unsatisfactory rate. And all the while, though running payments deficits, the United States was accumulating more and more *net* assets abroad, short-term and long-term combined. Indeed, the large purchases by U.S. citizens of capital assets abroad was one major cause of the deficits.

THE IMF LENDING OPERATIONS

After its founding in 1947, the IMF for many years played only an insignificant role in terms of lending operations.[2] As late as 1957, total loans ("sales" in the Fund's verbiage) had aggregated only $1,360 million, of which $636 million had been loaned to advanced countries, $495 million to underdeveloped countries, and $220 million to partly developed countries like Yugoslavia, Czechoslovakia, Finland, and Australia. Beginning with 1957 (the year of the Suez crisis) lending operations increased substantially. By the end of April, 1963, the cumulative total had reached $6.8 billion,

[2] See the Annual Reports of the International Monetary Fund, 1949–1963, but especially 1956–1963.

of which $2 billion were still outstanding on April 30, 1962, and $1.7 billion on April 30, 1963.[3]

At first, while most currencies were inconvertible, the borrowing countries wanted dollars. By April 30, 1958, aggregate currency sales had amounted to $3,016 million, of which $2,767 million were dollars, $192 million (valued in dollar terms) were in sterling, $26 million in German marks, $15 million in Canadian dollars, $11 million in Belgian francs, and $5 million in Dutch guilders. In short, 92 per cent of the total currency sales from March 1, 1947, to April 30, 1958, consisted of dollars. Thereafter other currencies began to be employed as directed by the Fund management. In the year ending April, 1959, 22 per cent of aggregate sales was in sterling and marks; in the year ending in April, 1960, 35 per cent was in sterling, marks, French francs, and guilders. In both 1961 and 1962 dollar drawings had fallen to 36 per cent of the total, and by 1963 to 25 per cent. In the years ending April 30, 1962 and 1963, the distribution ran as shown in the table at top of page 93.

If we take the widest possible view of the IMF assistance programs and include not only actual loans but also standby arrangements which make loans available at a moment's notice (and can therefore be regarded as potential loans), we arrive at an aggregate which is called "Fund Financial Assistance." Actual loans reached a total, as noted above, of $6.8 billion by the end of April, 1963; but aggregate financial assistance, including standby arrangements, amounted to $10.9 billion. Of this amount $6.3 billion had been made available to ad-

[3] These loans are typically short-term loans. Of the $2 billion outstanding in 1962, $1.5 billion had been outstanding less than twelve months and only $250 million more than two years. Of the $1.7 billion outstanding in 1963, $555 million had been outstanding less than twelve months, and $435 million over two years.

Table 5-1. IMF Currency Sales

	1962 (in millions)	*1963 (in millions)*
Dollars	$777	$140.6
Marks	414	105.8
French francs	326	95.0
Lire	185	10.0
Belgian francs	102	20.0
Sterling	101	163.6
Yen	80	
Canadian dollars	75	
Swedish kronor	35	
Netherlands guilders		30.0
Spanish pesatas		7.5

vanced industrial countries and $4.6 billion to the primary producing countries, including some partially developed industrial nations.

Aggregate Fund assistance[4] to seven advanced industrial countries amounted to the following totals for the entire period 1947–1963. No other advanced European country received any assistance whatever. The United Kingdom was far and away the leading recipient.

[4] This consisted largely of standby arrangements.

	Millions
United Kingdom	$4,600
Japan	554
France	519
Canada	300
Netherlands	213
Denmark	44
Norway	10

Of the primary producing countries, 41 received assistance. The larger ones are as follows:

	Millions
India	$550
Argentina	525
Brazil	468
Australia	325
Mexico	252
Columbia	206
South Africa	173
Chile	170
Turkey	164
Indonesia	153
Peru	125
Iran	116

Financial assistance to advanced industrial countries have been concentrated in three periods: 1948 to 1949, 1957 to 1958, and 1962. The average for each period is as follows:

	Billions
1948–1949	$0.6
1957–1958	2.6
1962	3.4

In the period 1948–1949, the largest beneficiaries were the United Kingdom with $300 million, France with $125 million, and the Netherlands with $75 million. From 1950 through 1956 no assistance of any consequence was rendered to the advanced countries, the aggregate being only $175 million for the entire period. European countries were managing their own payments problems without financial aid chiefly by means of exchange and import controls.

The sudden emergence of Fund aid in 1957 to 1958 was in large part caused by the Suez crisis. Fund assistance to the

United Kingdom in this period totaled $1,300 million and to France, $394 million. In addition France received a special credit from the European Payments Union and from the U.S. government. Moreover, the U.S. Import-Export Bank made loans to the United Kingdom and to Japan. On top of all this, the French franc was devalued by 16⅔ per cent and this led to speculative capital movements which created a crisis for sterling and the Dutch guilder, resulting in heavy outflows of funds.

After 1958 no help was sought by any of the industrial countries until 1962. In the fiscal year ending on April 30, 1962, however, Fund assistance reached a record high of $2.3 billion for the developed countries alone, of which $2.0 billion went to the United Kingdom. Fund assistance in 1963 amounted to $1.8 billion, of which $1.0 billion went to the United Kingdom.

In the years 1961 to 1963 the United Kingdom suffered serious deterioration in its payments position. The speculative movements induced by the prospect of possible further upward valuation of the German mark and the Netherlands guilder fell heavily on sterling, and a general world monetary crisis seemed imminent. European central banks were aroused and granted $900 million short-term credits, the so-called Basle arrangements. All told the United Kingdom made drawings on the Fund amounting to $1,500 million in nine different currencies—the largest drawing ever made on the Fund. In addition the Fund made available, on a standby basis, substantial additional credits to be used if necessary.

THE GENERAL ARRANGEMENTS TO BORROW

The 1961–1962 crisis also initiated the special arrangement concluded in Paris, December, 1961, between the Fund and ten leading industrial countries—the so-called Paris Club or Group of Ten which was finally ratified and put into effect in October, 1962. Under this arrangement the contracting countries stand ready to loan their currencies to the Fund up to specified amounts whenever the Fund and these countries agree that additional resources are needed to support the international monetary system.[5]

DISTRIBUTION OF FUND ASSISTANCE

While Fund assistance to the industrial countries has been concentrated in three periods and has been made to only a few countries—indeed mainly to only five, namely, the United Kingdom, France, Canada, Japan, and the Netherlands—assistance to the primary producing countries has been widespread and more evenly distributed over time. In the period 1947 to 1956, the average assistance per year was

[5] The ten countries and the resources pledged by each are as follows:

	Millions
United States	$2,000
United Kingdom	1,000
West Germany	1,000
France	550
Italy	550
Japan	250
Canada	200
Netherlands	200
Belgium	150
Sweden	100

It should be noted that no country is under obligation to advance funds unless, at the time a request is made, the country agrees with the IMF that support is urgently needed.

The IMF announced in June, 1964, an agreement by which Switzerland will join the Paris Club on a consulting basis.

$80 million. For the period 1957 to 1963 this was stepped up to $570 million per year, but was especially large in 1961 and 1962.

The figure of $2.0 billion outstanding in the banner year 1962 may be compared with the Fund's aggregate resources of $3 billion in gold and $6.5 billion in the convertible currencies of leading industrial countries. One may ask why an organization with such large resources (not counting the supplementary resources referred to above) should not be doing a larger lending business.

LENDING POLICIES LIBERALIZED

Still, credit should be given where credit is due. The Fund has in fact been liberalizing its lending policies. In recent years it has initiated and greatly extended the new standby arrangements under which members are assured of an agreed upon amount of emergency aid, needed over and above the ordinary drawing rights. These new standby arrangements have grown rapidly in recent years reaching around $1.25 billion dollars both in 1962 and 1963.

In addition the Fund has increasingly liberalized the granting of waivers. Any drawing or standby arrangement exceeding 25 per cent of a member's quota within any twelve-month period or any drawing or standby arrangement that would increase the Fund's holdings of a member's currency to more than 125 per cent of its quota requires the grant of a waiver. In the fiscal year ending April 30, 1962, waivers were granted in each case in which the Fund's resources were used. In the 1963 fiscal year, waivers were granted in all but two cases. The provision permitting Fund holdings of a member's currency to increase to 200 per cent of its quota was first introduced in May, 1962. In the fiscal year 1963, three members were granted standby arrangements under which the Fund's holdings of their currencies could be increased to 200 per cent. Half of the standby arrangements granted were for amounts which could increase the Fund's holding of the currencies in question to 175 per cent, or more, of their quotas.

BERNSTEIN'S PROPOSALS

Edward Bernstein, one of the leading world authorities on the history and continued operations of the Fund (formerly for many years the director of the Fund's Research Department), has been, as is well known, a persistent advocate of a more liberal lending policy. He argues that members should include as part of their gross international reserves not only the so-called "gold tranche" (the part of the member's quota paid in gold),[6] but also the "credit tranches," namely, their full drawing rights. This practice would imply that a member must be accorded the automatic right to borrow in each twelve-month period the 25 per cent of its quota provided in the Fund agreement without being subjected to any delay. The policy of the Fund has been to recognize only the drawing upon the gold tranche as an unconditional right. Thereafter the drawings require justification and must await

[6] Each member country, upon admission to the Fund, must make an initial contribution in gold amounting to 25 per cent of its quota, or 10 per cent of its gold holdings, whichever is smaller. The remaining part of the member's quota must be paid in terms of the country's currency, either as a deposit account or as a non-interest-bearing obligation of the government. Whenever a member draws on the Fund, it must deposit an additional amount of its own currency with the Fund equal to its drawings upon the Fund. Thus while the *composition* of the Fund's holdings will change whenever it makes a loan to any member, the aggregate assets held by the Fund remain intact. As time goes on, the loans made are likely to be of such a character that the Fund's holdings of strong currencies will be reduced while its holdings of weak currencies will increase.

prior approval. If a member's full quota in the Fund were to be included in its reserves, as Bernstein advocates, it must have the unrestricted right to draw the full amount. Bernstein, moreover, argues that a member should be permitted in the first twelve-month period to draw not only the gold tranche but also the first credit tranche, namely, the second 25 per cent of the quota. Thereafter the drawings should be limited to 25 per cent of the quota in each twelve-month period unless special waivers (as is in fact currently the practice) are granted.

Drawings within these limits, says Bernstein, should be freely permitted to any member that has not been declared ineligible to use the resources of the Fund. Larger drawings should be permitted only on terms and conditions agreed upon with the Fund. Each member would of course understand that drawings upon the Fund are not to be looked upon as long-term credits. They are short-term loans that must be repaid at least within three to five years. Occasionally a few members have abused their rights, but the aggregate quotas of such members, Bernstein asserts, have been small and have affected very little the asset position of the Fund. In the case of extreme misuse of the Fund's resources, the member's right to draw upon the Fund could be suspended.[7]

THE UNITED STATES AS SUPPLIER OF FUNDS

As noted above the United States has supplied by far the largest quota of currencies actually loaned out by the Fund but has made little use of its drawing rights on the Fund. In the survey of the Fund's financial operations given

[7] See Edward M. Bernstein, *Hearings before the Subcommittee on International Exchange and Payments,* 87th Cong., 2d Sess., pp. 217–218.

above one would scarcely learn that the United States has been passing through very serious crises in its own international payments position. During these crisis years the Fund has indeed been of invaluable assistance to many countries and this, of course, has been of immense help indirectly to the United States. It has also helped to innovate additional approaches. But by and large the United States has managed its own difficulties. Some have argued that this is a mistake. It is said that the United States should include its quota of drawing rights on the Fund in its listing of exchange holdings. Instead of being afraid to use the Fund lest drawings indicate a weakness, the United States should draw on the Fund simultaneously whenever its own resources are drawn upon.

The United States has, largely on its own, developed international arrangements which help to strengthen the position of the dollar. It has introduced only to a limited extent restrictive measures designed to improve the trade balance quickly. The major effort has been to develop through various channels a counterflow of funds to offset our large public transfers of grants, loans, and military expenditures abroad.

In addition to *basic* imbalance, the United States also has had to grapple with emergency crises of an episodic nature such as the speculative short-term capital movements engendered by early fears that the incoming Kennedy Administration (January, 1961) might resort to dollar devaluation; the revaluation of the German mark and the Dutch guilder in 1961; the sterling crisis of 1961–1962; the stock market collapse of May, 1962; the Canadian devaluation in 1962; and the Cuban crisis of October, 1962.

So far, the measures taken by the United States relate primarily to these episodic events rather than to the more stable basic items in the payments imbalance. Yet the new measures point the way toward a systematic development of international monetary machinery capable of dealing not only with emergencies but also with the longer-run problems.

In the absence of an international monetary mechanism, the development of cooperative action between the monetary authorities of the United States and leading industrial countries to deal with emergency situations must be acknowledged as a major, if indeed not revolutionary, advance. These are the beginnings of organized international credit facilities.

NEW DEVELOPMENTS

This development has proceeded along three lines: first, foreign exchange transactions; second, swap arrangements between the Federal Reserve System and foreign central banks; and third, the funding of some part of the excess dollar holdings of foreign central banks by means of the sale of medium-term bonds to foreign governments and their monetary authorities.[8]

First, there was the decision to enter into foreign exchange transactions with a view to counter any run that might be made against the dollar. Operations by the U.S. Treasury began in March, 1961. And exchange operations involving transactions directly with foreign central banks were begun by the Federal Reserve System in 1962. Close collaboration between the Treasury and the Federal Reserve is ensured

[8] See Robert V. Roosa and Charles A. Coombs, "Emergence of an American Balance-of-payments Policy," *Factors Affecting the U.S. Balance of Payments*, Joint Economic Committee, 87th Cong., 2d Sess., 1962, part 5, pp. 325–351. See also Robert V. Roosa, "U.S. Borrowings of Foreign Currencies," *Hearings before the Joint Economic Committee*, 88th Cong., 1st Sess., pp. 96–101; *Monthly Review* of the Federal Reserve Bank of New York, August and October, 1963, and March, 1964.

by the fact that an officer of the New York Federal Reserve Bank conducts the exchange operations for both the Treasury and the Reserve System.

The United States had not engaged in exchange transactions since the thirties for the simple reason that for two decades the United States had faced no balance-of-payments problem. The Treasury had no reserves of foreign currencies to fall back on. It began operations by borrowing foreign exchange from some countries and later by purchases whenever the market was favorable. In March, 1961, at the time of the German mark revaluation there developed a heavy outflow of funds from the United States to Germany. In this crisis the U.S. sold $350 million forward marks against dollars to help check the speculative rise in the price of marks and conversely to support the dollar. In the July, 1961, Berlin crisis, foreign exchange operations helped to check the speculative flow of dollars that was pouring into Switzerland. Early in 1962 the United States transacted sales of guilder and Italian lire. All told these operations in 1961–1962 amounted to about $1.5 billion. On the occasion of President Kennedy's assassination sizable offers of foreign currencies were placed to stabilize the market. The intervention of the U.S. Treasury through the Federal Reserve in the private forward exchange market is in effect a way of giving guarantees to private holders of dollars.

These operations served in some measure to allay fears about the dollar and helped to restrain foreign private holders of dollar balances from unloading their holdings upon their central banks. Foreign private banks and corporations have typically in recent years held some seven to nine billion dollar balances. Obviously it is of the greatest importance to prevent this vast volume from piling helter-skelter under the impact of speculative movements into the laps of foreign central banks where a large part of the holdings will almost certainly be rapidly converted into gold. The more that U.S. holdings of foreign currencies can be employed as working balances for international transactions, the more the dollar holdings will be protected against gold drains.

A second line of defense initiated by the United States is the so-called swap arrangements between the Federal Reserve System and European central banks. These are strictly bilateral arrangements. Nevertheless a general network of swap arrangements between a number of the central banks in the leading industrial countries form at least the beginning of an international fabric of credit facilities. These bilateral swaps involve the mutual holding of each other's currencies. By the end of February, 1964, twelve such arrangements had been executed aggregating a total of $2,050 million. The amounts for the most important were $500 million with the Bank of England, $250 million with Canada, $250 million each with West Germany and Italy, $150 million each with Switzerland and the Bank for International Settlements, and $100 million with France and the Netherlands. Note should especially be taken of the sharp increase in the Bank of England–Federal Reserve swap from $50 million to $500 million in May, 1963. The New York Federal Reserve Bank *Monthly Review* referred to this development as a milestone in the evolution of international financial cooperation.[9]

Swap agreements can cushion temporary shocks, but longer-term arrangements may be needed to protect against persistent pressures. Special note should therefore be taken of a

[9] Short-term credit arrangements have also been negotiated between various European central banks. Thus a short-term credit aggregating $900 million was extended by a number of countries to the Bank of England during the sterling crisis of 1961—the so-called Basle credits. In order to repay these short-term borrowings, however, Britain was compelled to make the large drawings on the IMF in 1962. Again $250 million was made available to the United Kingdom in the sterling crisis of February, 1963.

third development—the emergence of a new system of international credit facilities in terms of longer-term funding arrangements. Under the swap agreements, central banks undertake to exchange each other's currencies for a limited period, say three months or at the most six months. But when large amounts of dollar holdings accumulate in a foreign central bank, and when the prospects are that this will continue for some time, the foreign central bank may prefer to fund the excess liquid dollar holdings into longer-term U.S. securities. We discuss this development below under the heading "The So-called Roosa Bonds."

Indeed the whole problem of excess dollar holdings by foreign central banks, private banks, and traders could quite well be managed if the United States could successfully, and on reasonable terms, float long-term bonds in the various European capital markets amounting, let us say, to around $5 billion. The foreign currencies obtained for the sale of these securities could then be used to liquidate $5 billion of the excess short-term dollar holdings. A short-term debt would thus be funded into a long-term obligation which would not readily be convertible into gold. Alternatively, the problem would be solved if foreign central banks would sell their excess dollars in exchange for long-term U.S. securities. The Roosa Bonds point in this direction.

EUROPEAN CAPITAL MARKETS

This promising way of escape however is largely precluded by the fact that the European capital markets cannot be depended upon to take large issues of foreign bonds. Presumably it could be done if the U.S. security issue in question paid a sufficiently high rate of interest and if it was denominated in foreign currencies so as to ensure no loss to the buyers in the event of a dollar devaluation. But foreign countries might not be pleased to see large investment funds diverted away from their own capital needs, and American taxpayers would scarcely be pleased to offer foreigners rates of interest higher than they themselves receive. This is especially true since taxpayers increasingly feel that Europeans ought to carry more of the load of foreign aid, thereby preventing the piling up of excess dollar holdings in the first place.

European capital markets present grave shortcomings. In West Germany 70 per cent of the total bonds issued are mortgage and communal bonds. The housing boom, supported by government concessions and subsidies, drains off a large part of potential investment funds. The net effect is a high rate of interest (around 6 per cent) which virtually precludes the placement of strong foreign securities in the German market. In France strict government regulations account at least in part for the fact that no foreign securities outside of the French Zone have been offered since World War II.

In Italy small flotations of the International Bank for Reconstruction and Development, the European Investment Bank, the Inter-American Development Bank, and the European Coal and Steel Community represent a recent development. None of these placements was very successful since the rate of 5 per cent compared unfavorably with the Italian government securities offered at 5½ per cent. Foreign issues are subject to official approval. In the Netherlands all foreign issues must be cleared by the central bank.

In Switzerland the central bank controls the volume of new foreign bond issues, which by European standards is considerable. However, the large increase in issues in recent years is related to the large inflow of capital from abroad caused by recurring international crises.[10]

[10] See the Survey of European Capital Markets in *Hearings before the Joint Economic Committee on U.S. Balance of Payments*, 88th Cong., 1st Sess., July 8–9, 1963, pp. 139–142.

THE SO-CALLED ROOSA BONDS

The experience of recent years shows, however, that something can be done (and indeed in considerable measure) to fund the overhang of excess dollar holdings. Thus in 1962 when the Bank of Italy was accumulating large amounts of dollars the United States offered to absorb the excess holdings by issuing three-month certificates denominated in Italian lire. After several renewals of these certificates, an agreement was reached to fund the three-month certificates into fifteen-month bonds. Similarly the U.S. Treasury and the Bundesbank agreed to fund some part of the dollar holdings of the German Central Bank. In this case the medium-term bonds issued carried the privilege of conversion into ninety-day certificates if, later on, heavy drains upon German reserves should develop.[11] This conversion privilege proved to be a further attraction and was later incorporated in U.S. issues to the central banks of Italy, Austria, and Belgium.

A special case of placing U.S. securities in Europe was the Treasury arrangement with the Swiss government. The Swiss Confederation, having had several years of budget surplus, had found investment outlets in short-term foreign securities including U.S. Treasury bills. Since this involved frequent renewals, a medum-term bond denominated in Swiss francs was substituted for the short-term Treasury bill. Later a similar arrangement was made with the Swiss National Bank under which a medium-term convertible bond denominated

[11] See *Monthly Review*, Federal Reserve Bank of New York, August, 1963. Actually this conversion privilege was incorporated in the Agreement because of a technicality in German law which limited the maturity of Ceneral Bank assets to 90 days. See also the Fowler Report of Apr. 27, 1964, "A Report to the President from the Task Force on Promoting Increased Foreign Investment in U.S. Corporate Securities and Increased Foreign Financing for U.S. Corporations Operating Abroad."

in Swiss francs was substituted for eight-month certificates.

By 1964 the placement of medium-term bonds abroad by the U.S. Treasury had reached a total of $760 million. Increasingly the maturities have been lengthened from the original fifteen-month and eighteen-month bond to two-year bonds.

Combining the Federal Reserve swap holdings of foreign currencies with the U.S. Treasury bond issues, we have a total operation, as of March, 1964, of $2.0 billion. Compare this with the Fund's $2 billion loans outstanding at the end of its banner fiscal year, 1962. Note also that the U.S. operations grew to these dimensions in the short space of two years.

These developments under U.S. leadership have built up a system of bilateral credit arrangements between the highly developed countries.[12] The United States has been evolving instrumentalities outside of the province of the IMF, but with its support and collaboration. These developments raise interesting questions about the future evolution of the international monetary structure. In particular the U.S. special convertible bonds, denominated in foreign currencies, point the way toward a measure of international financial integration which goes far beyond anything hitherto attempted.

In addition to the new developments between the monetary authorities of the United States and foreign countries, note should be taken of an extremely significant transaction between the United States and the Fund which could become a procedure of major importance. I refer to the sale of gold in recent years by the IMF in return for U.S. government securities carrying a gold-value guarantee. The

[12] In 1961–1962 the United States, United Kingdom, Switzerland, and the Common Market countries set up a joint central bank pool to help stabilize the price of gold on the London gold market. The Bank of England acts as the buying and selling agent for the pool. The mere fact that the pool is operating tends to check speculative activity.

1956 Annual Report of the IMF showed an investment of $50 million in U.S. Treasury bills. The aggregate investment by the Fund in U.S. securities was increased to $200 million in 1959, to $500 million in 1960, and to $800 million in 1961. From the standpoint of the IMF this transaction converts a part of an unearning gold stock into an interest-earning asset. From the standpoint of the United States this borrowing process is a means of replenishing its gold stock. In effect, U.S. government securities have been monetized and the aggregate supply of international reserves has been increased. The highly important significance of all this is that it suggests a basis for open-market operations by the IMF.[13]

[13] I am indebted to Prof. James Tobin for stressing the importance of this transaction as a precedent for possible future developments.

chapter six

NEW PROPOSALS

CURRENT DEVELOPMENTS

There is no need to dismantle existing structures. The IMF need not be buried. We can leave it entirely intact, continuing to experiment and to expand its operations. The post-war monetary difficulties would have been far more disturbing without it, and it is increasingly exhibiting an awareness of the needs of today and tomorrow.

Moreover, we welcome the bilateral arrangements between central banks, the operations of central banks and treasuries in the foreign exchange markets, and the increasing efforts of the monetary authorities, particularly of the United States, to acquire larger holdings of foreign currencies. All these things constitute first steps toward achieving the goal of a more integrated international financial community.

In earlier chapters we have discussed among other things various ways in which gold complicates the U.S. balance-of-payments problem and the gold reforms which might minimize or even remove altogether the disturbing effects that flow from our current mismanagement of gold. In the present chapter I propose to push this analysis a bit farther. In particular I shall raise the question of whether man-made institutions can create an international unit which could emancipate us from the restraints imposed by gold. In our domestic economy we have largely freed ourselves from its shackles; Federal Reserve credit has become the real backing supporting our monetary base. The creation of Federal Reserve credit is the modern alchemy. Central bank credit is "as good as gold," or should we say "better than gold."

NEW OFFICIAL STUDIES

We have come a long way but not far enough. At first disputed, this has now at long last become the accepted official opinion of the international banking community. Thus in the 1963 annual meeting of the Fund it was decided to undertake, in cooperation with the Group of Ten, a study of the problem of international liquidity and ways and means of remedying the weaknesses of the current two key-currencies system.

What these studies will finally come up with is not clear. See, however, comments on the Tokyo Reports in Chapter 10. In this chapter we shall consider unofficial proposals. Some add new dimensions to existing institutions while others aim to replace them. To introduce a variety of ideas,

I propose to outline first a plan of my own for which I claim no particular originality.

THE GROUP OF TEN

I suggest that we need to build a new monetary mechanism around the so-called Group of Ten. The General Arrangements to Borrow concluded between the Fund and the ten leading industrial countries built an important new foundation pillar into the international monetary structure. What was significant was not so much the fact that under this arrangement the Fund could (if members agree) borrow supplementary resources up to $6 billion. More important was the fact that, quite apart from the additional international liquidity thereby created, this arrangement introduced a new approach to the problem of international monetary reserves. Recognition was here in effect given to the fact that the liquidity problem requires something more than the window dressing involved in agreements providing larger and larger quotas for a 100 or so members of the Fund. An adequate expansion of international liquidity on as solid a financial base as is provided by the Federal Reserve System (to take only one example from the strong-currency countries) cannot be achieved simply by enlarging the pool of 100 currencies of which only a handful are usable for international exchange. An international medium of exchange cannot be based on loans and investments in the underdeveloped economies. It must be founded on strong currencies. The General Arrangements to Borrow created a working group of ten strong-currency countries. The arrangement provides, so to speak, an economic cabinet within the IMF.

This development suggests a new governing board consisting of the managing director of the Fund and delegates representing the monetary authorities of the Group of Ten.

Upon this board should be placed the responsibility to operate the monetization machinery needed to make the gold-exchange standard work.

The new governing board would have a very special function to perform, one that vitally concerns every country in the free world. It would leave to other institutions and programs the vast problems of development. The underdeveloped countries are indeed members of the IMF, and rightly so, since the universal problems of short-run balance-of-payments disequilibria apply to them no less than to the advanced countries. But the underdeveloped countries have deep-seated problems that lie quite outside of matters relating to a secure and adequate international medium of exchange. Indeed a vastly expanded program operating under the aegis of the United Nations should be high on the agenda of international cooperation.

AN INTERNATIONAL DOLLAR

A basket of ten currencies, however, would make an awkward monetary unit. The IMF, operating jointly with the Group of Ten, can create a new international unit based on the financial security of the ten leading industrial countries. We need an "international dollar." We already have a U.S. dollar and a Canadian dollar. Why not an international dollar solidly based on the financial resources of the major industrial countries?

A MODEST FIRST STEP

To this end I propose the following plan which incorporates ideas derived from several sources including especially proposals by Prof. S. Posthuma of the Netherlands Bank and Prof. Xenophon Zolotas, governor of the Bank of Greece.

Plans with at least similar features have also been offered by Sir Oliver Franks, the Rt. Hon. Reginald Maudling, and Dr. Edward M. Bernstein. There are, however, in some respects important differences, the details of which need not concern us here. My proposal is a "modest first step"[1] along lines that appear to command widespread approval. It is a program limited in character and built upon already established institutions.

The proposal is as follows: Let the IMF adopt as an appropriate goal for a workable gold-exchange standard a maximum gold ratio of 60 per cent. Such a declaration would give recognition to the fact that the current wide differences in gold ratios do not reflect "an equitable distribution of the burdens of international monetary cooperation."[2] This goal could, of course, not be achieved at once. It would be a goal to work toward. Under such a rule the high-gold-ratio countries would undertake not to accumulate any more gold until their respective gold ratios had been brought down to or below the 60 per cent maximum.

This would mean, for the high-gold-ratio countries, a gradual evolution toward a genuine gold-exchange standard in place of their current heavy reliance on gold. In the event that the gold countries continued to run payments surpluses, they would have to be content to accumulate more and more reserve currencies. This we can be certain they would not like, and agreement on these lines can be counted out as highly improbable. So what to do?

[1] The phrase comes, perhaps somewhat unexpectedly, from Prof. Robert Triffin in his contribution to Seymour Harris (ed.), *The Dollar in Crisis*, Harcourt, Brace & World, New York, 1962, pp. 292–293 in which he indicates that he is prepared to approach the problem along step-by-step evolutionary lines. I am not implying that he necessarily will agree with my own formulation of the first step.

[2] Quoted from the French Finance Minister, M. d'Estaing, at the IMF meeting in 1963.

A way out of this difficulty would be to follow the lead given by Professor Zolotas. Permit the holders of reserve currencies to deposit their dollar (and sterling) balances in exchange for new international units with a new division organized within the IMF. We might call it the International Reserve System, the IRS. The IRS would then hold the dollar and sterling balances, which under the Fund Articles of Agreement would carry a gold-value guarantee.[3] The IRS would then invest the dollar and sterling balances in long-term, interest-bearing U.S. and U.K. government securities. The IRS would have monetized the long-term securities in question into new international units denominated as international dollars.

The IRS would, however, at this stage not be permitted to play the role of a full-fledged international bank. It would not be permitted to engage on its own initiative in open-market purchases of the government securities of the Group of Ten. It would not be permitted to issue international dollars based on loans to the less-developed countries. The IMF would continue its present function of short-term lending to help all its members over their balance-of-payments difficulties. The IRS would accept deposits of reserve currencies and issue international dollars in exchange.

Reserves held in the form of international dollars would be freed from the risk of possible devaluation and they would earn interest. They would be available at any time for international trade or investment transactions. Interest earnings would derive from the fact that the IRS would invest its dollar and sterling holdings in time deposits or in government securities. IRS members would find the international dollar as good as gold, and in fact, as an interest-earning asset, better than gold.

[3] Because of the guarantee, the United States might conceivably wish to limit the amount of funds which the IRS could invest in time deposits and U.S. securities, but this is scarcely probable.

A BOLDER NEXT STEP

Sooner or later the next step might prove to be in order. If and when it becomes evident that more international liquidity is needed (i.e., more than the amounts fed from the deficits of reserve currency countries or from the normal processes of borrowing in the capital market of surplus countries) the Group-of-Ten Agreement might then be amended to permit the IRS on its own initiative to invest in long-term government securities of any of the ten leading countries but only with the consent of the country in question. Alternatively the country in question might take the initiative. On the basis of this investment the IRS would credit the participating country with new international dollars. The IRS would then have become a full-fledged international credit-creating bank, but controlled, as Professor Zolotas suggests, by the governing board representing the Group-of-Ten countries.

Admittedly there is a danger that such a governing board might become weighed down by bureaucratic procedures and that quick action at decisive moments could not easily be taken. One cannot help being impressed with the efficiency of the informal methods of international collaboration that have been developed by leading central banks in recent years. "One cannot over-emphasize the importance of being able to move quickly—on the basis of telephone consultations if necessary—against speculative pressures before they gain momentum. In our view, the central bank and intergovernmental defenses developed during the past two years should be regarded as a permanent reinforcement of the international financial machinery."[4]

This danger is however less serious in my proposal than in those of some others since in my plan countries are free to ac-

[4] C. A. Coombs, M. Iklé, E. Ranalli, and J. Tüngeler, "Conversations on International Finance," *Monthly Review,* Federal Reserve

cumulate foreign exchange on their own without being restricted by prescribed uniform ratios.

BERNSTEIN'S PLAN

A new plan by Edward M. Bernstein was published November 13, 1963, in the *Quarterly Review* of Model, Roland & Co., a member of the New York Stock Exchange dealing in foreign securities. This proposal, like my own, is concerned exclusively with the establishment of a strong international monetary system. It does not mix this up with development programs. Accordingly the plan devolves upon a limited number of leading industrial countries.

Bernstein's plan, unlike my own, is modeled on the IMF quota system of participation. Each participating country would contribute its *own* currency (according to an agreed upon schedule of quotas) to a pool of currencies which the IMF would hold as trustee. Bernstein suggests an initial aggregate quota of $3.5 billion, of which the United States' share would be about $1.7 billion. In return each country would be given a credit on the books of the trustee denominated in reserve units, a new international unit equivalent in value to the U.S. dollar. Thus the trustee would hold initially $3.5 billion in currencies of the eleven[5] countries, and they in turn would hold $3.5 billion of reserve units. The currencies so held by the trustee would be guaranteed against exchange depreciation.

The aggregate gold holdings of his eleven countries amounted in 1963 to about $32.0 billion. Accordingly the $3.5 billion of new reserve units would permit each country to hold 1 reserve unit for every 9 dollars of gold. International reserves should not be increased too rapidly, hence the relatively small initial increase of $3.5 billion. New reserve units would be created from year to year until, finally, the aggre-

[5] Bernstein suggested adding Switzerland to the Group of Ten.

gate reserve units would be equal to one-half of the total gold holdings. This would amount to about $16 billion of reserve units backed by a pool of currencies of which the United States would contribute $8 billion, all subject to the gold-value guarantee embodied in the IMF charter.

Under this agreement, participating members could not demand 100 per cent payment in gold in exchange for their holdings of foreign exchange. In the initial stages, holders could demand only 90 per cent in gold and 10 per cent in reserve units. This proportion would be reduced in successive stages until ultimately the ratio would be two-thirds gold and one-third reserve units. Thereafter the ratio could be further adjusted so as to permit a continued adequate increase in aggregate international reserves.

The participating countries would be free to hold their own international reserves in any form they wished—gold, foreign exchange and reserve units. But holdings of gold would have to be matched by a minimum amount of reserve units. Holdings of foreign exchange would be exempt from this regulation.

This means that no creditor country (if a participating member) could demand full conversion into gold. Looked at from the standpoint of a deficit country, its gold holdings would go 50 per cent farther in debt payment. Its gold holdings would ultimately have been increased by 50 per cent. The new reserve unit is made, one may say, legal tender for international payments up to one-third of any international indebtedness between official monetary authorities.[6]

[6] Bernstein had already anticipated his more recent proposal in the *Hearing before the Joint Economic Committee*, 87th Cong., 2d Sess., December, 1962, p. 226. "Each of these countries would deposit with the International Monetary Fund certain amounts of its own currency and get credit in these reserve units. They would then pass the reserve units to each other along with gold as a composite standard. As these would be held by the International Monetary Fund they would carry an exchange guarantee."

Under my plan, countries that hold more than 60 per cent of their aggregate reserves in gold cannot add to their stock of gold. Of the foreign exchange holdings, a minimum of one-half might be in international dollars. The rest could be in U.S. dollars or any other convertible currency. Alternatively my plan might be completely voluntary, permitting Group-of-Ten members to hold reserves in any form they might wish—gold, international dollars, or convertible currencies. In view of the exchange guarantee plus their interest-bearing quality, international dollars might well be preferred over all other forms of reserve holdings.[7]

POSTHUMA'S PLAN

Professor S. Posthuma of the Netherlands Bank stresses firmly the importance of an exchange guarantee in any monetary reform. He puts the matter very bluntly as follows: "Central banks cannot be expected to hold considerable

[7] The extraordinary large holdings of gold by the Common Market countries and Switzerland is supposed to be indicative of astute and prudent investment policy. But is it? Let us compare the record of the Netherlands and Sweden in 1958 to 1963. Holland's holdings of gold averaged $1,400 million in this period, Sweden's $185 million. Holland's holdings of foreign exchange averaged $250 million, Sweden's $415 million. Holland's aggregate reserves averaged $1,650 million, Sweden's $600 million. Holland's reserves were therefore 2¾ times the Swedish reserves. If we now multiply the Swedish items by 2¾ in order to make them comparable to Holland's, Swedish gold holdings would then amount to $510 million compared with Holland's $1,400 million. On a comparable basis, therefore, Holland was losing interest each year on about $900 million of gold in which amount Sweden was earning about 3.5 per cent per year. It is, I think, fair to say that Sweden's policy with respect to the composition of her international reserves represents not only a high degree of international cooperation but also a prudent investment policy. It would require very large periodic devaluations of the dollar for the Netherlands' reserve investment policy to match that of Sweden in terms of financial prudence.

amounts of foreign currency without being quite sure that these holdings will never devaluate in terms of either gold or their own currency." Referring to the medium-term U.S. bonds (which we discussed in the preceding chapter) denominated in the currency of the holder, he concludes: "There seems to be no reason, however, why this should not be systematized in that such a guarantee should apply reciprocally to any conventional holdings of foreign currencies in the possession of central banks."[8]

Professor Posthuma is doubtless realistic when he says that central banks will not agree to limit their gold holdings unless the foreign exchange alternative carries an exchange guarantee.[9] As compensation for renouncing the unrestricted right to convert all holdings of foreign exchange into gold, the creditor countries must have an exchange guarantee. "No country whose currency forms part of the reserves of other countries can therefore expect that it will be released from its conversion obligations without giving a guarantee that it will not alter the exchange rate of its currency."[10]

[8] S. Posthuma, "The International Monetary System," Banco Nazionale del Lavoro *Quarterly Review*, no. 66, September, 1963, p. 15.

[9] West Germany, Italy, Switzerland, Belgium, and the Netherlands added collectively $3.6 billion to their gold stocks from 1958 to 1963 while they actually reduced their aggregate holdings of foreign exchange.

Professor Posthuma might well have raised the question, however, whether investment of so large a proportion of reserves in gold, an unearning asset, is really a prudent investment.

[10] Professor Posthuma plays no favorites. Note the following: "It will be readily apparent that not only the claims on the United States, but also the claims of the United States on other countries would have to be similarly secured against the exchange risk."

Finally, this firm statement on the position of the gold countries: "No sovereign government will be able to justify to its people the renunciation of its conversion rights without adequate cover against the risk of an alteration in the exchange rates of the currencies concerned." See his Kiel University Lecture, July 19, 1963, pp. 13, 20.

I heartily agree (see Chapter 3) with Professor Posthuma that every country whose currency constitutes a part of international reserves ideally should give an exchange guarantee. It may, however, prove difficult to persuade the U.S. Congress (and European parliaments) to give a unilateral guarantee. It might be possible to achieve much the same result by operating through a division of the IMF and so obtain automatically an exchange guarantee for international dollars issued under the cover of the Bretton Woods formula. For this reason this suggestion may perhaps be more practical than that suggested by Professor Posthuma.

The fiduciary component is suspect. This is at the center of the issues that confront us in our current international monetary problems; every reform proposal (whether a modest first step or an extensive overhauling) contains some element of an exchange guarantee. To this there is not, I believe, a single exception. No fundamental improvement of the international monetary system is possible without attacking in some manner the problem of improving the quality of the fiduciary component of the gold-exchange standard.

An exchange guarantee of some form would end a deficit country's fears of gold drains and a creditor country's fears of devaluation. This alone would go a long way toward solving the problem of adequate international liquidity. Without an exchange guarantee to bolster the fiduciary component of the gold-exchange standard, the amount of international liquidity needed to protect the dollar from gold drains would be enormous. With an exchange guarantee, relatively little liquidity is needed. It is a great mistake to regard the demand for liquidity simply as a function of the volume of world trade. The volume of trade does determine, within limits, the transactions demand. But liquidity preference also involves the speculative motive. The demand for international liquidity is in no small measure a function of the acceptability of the fiduciary component.[11] To the extent that the fiduciary component is endowed with a gold-value guarantee, the liquidity preference schedule will be shifted downward.[12]

There remains nevertheless in a growing society the problem of adequate liquidity. In addition to the various currently available methods to increase the quantity of international reserves such as key-currency deficits, enlargement of IMF quotas, swap agreements, etc., there are at least three possible ways of adding to the volume of reserves:

1. A rigid control of gold ratios, which would be adjusted from time to time to permit sufficient expansion of the fiduciary component to provide adequate international liquidity.
2. Establish a new, international credit-creating institution, an international central bank.
3. Return to a full gold standard but increase the price of gold from time to time sufficiently to provide adequate international liquidity.[13]

The Posthuma proposal falls under the first of the three methods outlined above.

Professor Posthuma notes that in 1962, of the total reserves of OECD countries (excluding Switzerland) plus Japan, the

[11] Note should also be made of the fact that if reserve currencies carried the exchange guarantee not only would there be less need for liquidity, but, in addition, the removal of exchange risk would greatly facilitate balance-of-payments adjustments via capital flows. See James C. Ingram, *Regional Payments Mechanisms*, and J. O. Blackburn, "Regional and National Balance of Payments, Once More," *Economia, Internazionale*, November, 1963.

[12] Bent Hansen, in his Lectures on International Liquidity (Central Bank of Egypt, 1962), gives an illuminating discussion in Keynesian liquidity preference terms of the transactions demand for international reserves and the speculative and precautionary demand for reserves.

[13] Bent Hansen, *ibid.*, argues convincingly that a once-for-all big jump in the price of gold would be disruptive, while a step-by-step increase would almost certainly bring about heavy speculation in future increases.

ratio of gold to the fiduciary part was about 60:40. In order to keep this ratio constant he suggests that U.S. future deficits should be covered in gold and dollars in the 60:40 proportion.

In the case of future U.S. surpluses, however, European deficit countries would be allowed to pay 100 per cent in their own currencies until the United States had reached the standard 60:40 gold–foreign exchange ratio.

Once the standard ratio has been achieved all around, deficit countries would pay in: (1) gold, (2) foreign currencies, and (3) their own currency, in the proportion 60:40:40. If international liquidity proved to be inadequate, the gold percentage should be reduced.

Under Posthuma's plan this composition of the international reserves of the participating countries would be adjusted through a complicated "settlement center" system of accounting control (described in the annex to his *Quarterly Review* article) so as to yield eventually a uniform gold–foreign exchange ratio.[14]

[14] In reading Professor Posthuma's able lecture at Kiel University I could not help noting the fact that in discussing the U.S. deficits he never even mentions the $6.5 billion of U.S. annual loans, grants, and military expenditures abroad, and he neglects to point out that if the Common Market countries plus Switzerland would finance themselves instead of coming to the New York market for funds, the U.S. deficit would be substantially reduced. He speaks about "measures that will cause U.S. exports to rise relatively more steeply than Western European exports" but does he really think that drastic measures of this character would be welcomed in Europe? He refers to autonomous domestic inflation in the deficit country in a manner that strongly implies that he believes the U.S. deficits are due to U.S. inflationary developments. As is well known, price statistics do not support this view. He appears to believe that the surpluses of European countries leave them only the alternatives of (1) inability to live up to their means or (2) opening the door to inflation, forgetting that if they would import more they could raise their consumption and investment standards, and that imports are anti-inflationary.

CRITIQUE OF THE POSTHUMA AND BERNSTEIN PLANS

Both the Posthuma and the Bernstein gold-ratio plans could be implemented in radically different ways. The ratio could simply be employed as a *maximum* gold ratio or it could be employed as a *prescribed uniform* ratio. In fact they are employed by the authors of these plans as prescribed uniform ratios. This I think is an unwise procedure.

The prescribed uniform ratio requires continuous surveillance over the composition of the reserves held by each participating country. It is not probable that the participating countries will agree to any such regimentation.

A major purpose of Professor Posthuma's plan is to maintain a rigorous control over the volume of international reserves with a view to preventing either an excess or deficiency of reserves. Underlying this is the view that domestic price stability in the participating countries is closely determined by the volume of international reserves and fluctuations in these reserves. This was true in the old days of the automatic gold standard but under modern central banking this is no longer true, or at least no longer need be true. Today, central banking can effectively isolate the volume of domestic credit from the impact of increases and decreases of foreign reserves. That some central banks have not managed this problem very well in recent years (*vide* West Germany) is no convincing argument. In some cases modernization of central banking and debt management techniques may well be necessary. The international monetary system however should not be controlled by institutional imperfections that still remain in certain countries.

Under modern central banking techniques, there is no reason why excess international reserves should cause any unmanageable domestic monetary problems. Excess international reserves are undesirable for quite other reasons. It is true that they create, along with other day-to-day disturbances, monetary problems that have to be faced and managed and, therefore, from this standpoint can be regarded as a disturbing nuisance which should as far as possible be avoided. But there are more substantial reasons why surplus countries should strive to prevent excess reserves. Persistent unwarranted surpluses mean that the country in question is not using its resources to the best advantage. Its consumption and investment standards are below the level of its full productive potential. Such a country ought to import more for larger imports restrain inflationary pressures. It ought perhaps to invest more abroad. It is in these terms that any excess of reserves should be appraised.

There are indeed valuable features in the Posthuma plan, and these could be achieved without regimenting the participating countries into a common mold. There is no need for any rigorous predetermination of the desired amount of international reserves. Professor Posthuma himself admits that no one can tell in advance what the appropriate aggregate reserves should be. Individual countries should be free to acquire such international reserves as they believe they need. They may indeed wish to borrow from an international monetary institution. But they should not be prevented from acting on their own.

The valuable features of the Posthuma plan are quite otherwise. The exchange guarantee which he urgently recommends is commendable. It could be all-inclusive (I approve) or it could be restricted to special arrangements such as the Roosa Bonds. Again it could be implemented in part via the Roosa Bonds and in part by the voluntary conversion of foreign exchange holdings into gold-guarantee certificates bearing no interest, as recommended by Signor Lolli, vice-president of the Banco Nazionale del Lavoro, or bearing a low rate of interest as was suggested in Chapter 3.

Bernstein's plan is much more flexible. While it also sets out a prescribed uniform ratio, this ratio applies only to reserve units, not to foreign exchange reserves. In his proposal, reserve units constitute only a part of aggregate fiduciary reserves. Participating countries would therefore be free to expand their international reserves on their own. The prescribed uniform ratio of gold to reserve units (Bernstein) would accordingly not rigorously limit aggregate reserves as in the Posthuma plan.

Nevertheless, I would make two criticisms of Bernstein's prescribed uniform ratios. First, in lieu of his scheme under which the reserve units are *periodically* increased by rather large jumps, I propose a continuous process of adjustment.[15] Second, as also with respect to the Posthuma plan, I am not at all happy about the extreme regimentation which prescribed uniform ratios would impose.

Here again, if the *maximum* gold ratio[16] approach were adopted, I can see some very useful features in the Bernstein approach. It does provide a supplementary method of increasing reserves. And a maximum gold ratio would help bolster the fiduciary component of international reserves and so help to minimize gold drains. If Bernstein would also permit participating countries to deposit their holdings of foreign exchange with his reserve unit institution, I can see much

[15] Instead of periodic quota increases of $3.5 billion or so, increases in international dollars should be subject to day-to-day management in just the same manner that the quantity of Federal Reserve credit is controlled by the Federal Reserve System in the United States.

[16] Actually any rigid ratio linkage to gold is dangerous since if gold production should prove to be quite inadequate, the fiduciary component should grow much more rapidly in order to provide adequate total monetary reserves.

good in his approach. His plan does have the special merit that it proposes specific joint action without waiting indefinitely for the individual country to act. But once the ice is broken why not let the individual country borrow reserve units if and when it needs them?

THE INTERNATIONAL RESERVE SYSTEM

Under an International Reserve System such as I proposed above, in which the international dollars are endowed with an exchange guarantee, countries would no longer need to hold large stocks of gold in their reserves. The problem of an equitable distribution of gold would no longer be a matter of concern. All countries would be free to hold their reserves in any form—gold, international dollars, or foreign currencies. All participating countries would agree to maintain the value of their currencies within fixed buying and selling points around par. Perhaps these points should be widened to permit greater flexibility and thereby ease the long-run adjustment process. Parity would be expressed as now in terms of gold or in terms of the U.S. dollar of the "weight and fineness in effect on July 1, 1944," as in the Bretton Woods Charter. The IRS would accept gold deposits and give international dollars in exchange. These dollars could in turn be redeemable in gold.

Whether or not such a system would finally absorb all the world's monetary gold is a question that no one can answer. Nor is it important. It is indeed true that if all the gold should be so concentrated, some two-thirds of the IRS assets would at first consist of gold, an unearning asset. This would compel the IRS to pay a lower rate of interest to its depositors. But these depositors would in turn be freed from the cost of carrying gold as part of their international reserve. As world trade expands and more international reserves for whatever reason are needed, the IRS would necessarily increase its holdings of the government securities of the participating countries relative to its holdings of gold.

OTHER PROPOSALS

The Maudling and Zolotas plans also limit their respective proposals to major trading countries. The plans are not spelled out fully, but the basic ideas are, I believe, reasonably clear. Maudling's plan[17] suggests that a mutual currency account be set up in the Fund. Countries with a surplus in their balance of payments could continue to acquire the currencies of deficit countries but they could use these currencies to acquire a claim in the Fund in the form of a mutual currency account. Precisely how this mutual currency account could be drawn upon and for what purposes is not explained in any detail. It could at any rate be drawn upon should the country in question encounter a deficit in its payments balance.

Zolotas's proposal[18] is essentially along similar lines, but is set forth more explicitly. Excess holdings of currencies (e.g., dollars) could be sold to a new institution or department in the IMF in exchange for either a pool of strong currencies or for a deposit in terms of an international unit. These deposits would enjoy the protection of the gold exchange guarantee as provided in the Bretton Woods Agreement. The new deposits would be as freely usable and transferable as the exchange holdings of key currencies. The reader will readily observe that my own plan is nothing more or less than an elaboration of the Zolotas proposal.

[17] *Summary Proceedings*, Annual Meeting, International Monetary Fund, 1962, pp. 61–68.

[18] *Ibid.*, pp. 108–116; and 1963, pp. 91–99.

Sir Oliver Franks[19] has proposed (also accepted by the Radcliffe Commission) that members of the IMF could deposit with the Fund their holdings of dollars, sterling, or gold, and receive in return deposit balances.

THE MAXWELL STAMP PLAN

We are now prepared to see how the full-fledged Triffin plan and the Maxwell Stamp plan differ from the proposals discussed above. The Stamp plan[20] is the clearest case. Stamp proposes that the Fund be empowered to issue certificates up to a specified amount in any one year to any of the international agencies engaged in financing development programs in the primary producing countries, including the International Bank for Reconstruction and Development and the International Finance Corporation, and through it to assist private enterprise. The certificates would then be allocated by the international agencies to such underdeveloped countries as might be prepared to take them in exchange for their own obligations. These certificates (which are obligations of the Fund and backed by the securities of the underdeveloped countries) could then be used to pay for capital equipment and other needed imports from the leading industrial countries. Industrial countries would be under no compulsion to accept these certificates if they doubted their exchange value and the marketability of the securities upon which they are based. They might be induced, however, to accept them in view of the resulting stimulus to their exports.

Under this scheme the financial assets behind the certifi-

[19] Sir Oliver Franks's Annual Statement to Shareholders of Lloyds Bank, 1958.

[20] Maxwell Stamp, "The Fund and the Future," *Lloyds Bank Review*, October, 1958. See also "Changes in the World's Payments System," *Moorgate and Wall Street*, Spring, 1961.

cates would doubtless have a low market rating.[21] Their value would essentially depend upon the willingness of the various central banks in the industrial countries to accept these certificates in payment for exports on the assumption that they would generally be acceptable by most members of the Fund as international media of exchange in lieu of gold and key currencies. To be sure, the amount of the issue would presumably be limited.

In the event that such certificates proved to be acceptable they would have an expansionist impact upon the leading exporting countries, adding further inflationary pressures to those already present in these economies. Such a development might, therefore, call for counter fiscal and monetary restraint on the part of the participating industrial country.

It is difficult to see how this plan could have any chance of acceptance by the leading countries although it offers a seemingly painless way to raise funds for development in contrast to the painful process of tax-supported appropriations for foreign aid in the regular governmental budgets. Growing economies must of course use credit expansion in the domestic sphere and there is no *theoretical* reason why a part of the appropriate credit expansion might not be allocated to foreign aid. Moreover the foreign aid loans now made by the United States are no better backed by marketable securities than these certificates would be. It must not be overlooked, however, that the U.S. dollar is not based on these securities. An international dollar needs equally firm backing.[22]

[21] In his *Moorgate and Wall Street* article the scheme discussed above is called Plan A. In this article he also introduced a Plan B under which the Fund certificates would not be given away to underdeveloped countries but would be exchanged for strong currencies (e.g., German marks) which in turn would be loaned to key-currency countries when needed. He still regards Plan A as his ideal and I have therefore concentrated my comments on it.

[22] The Subcommittee on International Exchange and Payments (87th

KEYNES'S CLEARING UNION

It may be noted that Keynes's clearing union was in essence similar to the Stamp plan. This is true because, while his plan imposed limits on the drawing rights of the debtor or deficit countries, it fixed no limits (except the aggregate of deficit countries' quotas) upon the obligations assumed by the creditor or surplus countries. The outstanding creditor or surplus country in those days was of course the United States. The global drawing rights (excluding the United States) amounted to about $30 billion. Thus, in effect, the United States might have had to supply dollars to this amount. While in the end the United States has supplied much more than that (by 1963 about $90 billion) for the reconstruction and security of the free world, in 1943 (the date of the clearing union pamphlet) any such sum was regarded as fantastic and was wholly unacceptable to the U.S. Congress.

Keynes to be sure, while admitting that the gates were wide open as far as a creditor country (e.g., the United States) was concerned, argued that this did not mean that the creditor country was helpless. The growth of credit balances, he contended, would not impose any unmanageable maximum liability outside its own control. The liability, he said, was determined, not by the aggregate quotas of other countries, but by its own policies. A creditor country could use its

---

Cong., 1st Sess.) has made a somewhat similar proposal. Under a new agreement with the IMF, member countries would stand ready to purchase up to a specified amount, interest-bearing obligations of the Fund having maturities up to four to five years. Members purchasing these obligations would be permitted to use them in international payments along with gold and foreign exchange reserves. The Fund would, through the sale of these obligations, organize a pool mainly of strong currencies which could be loaned out to countries having prolonged balance-of-payments difficulties. The Fund could also make loans to underdeveloped countries.

credit balance to buy the goods or securities of the debtor countries. This is true, but the argument scarcely applies to the underdeveloped countries where securities are often not credit worthy, and whose supply of goods is very limited. Keynes's argument would have been more convincing had his clearing union membership consisted exclusively of advanced industrial countries. In dealing with the underdeveloped debtor countries there might be no escape for the surplus country except to keep on piling up credits that are not marketable, or else to refuse to continue to honor one's obligation as a creditor country.

THE TRIFFIN PLAN

Triffin's brilliant contributions have become world famous, and have aroused an immense amount of useful discussion. While future monetary reforms may well prove to be substantially different from Triffin's proposals, much credit should nevertheless be given to his provocative, original, and highly educational writings.

Triffin's plan is broad-gauged and is designed to build anew the international monetary mechanism. This is perhaps its most serious handicap and explains why it has aroused so much opposition. It discards the IMF in its present form—an institution built up with great difficulty and which is doing useful work. Of course Triffin is not alone in thinking that the IMF is obsolete. It has many critics, but most would not wish to dismantle it altogether.

With Triffin the whole mechanism is to be changed. It is not a question of adding a new department or an affiliated institution while retaining all the present functions of the Fund.

Gold is retained as a part of the international reserve but official foreign exchange holdings of convertible currencies are entirely eliminated (except possibly minimum operating balances). The IMF is transformed into a new international central bank.

Twenty per cent of a member country's gross international reserves must at once be transferred to the international bank either in gold or foreign exchange. The United States would pay practically all of this 20 per cent in gold since the United States holds virtually no foreign exchange. And all the high-gold-ratio countries—those with over 80 per cent gold ratios—would have to pay substantial amounts in gold. Countries with over 20 per cent of their reserves in foreign exchange would make no gold payments. All told the new international bank would acquire about one-eighth of the free world's monetary gold. For the most part, however, gold would still be held by the member countries. But all official foreign exchange holdings (except possibly minimum balances) would, under the new arrangement, be deposited with the bank. The new international central bank would possess all official foreign exchange holdings and in addition a substantial part of the world's gold.

Today, international monetary reserves consist almost exclusively of gold plus dollar and sterling balances. The foreign exchange holdings therefore consist of solidly backed currencies. These foreign holdings of dollar balances consisting of Treasury bills and notes and other U.S. government securities are backed by dependable marketable assets. No one questions this. If foreigners wish to transfer dollar holdings into gold or other currencies it is not because they doubt the *soundness* of the assets behind the dollar balances. It is because they may fear an official increase in the U.S. dollar price of gold. These two things are often confused in the public mind. The assets behind the dollar balances are never subject to question, only the dollar *price* of gold. And the same applies, of course, to the sterling balances.

According to the Triffin plan, the new international bank would start off with gold and dollar and sterling liquid assets. But the dollar and sterling assets would gradually be liquidated, under his plan, at the rate of about 5 per cent per year. Future assets of the new bank would therefore increasingly be determined by the loan and investment policy of the new institution. The new bank could make loans to member countries, developed or underdeveloped, for the purpose of helping such members over critical payments difficulties. Such loans would simply take the place of the current drawings on the Fund. The new international bank could, however, also engage in open-market purchases of the securities of member countries, but only with the consent of the country in question.

The Triffin bank, besides making direct investments in the government securities of both advanced and underdeveloped countries, might also purchase the securities of the International Bank for Reconstruction and Development together with its various affiliated or related institutions.

The Triffin plan seeks, essentially, to achieve two purposes at one stroke: (1) to provide adequate international liquidity and (2) to ensure substantial aid for the development of industrially backward countries. The liquidity aim is the one that has received the greatest attention and is also the one primarily in the mind of Professor Triffin himself. As I see it, however, the most challenging part of his proposal is the mechanism which it offers to finance foreign aid. As is well known, the United States has shouldered the overwhelming part of this burden, and continues to do so despite considerable prodding of its rich European allies. The Triffin plan could, so it would seem, virtually take over the bulk of the development program, at least within the limits of suggested expansion, say somewhere between 3 to 6 per cent of aggregate international reserves.

"Virtually take over" is perhaps too strong. The bank could not *directly* force any advanced country to supply funds for foreign aid. Indirectly, however, it could accomplish much the same thing without the consent of the government in question. The Triffin type of bank could on its own initiative purchase the securities of the International Bank for Reconstruction and Development or the securities of underdeveloped countries (where consent in either case would presumably readily be granted). Such purchases could create new funds for development purposes. These funds would then be employed to purchase equipment, etc., from the advanced countries. Upon receiving these deposits the advanced countries in question would in effect have undertaken to supply the *real* funds for development. The assets behind the new deposits thus employed, as in the Maxwell Stamp plan, would be the government securities of the underdeveloped countries.

At first, as we have seen, the Triffin bank assets would consist largely of U.S. and U.K. obligations. These would, however, be progressively liquidated under the 5 per cent per annum liquidation formula. Thus more and more the assets of the bank would consist of the government securities of the underdeveloped countries, securities which admittedly have questionable marketability. This could sooner or later militate against acceptance by the advanced countries of the new bank's deposit issues. The difficulty is that foreign aid and business finance are wrapped up in the same bundle as if they were one and the same thing.

Professor Triffin has himself, in his reply[23] to Altman's criticism (paragraphs 42 to 47),[24] admitted that this part of the discussion constituted the most solid argument of his critic. The paragraphs in question emphasized the fact that the in-

[23] International Monetary Fund, *Staff Papers*, vol. 8, p. 193, May 1961.

[24] *Ibid.*, pp. 171–174.

vestments of the Triffin bank would more and more consist necessarily of the securities of the underdeveloped countries. Triffin's reply, in effect, was that this is exactly what is wanted. In other words, we do not want to carry coals to Newcastle. And one could perhaps add that when the United States makes foreign loans, it itself accepts without question the obligations of underdeveloped countries. But there is a world of difference. The U.S. dollar is not based on these loans, as witness the assets of the Federal Reserve Banks. Every advanced country requires its central bank to hold unimpeachable assets against its liabilities. An international bank, if it is to succeed, must meet equally high standards.

Triffin's reply to Altman, referred to above, was published in May, 1961. Later in his contribution to the Seymour Harris volume on *The Dollar in Crisis* he made a more extended rebuttal in which he again acknowledged that a "more valid objection of Mr. Altman related to the composition of the Fund's assets." He reiterated that the expansion of the Fund's loans and investments should normally be expected to direct capital mostly to underdeveloped countries. But he called attention to the fact that in his *Gold and the Dollar Crisis* he had suggested that such development projects be financed only indirectly "through purchases of IBRD bonds or other securities of a similar character." This however would offer a very limited scope for investment. As is well known the IBRD is a "hard loan" institution and its aggregate loans covering a period of over fifteen years amount to only $6 billion. Perhaps in recognition of this fact, in the Seymour Harris volume, Triffin suggests that the Fund's investments could be "channeled to a greater extent towards older financial centers such as Frankfurt, Amsterdam, Paris, etc. and to London and New York."

Yet he clearly feels unhappy about this concession to his critics. The concession is made to "get around the taboos still prevalent in some circles about the nature of the assets which it is proper for monetary institutions to acquire." And in his *Gold and the Dollar Crisis* he said that the new Fund's resources would normally be employed in "markets where need for international capital is greater than in the United States and the United Kindgdom."[25]

This statement is highly revealing. It makes it quite clear that Triffin believes that ideally it is a primary function of a credit-creating international institution to provide capital to countries that are capital poor. It is my view, on the contrary, that its function is solely to provide an adequate international medium of exchange.[26]

HART-KALDOR-TINBERGEN PLAN[27]

This plan aims to solve at one stroke both the problem of commodity price stabilization and the problem of world liquidity. It is a modernized version of Benjamin Graham's multi-commodity standard for national currencies as ex-

[25] Robert Triffin, *Gold and the Dollar Crisis: The Future of Convertibility*, Yale University Press, New Haven, Conn., 1961, p. 117.

[26] It is always dangerous to report recollections of oral statements made by a famous individual, and such statements are usually (and quite rightly) taken with a grain of salt. Nevertheless, for what it may be worth, I recall a statement by Keynes made in the course of a casual conversation to the effect that he hoped the IMF would be businesslike in its loan policies, and that the World Bank would boldly assume risks. This statement I subscribe to. The World Bank bonds are backed by strong governments and their value rests in the final analysis on parliamentary appropriations. The World Bank could have been a more vigorous instrument of foreign aid. It has chosen however to be a conservative investment bank. A credit-creating central bank, however, cannot afford to be a foreign-aid, soft-loan agency.

[27] Albert G. Hart, Nicholas Kaldor, and Jan Tinbergen, *The Case for an International Commodity Reserve Currency*, A Memorandum Submitted to the United Nations Conference on Trade and Development, Geneva, March 28 to June 15, 1964.

pounded in his *Storage and Stability* (1937) and *World Commodities and World Currency* (1944).

The essential elements of this highly complicated scheme I have summarized as follows:

1. The IMF should establish its own currency called "bancor." Bancor operations should be completely separate and distinct from the existing system of IMF drawing rights which are denominated in national currencies.
2. Initially the IMF should issue $30 billion of bancor in exchange for $5 billion gold, $5 billion obligations of member countries, and a $20 billion bundle of commodities (thirty or so) suitable for storage.
3. This bundle of commodities would be purchased in the open market and from stocks held by member countries. They would be purchased at a "declared value" which means the average world price within the two preceding years.[28]
4. Member countries would agree to accept bancor in equal terms with gold. Only central banks would be entitled to hold bancor balances.
5. The convertibility of bancor into both gold and commodities should ensure that the price level of commodities as a bundle would be stable in terms of gold irrespective of changes in the exchange rates of individual currencies.
6. Members should undertake to employ their newly acquired bancor to pay off short-term indebtedness to other members. Specifically creditor countries should convert their holdings of key currencies into bancor. The key-currency countries should help to induce such conversion by lowering the short-term interest rate paid to foreign holders. Since the current official holdings of dollars and sterling amount to about $22 billion, this conversion could

[28] In the event that the market price of a commodity should rise by 50 per cent above its declared-value price, such commodity would be excluded from the bundle. If the plan were adopted in period of general increases in primary product prices, the whole scheme would go into suspense.

absorb $22 billion of the newly created $30 billion bancor, leaving a net increase in world liquidity of $8 billion.

7. If creditor countries do not choose to take bancor, the key-currency countries should then freeze their holdings of bancor as cover for the foreign official holdings of their currencies. Such a freeze would absorb $22 billion bancor with the same effect on world liquidity as if the dollar and sterling holdings had been converted into bancor.
8. The target of a $30 billion bancor issue it is thought might be reached in say five years, depending on how rapidly the $20 billion commodity bundle could be purchased. If commodity prices were falling, as was the case from 1955 to 1962, the declared value would rule above the market price and this would facilitate a rapid accumulation of the target commodity bundle of $20 billion.
9. Purchases and sales of commodities against bancor between the IMF and its members would take place in terms of warehouse certificates of a currently declared bundle of commodity units.
10. Private traders could be depended upon to buy commodities in the open market whenever the market price was below the declared value price at which the IMF would stand ready to buy within the margin of official buying and selling parity rates.
11. The IMF would set up its own marketing organization which would engage in open-market operations in the various industrial commodity markets whenever the market value of any of the commodities included in the bundle moved outside the official margins. Such operations, however, would not prevent the prices of individual commodities from changing in relation to each other. If the price of a commodity (sugar in 1962) should rise 50 per cent or more above its declared value, it should be excluded from the bundle. The stabilization of the general commodity price index would moderate the fluctuations of individual commodities but relative price movements would continue to prevail.
12. The important thing to note is that when the market price of commodities is below the declared value (as would be

> the case when the price level of commodities was falling) the IMF would be issuing new bancor and adding to its store of commodities. An increasing volume of international liquidity would be exerting an upward demand pull on commodities. Once the market price of commodities reached the declared value level, further storage of commodities and further creation of bancor would cease. An automatic self-balancing mechanism would control both the volume of international liquidity and the price level of commodities. Any tendency of the prices of the bundle of primary products to fall would be met by an absorption of stocks by the Fund and an increase in the bancor income of primary producers through the issue of bancor in exchange for commodities. Any tendency for world primary product prices to rise would be met by a release of stocks, a limitation of the rise in the bancor income of primary producers, and a reduction in world liquidity.

The theory underlying the scheme appears to be (1) that continued growth and full employment in the industrial countries depend on an increasing supply of primary products and (2) that the all-important factor in the development of the primary producing countries is an adequate supply of foreign exchange.

Basic to the analysis are the terms of trade. Because of the low elasticity of demand for foodstuffs and for many natural raw materials (owing to synthetic substitutes), a given rate of growth of manufacturing production in the advanced countries generates a less than proportionate growth of demand for primary products. Moreover the rate of growth of primary production lags a considerable time behind the movement of agricultural prices. In a period of high prices, large new investments will be made in the primary sector and, after a lag, these will produce a larger output of primary products. When these come to market, prices fall, investment in the primary sector declines, and eventually output is reduced until finally prices are restored to a remunerative level.

The fall in primary prices causes a decline in the purchases of manufactured goods from the industrial sector and in the investment by advanced countries in the primary sector. The decline in exports from the advanced countries to the less-developed countries may more than offset the gain to industrialized countries from the low cost of raw materials. Historically, according to the authors, a period of falling raw material prices has often been associated with a slowing down in the rate of industrial growth.[29] It is precisely, so it is argued, when the supplies of primary products are rising that rapid industrial growth is possible. These statements, I submit, are subject to challenge.

The authors admit that primary production may outgrow the needs of the industrialized sector, but this leaves out of account, they say, the potential acceleration of industrialization in backward countries. And this potential acceleration is blocked by the inadequate increase in effective demand, specifically (if I understand the authors correctly) an inadequate supply of foreign exchange for the primary sector.

In the authors' view, the central advantage of this scheme of commodity price stabilization by means of an international commodity reserve currency is precisely that under such an arrangement an increase in primary production will automatically cause an increase in the bancor income of the primary sector and so increase the effective demand for industrial products. This is true because any excess of supply of primary products will be absorbed by the Fund in exchange for bancor. These bancor will be used to buy manufactured goods, the industrial sector will experience export surpluses,

[29] This has clearly not been the case with respect to Western Europe from 1953 to 1963, though the argument may have some merit with respect to the United States.

and this will accelerate expansion and growth. As they expand they will need more primary products which can now be drawn from the bulging Fund stocks. The system appears therefore to be self-balancing. Instead, the current adjustment process, which permits prolonged periods of depressed prices, cuts down on the growth of output of primary products, and this reduces investment in the primary sector and causes a decline in industrial exports.

Expansion of exports from the industrialized sector benefits both parties so long as there is slack in the economy of the industrial countries. Once full employment is reached, exports can expand only as domestic consumption and investment are reduced. If there is no curtailment, the money costs of exports will rise unless the exporting country appreciates its currency. In either case the cost of imports to the primary producing sector will rise, and these countries will tend to transfer their purchases to areas that do not yet have overfull employment. Once these also reach full employment, purchases will be directed to still less-developed countries. The authors argue that since the world as a whole is a vast underdeveloped economy, vast reserves of labor can be absorbed into manufacturing if only raw materials are available and if demand is expanding. It is alleged that the growth of world manufactures can be stepped up to match any likely increase in the supply of primary products. The authors do indeed admit that industrialization requires "other things besides labor, capital and raw materials" such as know-how and managerial ability. But they believe that the experience of Japan, Brazil, and Mexico show that know-how and managerial ability can be acquired fairly rapidly when the underlying conditions (which, however, are not spelled out) for industrial growth are favorable.

Thus they conclude that because industrial expansion is so much a matter of effective demand and because weakness in the markets for primary products makes for unfavorable business conditions in industrial countries, the opportunities for accelerated economic growth afforded by the technical progress in primary production tend largely to go to waste. These statements seem to suggest that they fear that the advanced countries are quite incapable of pursuing a deliberate program of full employment, though the well-known competence of the authors in modern monetary and fiscal policy would negate this conclusion. These countries need, so the argument seems to run, an automatic scheme which will provide at one stroke the right amount of liquidity, commodity price stability, rapid industrialization of backward countries, and full employment and growth in the advanced sector.

As the canny Vermonter would say: "Sounds awfully good; what's the hitch?" Does the scheme make sense? Synthetic substitutes could easily develop to a point at which natural raw materials become increasingly unimportant, in which case the continued accumulation of stocks in order to maintain an artificial value would become completely irrational. There are, moreover, other ways, far less complicated and more practical, to accomplish the goal of more stable export earnings for the primary producers, if the advanced countries are prepared to undertake such a program. I myself favor preferential trade treatment and support prices for the primary producing countries so that our aid would reach them through normal economic processes. Stock piling as a means to boost prices can, however, be wasteful, expensive, and frustrating, as the American farm program has demonstrated. New international agreements are not easily reached, and for this proposal adroit salesmanship would be required to arouse any enthusiasm among the industrially advanced countries.

The plan professes, moreover, to achieve the right amount of world liquidity. It assumes that the amount of international liquidity that would automatically be created in pursuit of a stable price level of thirty primary products would be the correct amount, but this assumption is not buttressed with convincing evidence. If the bundle were a weighted and all-inclusive assortment of the aggregate merchandise world trade, that would be one thing, and even this would get us involved in difficult and controversial monetary theory. But if the bundle consists of thirty storable commodities which in fact are becoming relatively less and less important in a growing world trade whose composition is rapidly changing, that is quite a different thing. For a bundle of thirty increasingly obsolete commodities to control the value of international money would be like the proverbial stub tail wagging a rapidly growing dog. The world trade in the bundle of thirty commodities is less than $20 billion in contrast to aggregate world merchandise imports of $130 billion.

The need for liquidity is by no means a simple function of world trade as a whole, much less of the trade in a bundle of thirty storable commodities. The amount of liquidity needed will depend upon a great many things including the extent to which foreign exchange is covered by an exchange guarantee, the extent to which central bank collaboration can squelch speculative raids, the success of programs to stabilize cyclical fluctuations, the extent to which strong capital markets in various centers can absorb foreign security issues, the growth of aggregate world trade, etc.

How much bancor or foreign exchange could be issued to the primary sector without creating general world inflation would depend, for one thing, upon the extent to which the advanced countries would be prepared to tighten their belts in order to make room for huge exports to the underdeveloped countries. Hart, Kaldor, and Tinbergen appear to believe that the one limiting factor that restrains industrialization and growth in the backward countries is a lack of bancor income, i.e., foreign exchange. Materials, labor, and even know-how and skills are either amply available or can readily be acquired. All that is lacking is effective demand, which in this context must mean foreign exchange. Have not the authors vastly underestimated the overwhelming obstacles to progress—many not of an economic character at all—with which the underdeveloped countries have to contend?

• *part two* •

SOME CONTROVERSIAL ISSUES

chapter seven

"CORRECTIVE MEASURES"

FINANCIAL DISCIPLINE

As is well known by anyone who has followed the balance-of-payments controversies, proposals to alleviate the pressure on the key currencies often encounter the objection that such panaceas are merely "soothing syrup," pain-killers that fail to reach the seat of the trouble. They give the patient a deceptive feeling of security. The warning signals are covered up. Internal domestic policies are freed from the constraints imposed by external discipline.

The problem relates essentially to the control of inflation

and the role that external discipline actually plays as a restraining influence. Ask any Western European how he explains the *relatively* moderate increases in wages and prices in a period of great expansion, full employment, and often even overfull employment, and he will almost certainly point to the restraint imposed by international competition.

As a government official or central banker what he has in mind is almost certainly the threat of a balance-of-payments deficit. If he is an industrialist he has in mind the fear of losing his export market. His concern is limited to his own business.

Now this is a difference worth noting. In my own thinking, I should like to remove as far as possible the restraints which the external discipline (i.e., the balance-of-payments discipline) imposes upon domestic full employment policies. There will still be plenty of reasons why we should pursue the goal of reasonable price stability, and in particular I do not want to eliminate either domestic or international competition. At first thought this may seem like begging the question, but I do not believe it is. Domestic competition can be vigorous and effective, but here there is no balance-of-payments discipline. International competition is a deep concern for each industry even though these industries are located in a country which never experiences any balance-of-payment problem. Obviously international competition and the external payments discipline are not one and the same thing. I believe that much confusion arises from the mistaken view that they are identical twins.

How does one explain the fact that the postwar price increases have been kept reasonably under control? Competition, both domestic and international, is certainly a part of the answer. A part of the answer is inertia and lags. A part is an awareness by business concerns that a stable price policy is good public relations. Neither business nor labor likes to face hostile public opinion. I am convinced from President

Kennedy's tussle with the steel industry in 1962 that public opinion can be marshaled with sufficient force so that both business and labor become more cautious. The government is something more than a tug-of-war between organized producers. In the United States at any rate there is a very large public that is in no sense a party to any collective wage bargain. In particular, the President, who alone represents the entire nation, can and often does stand out over and above the special interest groups.

We want and need competition, both domestic and international. But we do not want unfair competition. Domestically we try to suppress unfair competition. Internationally, unfair competition means, for one thing, competitive pressure imposed by a country that is deflating its costs and prices or is engaged in export dumping, export tax remissions, or export subsidies. Discriminatory controls have to be applied against such countries and indeed this is permitted by the Bretton Woods arrangements. Again, disrupting influences may flow from a country that is experiencing rapid inflation. Once the rate of inflation has really moved into the danger zone, such a country's currency is no longer acceptable as foreign exchange.

These are the extreme cases. They fall outside of the area of reasonable limits. In economics as well as in law we continually have to apply the "rule of reason," as the U.S. Supreme Court puts it. Beyond reasonable limits it is contrary to good public policy to permit the external payments balance to control domestic policy. Indeed, this is precisely why countries build up international reserves. These reserves free a country from being *rigorously* controlled, month by month and year by year, by the severe discipline of the external balance. The current debate about the external discipline relates purely and simply to whether we should increase the "international margin" still more to give us greater freedom from the rigorous restraints on domestic policy imposed by this discipline. This is what the current liquidity problem is all about. In the past we have been concerned with episodic and cyclical imbalances. Does this go far enough? Now do we not need to provide time for adjustment of structural imbalances? Greater freedom can be achieved by (1) improving the quality of the foreign exchange component, endowing it with an exchange guarantee and thereby removing the pressure of gold drains and (2) increasing the aggregate volume of actual or potential reserves. Within reasonable limits this is in the line of progress.

In the 1963 meeting of the IMF a new note was struck. Joseph R. Slevin, reporting for the *New York Herald Tribune*, had this to say:

> Free-world financial officers are barely hinting at something they used to shout about. The missing subject is financial discipline. It is the painful, orthodox cure for balance-of-payments deficits.
>
> Instead of financial discipline the talk now is of liquidity. The stress is upon giving a country generous credit so that it can eliminate its payments deficit gradually.

Shortly before the conference met, the Brookings Institution published a report on the U.S. balance of payments by Walter S. Salant, Emile Despres and others. This report stated unequivocally that "deflationary measures, the classical means of improving the balance-of-payments, reduce employment and real incomes—effects which are neither politically feasible nor economically desirable in a modern industrial country."[1] Deflationary measures, the report said, restrain investment and hamper modernization and innovation. Efficiency increases are more likely to be made in an atmosphere of general

[1] *Report on the U.S. Balance of Payments in 1968* by Walter S. Salant, Emile Despres, Alice M. Rivlin, Lorie Tarshis, Laurence B. Krause, and William A. Salant, The Brookings Institution, Washington, D.C., p. 246.

expansion and unrestricted foreign competition. Measures which might endanger economic growth and high employment levels should not be adopted for balance-of-payments reasons.

FREEDOM TO PURSUE DOMESTIC GOALS

It was a cardinal objective of the Bretton Woods Conference to develop, through the IMF and the Bank for Reconstruction and Development, international cooperation and collaboration so that balance-of-payments difficulties would not act as a deterrent to domestic full employment policies. The problem was to find a way to meet payments imbalances without having to resort to deflationary and restrictive measures.

To counteract temporary disequilibria, the IMF was equipped with funds (subscribed by member countries) which could be loaned to members confronted with balance-of-payments difficulties. If a country's exchange rate got structurally out of line (fundamental disequilibrium), it might be helped out of its difficulty by development loans made by the Bank for Reconstruction and Development. Finally the deficit country was permitted unilaterally to alter its exchange rate up to 10 per cent, and if a larger adjustment was necessary the country could ask permission from the Fund. In the case of a fundamental disequilibrium, however, the Fund could not deny the request merely on the ground that the country had followed unorthodox domestic policies. Bretton Woods permitted exchange restrictions on capital movements but not on current transactions. In effect it placed the burden of adjustment on the surplus countries since it permitted deficit countries to place restrictions on imports if necessary to safeguard their international reserves but only to the extent permitted by GATT agreements and with the advice and consent of the IMF. Bretton Woods expounded the view that full employment policies are not only good for the country in question but are also beneficial to its neighbors, to world trade, and to international equilibrium.

Throughout the interwar period, Keynes defended the principle of national independence from external influences. To promote this independence he suggested (1) official buying and selling operations in the foreign exchange markets, (2) exchange control when necessary with special reference to capital movements, (3) widening the spread between the official buying and selling price of gold, and (4) adjustment when necessary of the exchange rate. He constantly stressed the point that the burden of adjustment should primarily be assumed by the surplus countries. In his House of Lords speech in support of Bretton Woods he declared: "We are determined that . . . the external value of sterling shall conform to its internal value as set by our own domestic policies."[2]

But Bretton Woods, as events actually turned out, proved to be far short of the resources needed to cope with the herculean task of rebuilding and stabilizing the free world by cooperative financial effort. The Fund's resources, as finally negotiated, had been whittled down to around $8 billion. In reality (considering the postwar collapse in Western Europe) the only asset that could effectively be counted upon was the subscription by the United States of $2,750 million.

KEYNES'S CLEARING UNION

This was a far cry from the bold program (politically unacceptable to the United States) which was advocated by

[2] Seymour E. Harris (ed.), *The New Economics*, Kelley & Millman, New York, 1947, p. 374.

Keynes in his clearing union plan. Keynes's proposal would have permitted deficit countries to meet the balance-of-payments needs by making overdrafts in the clearing union up to the limit of their assigned quotas. Surplus countries (primarily, and indeed almost exclusively, the United States as things then looked) would have agreed under the plan to accept payment in the form of bancor, the proposed new international monetary unit to be issued by the clearing union and which was to become the sole means of settling international accounts. And since the aggregate quotas amounted (over and above the U.S. quota) to around $30 billion, this could have resulted ultimately in the United States being "forced" to extend credit in that amount to deficit countries. In short, the scheme in practice would have implemented an enormous program of foreign aid financed by the United States, not by year-to-year appropriations by the Congress, but by advance commitments which could have cumulated to around $30 billion.

MARSHALL AID

Considering the magnitude of the task of rehabilitating the postwar world, Keynes's plan was highly realistic in terms of economics but it was politically unacceptable to the United States. Political hurdles are however often swept aside by powerful historical forces. The flow of worldwide economic forces could not be dammed up permanently by the severely limited outlook of the U.S. Congress. As the hard facts of life unfolded it became evident that the Marshall Aid plan, first proposed in June, 1947, made sense. The signal was given by the Communist penetration into Greece, Turkey, Hungary, Romania, and Czechoslovakia. The Marshall Aid program set the pattern for the vast U.S. foreign aid which by the end of 1963 had cumulated to around $90 billion. The monetary and economic rehabilitation thus financed was essential for the preservation of the Western world.

There was no other way out. The Fund's resources were not intended for long-term rehabilitation. Nor could the Bank for Reconstruction and Development, depending heavily upon funds raised in the private capital markets, cope with the rebuilding of the economic systems of the free world. Indeed the cumulated total loans made by the World Bank up to the end of 1963 amounted to only about $6.5 billion. Contrast this with the $90 billion poured out in foreign aid, economic and military, by the United States. Thus it was, as events turned out, that the United States became the financial bulwark of the Western world and the dollar became the central pivot—the primary key currency—of the evolving new international monetary structure—the gold–dollar-exchange standard.[3]

Keynes was quite right. The rehabilitation of the free world could only be achieved through vast advances by the United States. But he *underestimated* the amount. Under his plan these advances would have been made through the clearing union and financed (at least this is the implication) automatically through an expansion of Federal Reserve credit which would have come into existence as and when American exporters deposited their bancor balances in commercial banks which, in turn, would send them to a Federal Reserve Bank to be credited to their deposit account. As it turned out the job was in fact done by the unilateral action of the United States financed, not by expansion of central bank credit, but by appropriations voted by the Congress.

The experience of the last fifteen years clearly reveals a

[3] Sterling continues to be the key currency for the sterling area built up around the old British Commonwealth, but the amount of sterling held as official foreign exchange balances has remained frozen at around $7 billion during the last decade.

very fundamental fact which has still not been fully grasped, namely, that the modern world cannot function without massive capital transfers. The United States has made gigantic grants and loans, so gigantic indeed that in recent years these outflows (supplemented increasingly by private capital outflow) have resulted in a piling up of excess dollar holdings. These excess dollar holdings are in some measure an indication of the failure of Western Europe to carry its part of the burden of foreign aid and military security. The surplus countries of Western Europe have not been balancing their international accounts by investing these excess dollar holdings abroad. Substantial international payments surpluses have not been offset by long-term international financing.

Spurious comparisons of aid provided by advanced countries have often been made which confuse the financial aspects of a continuing economic colonialism with genuine foreign aid. Properly speaking aid should be limited to government grants and loans to noncolonial areas and to government contributions to international development institutions like the World Bank. At first the United States was the only significant source of foreign aid so defined. Gradually this has changed and it is estimated that by 1963 the United States provided about 55 per cent of the aid to noncolonial areas.[4]

Experience shows that this matter cannot be left simply to the unilateral action of individual nations. No modern nation has succeeded in providing security for old age by leaving this up to the individual but instead has found it necessary to introduce collective action in the form of social security. So, too, we are learning that the necessary flow of capital offsets to persistent deficits of countries that carry a disproportionate share of the costs of international security requires new programs designed to bolster the gold-exchange standard.

[4] See *Economic Report of the President*, January, 1964, p. 157.

AN INTERNATIONAL CAPITAL MARKET

No system of fixed exchange rates can survive in a market free from exchange controls, import quotas, and the like without a fluid and effective capital market encompassing the area within which fixed exchange rates persist.[5] Take for example the twelve Federal Reserve districts in the vast area of the United States. Disequilibrating forces are continually at work making some districts deficit areas in their payments relation to the rest of the country. What holds the whole thing together? By far the most important single factor is the fact that all areas in the United States are integrated into a common capital market. Moreover, the Federal government plays a large role in dispensing funds—relief, reconstruction, development aid, social security, unemployment benefits, farm price supports, etc. The national unified monetary unit (which means a system of fixed exchange rates) covers the same area as the nationwide capital market and the Federal fiscal system.

Assume that the Ninth Federal Reserve District has a trade deficit with the New York District. The Minneapolis area imports too much and exports too little. A business firm in Mankato sends a $10,000 check to a New York firm from which it has purchased a supply of goods. This check is deposited in a New York bank and sent on to the New York Federal Reserve Bank for collection. The New York Federal sends it on to the Minneapolis Federal. The latter debits it

[5] "There is no reason why long-term loans should not be applied for this purpose. The whole idea of the current or the basic balance of a country as an indicator of the 'soundness' of its international position, and of the necessity for keeping the basic balance in equilibrium, ought to break down with rational and deliberate policies of the kind described here. . . . It may be a 'sound' policy to lend and borrow for long periods." Bent Hansen, Central Bank of Egypt Lectures, 1962.

against the Mankato bank's balance. Thus the liabilities of the Minneapolis Federal to the Mankato bank are reduced by $10,000 and offsetting this, it now owes the New York Federal $10,000.[6] The Minneapolis Federal can reimburse the New York Federal by means of a transfer of gold through the Gold Settlement Fund. Both the liabilities and the assets of the Minneapolis Federal will now have declined by $10,000. The Federal Reserve Board may then reallocate the various districts' holdings of gold and government securities so as to restore the gold reserve ratio of the Minneapolis Reserve Bank. For example U.S. securities could be transferred from the Minneapolis bank to the New York bank in exchange for gold. Thus the liquidity of the Minneapolis district would be restored. This would permit renewed expansion of Federal Reserve credit in the Minneapolis area, and thereby reduce the deflationary pressure. In the meantime, long-run adjustments such as the relocation of labor and industries to more prosperous and expanding areas will gradually be made.

Thus within the boundaries of a sovereign country we do not apply punitive measures and painful disciplines. We fill the trade balance gap with capital flows.[7]

Bank credit and governmental expansionist measures may facilitate the building up of new industries and the strengthening of old ones. Thus the adjustment is made, not by the process of "going through the wringer" (perverse restraints), but by means of the cooperating expansionist policies and collective action of the nation as a whole, namely, by offsetting capital flows made possible by an ample volume of

[6] The figure here used is for convenience only. It is of course ridiculously small. It would take far more to cause a gold transfer.

[7] For an excellent discussion of the role of the capital account in the balance of payments see James C. Ingram, *A Proposal for Financial Integration in the Atlantic Community, Materials Prepared for the Subcommittee on International Exchange and Payments*, 87th Cong., 2d Sess., 1962, pp. 177–207.

interregional liquidity. This process of expansion can and should be carried to the point of full employment, but not to the point of inflation.

Keynes had hoped for his clearing union a degree of financial integration akin but not yet equal to that achieved within the domestic economy of a sovereign nation. And Bretton Woods represented a modest effort toward this goal. The point that needs to be stressed is the enormous importance of an adequate flow of equilibrating funds between surplus and deficit areas if the process of going through the wringer—the so-called "corrective measures"—is to be avoided. What is needed is a pool of international compensatory funds adequate not only to offset temporary imbalances but also to hold the line while slow-moving, long-term adjustments are being made.

As long as the credit pool is relatively limited, as is currently the case, the available or potentially available credit reserves need to be supplemented by gold. Increasingly, however, as the international compensatory finance structure is built up and strengthened year after year, gold may come to play, bit by bit, a smaller role. Speculation in gold will more and more be brought under control. A larger and larger part of the burden of exchange stabilization will be carried by international compensatory finance. We may then at long last attain an international monetary system which is wholly "managed" and no longer based even partially on gold.

RESTRICTIVE MEASURES

In the nineteenth century, severe self-discipline—meaning, in fact, deflation of wages and prices—was the orthodox remedy (automatically enforced by the gold standard) for balance-of-payments deficits. This policy could indeed, and in fact did, restore balance in the international accounts in the days before World War I, though at the cost of widespread suffering and unemployment. Balance was not achieved without evoking riots and bloodshed. The history of violence in the American labor movement in the last quarter of the nineteenth century attests to that. But through it all, balance was, in fact, restored.[8] The gold standard and the corrective measures it imposed were taken for granted as an inevitable way of life. No one was to blame. It all operated under so-called natural law.

In the interwar period following World War I deliberate action was widely introduced to cope with balance-of-payments maladjustments. Things were no longer allowed to run their course. Government intervention was undertaken on a broad scale. But these "contrived" measures were perhaps even more restrictive in their effect on the international structure than the mechanism of the gold standard had been. In the interwar period deliberate policies were introduced which later came to be described as efforts to lift oneself out of the international morass by "beggar my neighbor" devices such as competitive devaluations, prohibitive tariffs, import quotas, exchange control, and other methods of discrimination against foreign countries. Both the prewar automatic constraints and the interwar deliberately contrived policies sought to remedy international imbalances via impoverishment—the former by self-impoverishment, the latter by impoverishing one's neighbors. In contrast Bretton Woods proclaimed boldly the view that international equilibrium can best be won when all member countries are prosperous.

[8] Professor Triffin has long held the view that tight money in the United Kingdom in the nineteenth century reduced capital outflow and cut down the industrial demand for primary products, forcing down the prices of raw material imports. This stimulated domestic consumption and reduced costs. Thus the adjustment was obtained at the expense of the primary producing countries.

Deflation, low capacity output with attendant high unit costs, a low level of public and private investment will not make a country competitive in world markets. To be competitive, a country must be operating at a high level of capacity. To be competitive, a country must be prosperous. To induce home investment and attract foreign capital, it must be a growing, expanding economy. In an atmosphere of growth, innovation can best flourish. Restrictive practices both by labor and by management tend to disappear under conditions of full employment. And finally, a high level of exports requires prosperous neighbors.

This was the optimistic clarion call of Bretton Woods. Countries with short-run, temporary imbalances were to be helped over the hump by the IMF rather than be forced to apply self-flagellation. Once over the hump, a full employment economy exchanging goods and services in a prosperous world would be in a strong position to adjust to long-run changes and so to cope with the imbalances continually emerging in a dynamic, ever-changing world.

THE "MIX" OF MONETARY AND FISCAL POLICY

The problem of reconciling domestic full employment and international equilibrium has, however, proved to be far more recalcitrant than was recognized in the Bretton Woods philosophy. In the absence of a world government and a truly international economy, the all-important regulative devices to harmonize domestic full employment with international equilibrium are monetary and fiscal policy. If these were properly coordinated internationally, all would be well. In fact, both policies are pursued by individual nations acting for the most part independently. So long as this is the case, what is the proper "mix" of monetary and fiscal policy that deficit and surplus countries should pursue in order to promote as far as possible both full employment and a payments balance?

The rule currently most commonly accepted is that monetary policy should be employed to promote a payments balance and fiscal policy to promote full employment. If a payments deficit country is also suffering from high unemployment and tries to cure this by means of a low interest rate, capital outflows will create a still greater payments deficit. Higher employment is won at the expense of a payments imbalance. If a country with a surplus in its balance of payments (which is flooding its central bank and its commercial banks with excess liquidity, thereby causing overfull employment and inflationary pressure) tries to restrain the boom by means of higher interest rates, the effect will be to draw funds in from abroad and so increase still more the payments surplus.

The answer for the former country is: Cure the payments deficit with a high interest rate and the unemployment with expansionary fiscal policy. For the latter country the answer is: Cure the surplus by means of a low rate of interest and the boom by means of a restricted fiscal policy.

All this sounds so easy, too easy. The world is neither simple nor logical. Problems are neither white nor black. Higher rates of interest will tend to deter investment and this militates against efficiency and competitiveness. High interest rates are a deterrent to young and growing businesses and to residential construction and tend to raise the cost of community capital goods such as schools and hospitals.

An ingenious partial way out of this dilemma has been initiated and implemented in the United States. Instead of a high, long-term interest rate designed to choke off European borrowings in the New York capital market, introduce an interest equalization tax (an excise tax on American purchases of foreign stocks and bonds) which would have exactly the same effect on foreign sellers as an increase in interest rates,[9] while at the same time it would leave domestic interest rates undisturbed. Another ingenious device, which has been employed with some success, is the following: Let the monetary authorities sell short-term U.S. government obligations and buy long-terms. This raises the short-term rates and lowers the long-term rates. Raising the short-term rates helps to keep short-term money at home, which helps the payments balance; lowering the long-term rate helps employment.

UNACCEPTABLE EXPEDIENTS

There is no lack of so-called corrective measures which can quickly cure a payments deficit. But most of these expedients are unacceptable "in the sense that they undermine the national and international objectives which it is the very purpose of the international monetary system to promote," as Prof. James Tobin has aptly put it. Indeed, "a major symptom of a shortage of international liquidity," he suggests, "would be—and perhaps already is—that countries resort to such expedients."[10]

So long as there is a shortage of liquidity, acceptable policies (policies that are not damaging to the world economy) cannot be applied to correct imbalances. Yet a country may find itself in a tight place. It has to meet its international financial obligations and it has to pay its bills. It can shop around for opportunities to borrow. The United States, as we have seen, has been doing just that. But all this may not

[9] The tax, to prevent circumvention, should be applied to bank loans as well.

[10] See *Hearings before the Joint Economic Committee*, November 12–15, 1963, p. 553.

be enough to meet *today's* problem. The United States has, to a limited degree, felt compelled to do things it has not liked to do—things that could have been avoided if adequate international liquidity had been available.

Let us illustrate this concretely. On July 18, 1963, President Kennedy sent to Congress a special message on the balance of payments. In this message he urged the enactment of the interest equalization tax, referred to above, to become effective as of the day following the message. In addition he suggested a further tying of foreign aid to U.S. exports, a further reduction in overseas military expenditures, and a further reduction in purchases of strategic materials abroad. The Administration made it clear that it regarded at least some of these measures as temporary. They were emergency expedients designed to buy time for adjustment. The danger always is, as the history of protection shows, that strong special interests will be fostered which tend to entrench themselves in a permanent structure.

PRICE STABILITY

Often the most ardent disciplinarians place primary emphasis upon price stability as the means to cure persistent deficits. As a matter of fact price stability presents no conflict between desirable domestic goals and international equilibrium.[11] While a rigidly stable price level is obviously not possible or even desirable, "reasonable" price stability is equally important both from the domestic and international viewpoints.

[11] Prof. Gottfried Haberler, in an article in *Lloyds Bank Review*, January, 1961, expresses the view that for the leading industrial countries the external financial disciple argument does not apply. "Their internal sensitivity to prolonged inflation . . . is a sufficient inducement to financial discipline."

Leading industrial countries fully recognize this fact. By and large most of the leading countries, at any rate (for a fairly full detailed discussion see Chapter 11), have on balance pursued a policy of fairly reasonable price stability since around 1953.[12] The decade 1953 to 1963 cannot be labeled one of wild inflation. With respect to the United States there has been no significant inflation since 1958, the year our balance-of-payments crisis began. Wholesale prices stood at 100.4 in 1958, and at 100.3 in December, 1963.

Here a sharp distinction should be made between a program to undo the past and a program to prevent future maladjustments. A program designed to deflate an established level of prices, to break down a cost-price structure by monetary and fiscal measures, is clearly destructive, and no modern country can tolerate it. But an appropriate mix of fiscal and monetary measures designed to prevent a *future* rise in the cost structure is a quite different matter.[13]

Throughout the advanced industrial part of the free world, countries have, in the postwar period, reached a tolerable stability of prices. World trade has been expanding rapidly, and international financial relations are subjected to more collaboration and cooperation than ever before. The IMF, together with the supplementary support of the Group of Ten and other arrangements, especially the new Federal Reserve and U.S. Treasury inventions of recent years—all

[12] Note the following from the 1962 Annual Report of the IMF, p. 42: "The Fund recognizes that the process of economic growth itself is likely to create pressures on resources that may lead to price increases and that not all price increases are incompatible with sound development."

[13] The cost structure will not rise, in the absence of unjustified increases in administered prices, if money wages rise in line with overall increases in per worker productivity. Or at least this is true unless the marginal capital-output ratio is rising, which appears not to be the case in the United States.

this has provided reasonable assurance that short-term disequilibrium problems are pretty well under control. The soil is now ready for new approaches with respect to long-term and persistent imbalances, especially those caused by noncommercial transfers and by abnormal capital flows due to the failure of Western Europe to develop adequate capital markets.

The Western world is rich enough in financial resources, if properly marshaled, to wait out the processes of adjustment which are inherent in the very nature of a dynamic, expanding enterprise economy. Looking toward the future we can devise governmentally contrived methods of international financial integration along the lines suggested in Chapter 6.

A CONCLUDING NOTE ON THE EXTERNAL DISCIPLINE

The points of view expressed by the numerous economists who have concerned themselves with current international monetary problems cover so wide a range that any effort to classify may appear to be presumptuous. Such an attempt could easily run into almost endless detail and refinements. Instead I have chosen to cut through endless differences in order to make the simplest possible classification on very broad lines.

Adopting this bold (and no doubt somewhat arbitrary) approach, I divide the sheep from the goats as follows: One flock includes all those who are very much concerned that international monetary imbalances will not defeat the domestic goal of full employment. The other flock includes those whose special concern is the maintenance of price stability and who are therefore loath to weaken the external discipline.

I do not, however, mean to imply that either one of these groups is unconcerned about the matter which is close to the hearts of the other group. I am dealing here with the *predominant* interest of each group. You will notice that I do not even say "primary" interest, I say "special" interest.

Those whose special interest is full employment are very much concerned with improving the international monetary mechanism so as to provide a wide "international margin" —wide enough so that there is ample scope for full employment policies without continually being confronted with balance-of-payments restraints. They ask for leeway within which to operate. They ask for ample time for the international equilibrating and adjustment processes to work. Those whose special interest is price stability are afraid or at least reluctant to widen the international margin lest this opens the door to very strong and perhaps uncontainable inflationary pressure.

This is the gist of the argument. Each side attempts to deny that it is hostile to the goals professed by its opponents. The full employment adherents stress that they also are concerned about reasonable price stability. They point out that reasonable price stability is a goal that any responsible modern society must seek quite apart from any balance-of-payments problem. The international restraint is not a necessary condition. The external roadblock to full employment is an evil that must be removed. Once it is removed there will still remain plenty of good reasons why the goal of reasonable price stability should be pursued.

The adherents to the gospel of external discipline believe that the goal of price stability is an overriding one and that it is, in the modern "power group" society, extremely difficult to achieve. It needs all the support it can get. A powerful restraining influence is the external discipline. Once this is completely removed, all hell will break loose. Moreover, this group will not accept the view that the goal of reasonable full employment is necessarily rendered impossible of achievement even though the external discipline is retained. Nor is it adamantly opposed to schemes which permit some reasonable widening of the international margin, some enlargement of the area within which one is free to operate.

Thus for some members of each group there is a considerable middle ground. For many it becomes a matter of emphasis rather than clean-cut and sharp opposition. It is like the Republican and Democratic parties in the United States. One can find opponents like Goldwater and Javits in one camp, and Hubert Humphrey and Byrd in the other. But one is more likely to find middle-of-the-roaders on each side.

The external disciplinarians make up a more homogeneous group, on balance, than do the libertarians. The libertarians can quite easily be classified according to the primary method by which it is sought to obtain relief from the severe external discipline. Class A wishes to achieve this end by means of an exchange- or gold-value guarantee, partial or complete. Class B wishes to achieve it by means of a greatly increased volume of international liquidity. Class A believes than once the fiduciary component of international reserves is made as good as gold by means of the guarantee, there will be little need for large increases in liquidity. Class B believes (perhaps discounting the political possibility of extensive exchange guarantees) that large increases in liquidity (plus machinery to ensure adequate increases in the future) are urgently needed to provide time for the slow-moving adjustment processes.

chapter eight

THE CASE AGAINST DEVALUATION

FUNDAMENTAL DISEQUILIBRIUM

There is perhaps no sector in the wide field covered by economics in which language is employed so loosely as in the discussion of fundamental disequilibrium, overvaluation, and balance-of-payments problems. Often the words are used to cover up a difficulty rather than to clarify a problem. The Bretton Woods charter employs the phrase fundamental disequilibrium. This was the easy way out. Any effort to define the term clearly and unequivocally would have led to endless controversy. And if a country experiences persistent deficits in its balance of payments over several years, many economists are prone to jump hastily to the conclusion that the currency is overvalued, or, conversely, if there is no deficit that the exchange rate is in equilibrium.

In this connection, I should like to quote some paragraphs from an article which I wrote many years ago, as follows:[1]

> In England in 1925–30 the overvalued pound was reflected not in a deficit in the balance of payments but in a serious deflationary pressure upon prices and wages, especially in the export industries, and in widespread unemployment. Similarly, in the period 1931–33, the depreciation of the currencies of many countries had no significant effect upon the American balance of payment position, but exerted a strong downward pressure upon American prices. American industries competing with import industries took their licking by meeting the price competition of depreciated currencies. But they held their own in the market. American imports did not rise.
>
> An exchange rate may be regarded as correct if it affords no "artificial" advantage in international competition. This means that when all of the productive resources of a country are fully employed, the exchange rate should not artificially divert certain industries to the foreign market. A correct exchange rate is one in which only those productive resources of the country are employed in exports that have a comparative advantage in the foreign markets on the basis of an economic, world-wide allocation of resources. The exchange rate of a country should be adjusted so that its cost structure will tend to be pushed neither downward nor upward by the given exchange rate. An equilibrium exchange rate is therefore one that represents a "parity" in the cost structure of the different countries.
>
> It would probably not be difficult to discover serious departure from an equilibrium exchange rate if all countries really enjoyed full employment. Under these conditions the "pull" of the foreign market in the case of an undervalued currency, or the price-depressant effect of foreign competitors in the case of an overvalued currency, would be fairly easy to detect. In the case, however, of

[1] See Appendix B, A Note on "Fundamental Disequilibrium," in my *America's Role in the World Economy*, Norton, New York, 1945, pp. 187–192.

varying degrees of employment in different countries and in various phases of a violently fluctuating business cycle, the cost-price-structure relationship within any one country is seriously distorted. Unit costs are abnormally high when utilization of capacity is low. Unit labor costs are high, though wage rates would in fact prove to be low if capacity were fully utilized. The distortion of the cost-structure under depression conditions, makes international comparisons difficult.

In determining whether the conditions of deflation and unemployment is caused, or at least intensified, by a wrong exchange rate, judgment must, of course, be applied to various matters. The country may be depressed by reason of a low volume of domestic-investment. It should not be utterly impossible to distinguish price-depressing effect, flowing from inadequate internal outlets for investment, from deflationary pressures from outside. Mere price deflation and unemployment is no proof of a disequilibrium in the exchange rate.[2]

The matter is obviously exceedingly complicated. In the nineteenth century the problem was in fact relatively simple. Government policy was pretty much restricted to protectionism, and customs duties remained for long periods relatively fixed. Within this framework automatic or spontaneous factors played the overwhelmingly dominant role. Wages in a competitive market were determined by the overall marginal productivity of labor. International cost-price rela-

[2] This last paragraph particularly applies to the United States in the period of semistagnation, 1958 to 1962. In my judgment this semistagnation was induced by domestic, not international factors. By 1958 the spontaneous postwar factors making for prosperity and high-level employment had largely been exhausted. The scarcities in the American economy were no longer automobiles and household appliances. The scarcities were schools, hospitals, medical schools, doctors, nurses, urban renewal, public recreational centers, etc. This required an enlarged Federal budget. Indeed an enlarged Federal budget was needed to mop up the enormous savings which a U.S. full employment economy generates. See my booklet: *The Post-war American Economy: Performance and Problems,* Norton, New York, 1964.

tionships were automatically kept pretty much in line. The wage-productivity guidelines were in the very nature of a free market economy in control. Labor was distributed between industries so as to yield approximately the same efficiency wage throughout the economy. The limited international mobility of labor ensured that, while the marginal productivity would vary greatly from country to country, production in the various industries would be pushed in each country to the point where the marginal cost was equalized (account being taken of transportation) more or less throughout the trading world. Product differentiation was relatively unimportant. The price system was in control.

The literature on international economics still reads very much in terms of this pattern. But consider how the world has changed. A persistent deficit in the balance of payments may nowadays be the product of a multitude of factors. A country's efficiency wages (productivity-wage ratio) may or may not have gotten out of line; but even though it has, this may not mean that the exchange rate is out of line. A country's balance of payments is nowadays buffeted about, not merely by the spontaneous forces formerly dominant in a laissez-faire society, but also by a variety of policy programs pursued by foreign countries and by the relevant country itself. On top of this is the dynamism of modern industrialism and the rapidity of changes in products and in processes of production.

If a country has been experiencing persistent deficits for some years it is of the utmost importance to inquire into the cause or causes. One cannot jump to the conclusion that the exchange rate is out of line. One cannot offhand equate persistent deficits with overvaluations. One cannot assume right away that the appropriate remedy is devaluation. Devaluation is a mixed species of protectionism and subsidy—protection to the import competing industries, export subsidy to exporters. Subsidies typically ensure continued support to inefficiency. Devaluation may indeed be, in certain circumstances, the correct medicine, as may also at times be true of subsidies. But devaluation in the modern complex economy is no longer the obvious solution.

One cannot judge whether the exchange rate is correct or not until one first inquires into many things such as the following:

1. To what degree is the economy operating at full capacity? This will have a profound influence on the country's international cost function and relative profit opportunities and outlook.
2. Has the mix of monetary and fiscal policy been directed toward the opening of investment outlets (public and private) together with taxation and borrowing policies which tend to equate saving and investment at full employment? This will profoundly influence the unit cost position of the country in question and also the capital flows. Both the trade account and the capital account will be affected.
3. Is the country in question bogging behind in the current swirling technological race involving new technique and product differentiation? Imagine our meeting the competition of the Volkswagen by bolstering our automobile industry with a devalued dollar.
4. In view of current and more or less forseeable trends, what spontaneous and contrived factors are likely to come into play in leading competitive countries? To base an exchange-rate policy on what has happened during the last six years without attempting to peer into the future might do in the nineteenth century, but not in the last half of the twentieth century.

In short, as the above listing suggests, more attention should be paid to income elasticities both with respect to their impact on the trade account and the capital account. And as far as price elasticities are concerned we should first examine cost-reducing techniques instead of running to cover under the overall blanket of a change in the exchange rate which, in addition to realignment of the price structure, also necessarily exerts a violent (and disrupting) wrench upon the domestic price system.

IS THE DOLLAR OVERVALUED?

The U.S. balance of payments is, as we have noted, essentially a transfer problem. The imbalance can be corrected in one of two ways: (1) an offsetting adjustment in the goods and services account so that the noncommercial money transfer becomes translated into a real transfer or (2) an offsetting adjustment in the capital account so that the money transfer becomes translated into an international redistribution of wealth holdings. To a degree some offsetting adjustments (feedbacks) have in fact been made in the goods and services account.

Some economists, as already noted above, have taken the hasty (and I believe oversimplified) view that the mere fact that the United States has run persistent deficits for some years proves that it is suffering from a fundamental disequilibrium which requires a devaluation of the dollar.[3]

[3] The term "overvaluation" implies a disequilibrium in the cost-price structure of a country vis-à-vis its competitors. But one must first ask: In what terms is overvaluation to be measured? Should one consider the relative prices of consumers' baskets, wholesale prices, or export prices? Should one also take account of the prices of stocks and bonds, i.e., relative profit rates and interest rates? And what about lags in the adjustment process? Not until the lags have worked themselves out can one realistically appraise the degree (if any) of overvaluation. There are perhaps few, if any, words in economics more slippery than the term overvaluation.

Those who stress overvaluation as the cause of a disequilibrium in the balance of payments tend to overestimate price factors and to underestimate non-price factors including: (1) product differentiation, (2) governmental transfers, and (3) the governmental inter-

Even if the United States were suffering a fundamental disequilibrium, it does not necessarily follow that the appropriate remedy is a devaluation of the dollar. Overly hasty action could be a big mistake. Many things can happen within a few years. The surplus countries might for a variety of reasons encounter balance-of-payments difficulties. They might deliberately take council in terms of international collaboration which could ease the problems springing from the United States noncommercial transfers. The feedback effect of the noncommercial transfers may in a few years substantially alter the structure of the exchange-market account. Imbalances caused by political transfers require time for adjustment.

THE ADJUSTABLE PEG SYSTEM

But now is there not something that can be done to ease the adjustment process? Is a permanently fixed structure of exchange rates the best way to promote adjustments? What are the merits of the system of adjustable pegs? Is a flexible system of exchange rates to be preferred? Or is there also here a possible way out via evolutionary development? These are the questions to which we address ourselves in this chapter.

The experience with devaluation of the currencies of leading industrial countries in recent years[4] has not been an

---

vention of competing countries such as export subsidies, etc. A country whose cost-price structure is in international equilibrium may, for example, experience deficits in its balance of payments due to deterioration in its position in the product differentiation race. In recent years Germany and Japan have been forging ahead in no small degree by reason of product differentiation.

[4] "It should, perhaps, be added that the experience of 1949 demonstrated that a large and sudden devaluation of the currency in welfare states of the West-European type is neither a wholesome nor an

altogether happy one. A devaluation by a major country reshapes the economic map of the world. It will almost inevitably induce substantial counterdevaluation, sometimes worldwide as in the case of the United Kingdom in 1949.[5] No country takes this step lightly. No major country will devalue until the accumulated evidence of a serious disequilibrium is overwhelming or until the mounting pressures have become too strong for further resistance. If the step has to be taken finally, it is important that it be adequate. It must be a major operation. It must be large enough to preclude the necessity of an early repetition. The devaluation is therefore almost certain to overshoot the mark so that a new disequilibrium is imposed upon other countries.

To be sure the Bretton Woods Agreement condemned competitive depreciation. But empirical knowledge is not sufficiently accurate by a wide margin to determine what the degree of disequilibrium may be. Accordingly, even with the best of international goodwill, a country cannot know exactly how much it can devalue without creating new maladjustment in the international cost-price system. And the competing countries seriously affected by the devaluation are also in the dark. Some will be compelled to devalue more

---

efficient means of curing a structural disequilibrium in trade and payments. Moreover, if it is not a part of a whole complex of other policy measures, it tends to have only temporary effects and can, in no event, be repeated often. This does not, of course, mean that adjustments of unrealistic exchange rates, or even the institution of flexible exchange rates, might not be useful as part of a wider effort toward currency convertibility." Gunnar Myrdal, *An International Economy: Problems and Prospects,* Harper, New York, 1956, pp. 80–81.

[5] I do not mean to imply that some readjustment at that time may not have been desirable. The figure fixed upon, however, did involve a very drastic readjustment. By now, fifteen years later, this may not make much, if any, difference.

or less in order to stay reasonably in line. But by how much? Others may perhaps need no adjustment whatever but this cannot be demonstrated unequivocally. And powerful exporting interests will always be at work in the first few critical hours after the devaluation has been announced, bringing strong pressure to bear upon the monetary authorities to follow suit or at least make a substantial counter-devaluation. This might not in fact be justified. But the temptation and urgency is strong as many a finance minister who has been placed in this critical position can testify. Major devaluations cannot in the nature of the case be depended upon to leave the international price structure in much better balance than before.

It is plausible to believe that the Bretton Woods formula was the only feasible one in the chaotic period immediately following World War II. It could be argued, but I doubt convincingly, that Bretton Woods might advisedly have plumped for floating exchange rates, giving time and market forces a chance to find the equilibrium rates. This might have been true had it been possible for Bretton Woods to build up a formidable international financial pool of reserves adequate to ensure a reasonable and viable degree of stability. This task was too much for the limited resources of the IMF as actually established. And no one familiar with the political realities of the time is likely to argue that a more ambitious scheme could have been approved.

Today, however, we can take a fresh look at the Bretton Woods formula. The IMF has had years of experience and much has been learned.

THE ROLE OF CREDITOR COUNTRIES

The Bretton Woods Agreement, instead of putting its stamp of approval upon devaluation as the cure for a fundamental disequilibrium, might advisedly have chosen to resist devaluations in the case of advanced industrial countries. It could have required the surplus countries to choose between various methods of adjustment (or some combination thereof) such as: (1) appreciation, (2) foreign investment of their payments surpluses, (3) opening their markets to imports, or (4) some moderate degree of price increases. Keynes might on balance have liked this. At any rate he always argued that it was the creditor or surplus country that should take the lead. But practical politics pointed another way. The United States was then the surplus country and Congress did not see eye to eye with Keynes.

STRUCTURAL DISLOCATIONS

Structural or fundamental disequilibrium may arise from dislocating trade developments. Trade disequilibrium of a structural character could be caused by revolutionary technological developments which might displace a whole industry and sharply affect the volume of exports. New developments abroad might seriously weaken the ability of domestic industries to compete successfully with imports. New products or shifts in consumer tastes may wipe out an established line of exports.

In such cases, devaluation might not correct at the precise point where correction is necessary. Devaluation cannot reach specific ailments. It operates overall on the whole economy. It produces violent shifts in the widespread gamut of price relationships. To submit the entire economy to such a wrench may not be the appropriate remedy. A direct attack on the *specific* problem might be feasible rather than a revolutionary readjustment of the whole internal price system, most of which (despite specific cases of maladjustment) might well be quite in line with the world price structure. Admittedly the structural changes may be so widespread that a realignment of the whole cost-price relationship may be called for.

If there does exist an overall, fundamental trade disequilibrium, a change in the exchange rate could help bring the cost-price structure in line with the world cost-price structure, given favorable price elasticities of imports and exports.[6] Alternatively, if the difficulty seems to lie in the capital account, a change in the relative profitability of investment and in the relative growth rates may improve the overall balance. Full employment and high investment particularly in the development of new industries could bring about equilibrating capital flows. A trade disequilibrium may indeed involve, among other things, international cost-price relationships. A private capital flow disequilibrium may involve international relationships with respect to the prospective rate of profit.

THE TRADE BALANCE VERSUS THE CAPITAL BALANCE

A persistent payments deficit can be attacked from two angles: (1) via the trading balance and (2) via the capital account. It is perhaps fair to say that there is a tendency in the literature to assume that the gap in the payments balance must be filled by an increase in the net exports of goods and services. There is no good reason why the problem should not also (and in certain circumstances even predominately) be attacked in terms of the private long-term

[6] Those who favor exchange rate adjustments tend to overemphasize the role of relative international prices and to underestimate the role of new products and product differentiation. The sudden appearance of the Volkswagen in the U.S. market was not due to a disequilibrium in the international price structure. What was needed was not exchange rate adjustment but merely the introduction of compact cars by the U.S. auto industry.

capital account. Policies directed toward improving the prospective rate of profits may go further toward curing a persistent deficit than anything that can be done to shift the trade balance. An adjustment of the exchange rate might indeed change the investment outlook. Other measures to improve the profit rate outlook include expansionist monetary and fiscal policies and investment tax incentives. In addition governmental measures in collaboration with foreign countries can promote new institutional mechanisms which facilitate capital movements across international borders. It is strange that bankers are so reluctant to take the lead in areas that constitute their own bailiwicks.

In the case of the current persistent United States deficits it is perhaps no exaggeration to say that we can scarcely hope to achieve any very large results via the trading balance route. The prospects are better via the capital account route. But this also will very likely prove to be inadequate to achieve equilibrium unless new international monetary mechanisms are adopted to facilitate investment, both governmental and private, across international borders.

To meet a private capital account disequilibrium by devaluation would give the structure of international prices for goods and services a severe wrench when in fact there may be good reason to believe that the structure as such is basically in balance. To offset the private capital transfer imbalance by a shift in exports and imports may in severe cases be necessary but it can scarcely fail to be highly disruptive. And it could well turn out that any improvement in the payments balance might be minimal. Even representatives of the financial community who might be expected to demand quick action affecting exports have stated that they have no easy hopes of our restoring balance-of-payments equilibrium through the trade account.[7] What chances are there that any

[7] *Hearings before the Joint Economic Committee*, 88th Cong., 1st Sess., July 29, 30, 1963, p. 332.

tolerable devaluation of the dollar would produce a sufficiently large net export of goods and services to balance our international accounts? Statistics on price elasticities have indeed been assembled and analyzed. But the authorities disagree. There is no firm foundation of knowledge on which to act.

As far as the primary producing countries are concerned, the price movements have been so violent that periodic devaluation such as we have been accustomed to are probably inevitable. In time a managed system of fluctuating exchange rates could perhaps evolve even for these countries.

A MANAGED SYSTEM OF FLEXIBLE EXCHANGE RATES

With respect to the leading industrial countries, discontinuous jumps in exchange rates, far from serving to stabilize, may substitute new imbalances for the old. The adjustable peg system under which we now operate should be replaced by something better.

Yet if nothing took its place, uncorrected disequilibrating developments of the cost-price structures of leading industrial countries could become serious. Devaluation by international agreement may on rare occasions be necessary. Moreover, an alternative to the adjustable peg system might be a moderate, and for the advanced countries, closely managed system of flexible exchange rates.

Such a system would be free to fluctuate within limits established by international agreement. This would require large pools of international finance to hold the rate in line within the designated limits.

Flexible rates operated within limits have one very great advantage over freely fluctuating rates. In practice such a system would not be very different for a system of fixed exchange rates. With adequate pools of compensating finance, the fluctuations could be kept under control. The adjustment process could be slow and gradual. The greater the disequilibrium and the longer the time required for adjustment, the greater the need for a pool of international funds large enough to cope with both the accumulated long-term pressures and temporary speculative movements.

The greater the disequilibrium and the longer the time required for adjustment, the greater will be the danger that large accumulations of excess currency holdings will pile up to the credit of the surplus countries. These excess accumulations in the absence of exchange guarantees may eventually put heavy pressures upon the deficit countries. Adequate stabilization funds with some moderate degree of flexibility of exchange rates is indicated—the first providing time for adjustment, the second facilitating the adjustment process.

Managed flexible exchange rates operating within fixed limits could be implemented in various ways. The most effective and least complicated might be an agreement between the leading industrial nations, members of the Group of Ten, to a plan, announced well in advance, that the buying and selling prices of gold would be gradually widened by no more than one-half of 1 per cent each time above and below par value. In the first period this would only apply to the United States since other countries already employ a spread of prices of three-fourths of 1 per cent above and three-fourths of 1 per cent below gold parity. The United States, however, sells gold at one-fourth of 1 per cent above parity (i.e., at $35.0875 per oz) and buys gold an one-fourth of 1 per cent below parity ($34.9125 per oz). At the end of the next period, however, all countries would establish a spread of 1 per cent above and below parity. Eventually the spread might be widened until it reached say 3 per cent above and below the gold parity price.

Gold speculators would not be able under such a plan to make profits out of possibly resulting changes in the market rates of exchange. Such changes could of course be expected. For, while the par value of gold in terms of all the member currencies would remain unaltered, the market value of any currency could fluctuate somewhere between the gold buying and selling points. From one period to another the market exchange rate of weak currencies might depreciate in terms of gold by one-half of 1 per cent, while the market rate of a strong currency might conceivably appreciate by one-half of 1 per cent each period. But under such a limited plan, the forward market would effect continuous adjustments which would completely wash out any chance of a one-way street to speculative profits.

Under this plan if strong pressures continue to be exerted on the dollar for example, this would keep the dollar market rate close to the ceiling selling price, while the surplus countries would tend to fluctuate more or less closely around the buying price. Accordingly, the dollar might eventually, by a slow and gradual process, have depreciated as much as 6 per cent against surplus currencies. This could make a slow and gradual contribution toward effecting a new equilibrium both on the trade balance and the capital account balancc.

The widening process could equally be implemented by increasing at intervals the selling price of gold by 1 per cent until eventually the selling price had been raised by a total of say 6 per cent.[8] The buying price of gold would however under this plan remain unaltered. This would be a concession to those who are fearful, for traditional reasons, of any weakening in the monetary function of gold. Under

[8] A plan somewhat similar to this was proposed by A. W. Phillips, "Employment, Inflation and Growth," *Economica*, pp. 1–16, February, 1962.

this plan also, the maximum depreciation of the dollar against the surplus currencies would be say 6 per cent.[9]

PROFESSOR MEADE'S PROPOSAL

A different program of gradual adjustment of the market exchange rate is the plan proposed by Professor Meade,[10] namely, an agreement between the leading industrial members of the IMF to the effect that the highly industrialized nations be permitted to change the par value of their currencies by no more than 2 per cent a year. This also could be implemented in small steps of one-half of 1 per cent each quarter.

The main difference between this method and widening the spread between buying and selling points is that the Meade plan would produce an appreciation of the dollar by a definite amount every time the par value was increased. Widening the gold points, however, would leave the adjustment completely to market forces, moderated by action of monetary authorities operating in the foreign exchange markets. The adjustment would likely be smaller and more flexible than in the case of the Meade plan.

The fact that the exchange rate could, under the Meade plan, be depreciated 2 per cent per year indefinitely might become a built-in feature in annual wage negotiations. If this should happen it would negate (as Prof. Gunnar Boe of

[9] It could be argued that all these wider gold point schemes suffer from the possibility that the drop of a currency to its lower limit might set up doubts that it will be able to stay within the permitted range and thus give rise to speculation. This, however, does not appear to be a serious matter, if one can judge by experience, with respect to the prevailing gold point margins.

[10] See J. E. Meade, *Hearings before the Subcommittee on International Exchange and Payments,* Dec. 12–14, 1962, Appendix, pp. 241–243.

Trondheim University, Norway, has suggested) the intended effect on international equilibrium. This possibility cannot be discounted, and it militates strongly against Professor Meade's scheme.

UNILATERAL DEVALUATION VERSUS INTERNATIONAL AGREEMENT

Should the time come when the United States has to chose between deflation and devaluation, the choice should unhesitatingly be devaluation. That time could come in the event of disequilibrium so serious that a persistent deficit develops in the exchange-market account—the market-oriented balance excluding government grants, loans, and military expenditures abroad.

No effective devaluation could be carried out unilaterally. To achieve any general improvement in international equilibrium a U.S. devaluation would have to be implemented in terms of an international agreement in which all the leading industrial countries—the Group of Eleven—would commit themselves not to engage in competitive devaluation. Without international cooperation and support, a U.S. devaluation would raise the roof, and the result would be not international equilibrium but international chaos. Thc famous Tripartite Monetary Agreement of 1936 between the United States, the United Kingdom, and France should serve as a beacon for any future major devaluation.

chapter nine

THE BROOKINGS GROUP REPORT

THE KENNEDY GOALS

The Kennedy Administration had set out to achieve certain economic goals which threatened, within certain limits, to come into conflict. These goals were as follows:

1. To reduce unemployment to 4 per cent of the labor force
2. To achieve an average growth rate of GNP in real terms of 4.8 per cent per year between 1960 and 1968
3. To maintain reasonable price stability, defined as an average increase per year of 1.5 per cent in the GNP price deflator

4. To maintain the stability of the dollar in relation to gold and stable European currencies

President Kennedy was understandably concerned to know whether the goal of preserving the stability of the dollar, if rigidly adhered to, would render impractical the goal of full employment as defined above. In the spring of 1962 he therefore asked the Council of Economic Advisers in co-operation with the Secretary of the Treasury and the Director of the Bureau of the Budget to consider the outlook for the U.S. balance of payments over the next several years. These officials, believing that a comprehensive and independent study was needed, asked the Brookings Institution to undertake such an appraisal.[1] The now famous Brookings Report, published in August, 1963, was the result.

THE BROOKINGS PROJECT

The project assayed the difficult task of making projections to the year 1968 with respect to the various factors that determine the U.S. balance of payments. This is precisely the kind of job that economists have to face up to if their profession is to play a useful role in the difficult task of decision making. It is all very well for "purists" to insist that such a task is impossible. But *men of affairs*—whether in business or in government—are forced to act, to take calculable risks. And in assuming these risks they have a right to ask for whatever illumination economics can provide, imperfect though this be. To undertake this task requires courage, and the authors of the Brookings Report have displayed both courage and skill. The value of the Report far

[1] The authors are however alone responsible for the Report. The authors are Walter S. Salant, Emile Despres, Alice M. Rivlin, Lorie Tarshis, Laurence B. Krause, and William A. Salant.

transcends the compass of the Report itself, for its publication has elicited appraisal and analysis from economists all over the world. From all this, much will be learned.

The Report singles out straightaway in the first chapter the heart of the problem, namely, the strategic importance of Western Europe for the U.S. balance of payments. This chapter presents a chart showing the movement of official gold and foreign exchange reserves of (1) industrial Continental Western Europe and Japan, (2) underdeveloped countries, (3) the United Kingdom, and (4) the United States. The chart reveals no change of any significance in the holdings of the underdeveloped countries and of the United Kingdom, a sharp increase in the official gold and foreign exchange holdings of Continental Western Europe, and a significant decline in the gold holdings of the United States.

WESTERN EUROPE VIS-À-VIS THE UNITED STATES

And so the Report concentrates on Western Europe and the United States. What will happen to the U.S. balance of payments will be determined, the authors insist, basically by: (1) the relative changes in the GNP growth rates of Western Europe and the United States and (2) the relative competitiveness of the United States and Western Europe, particularly changes in the GNP price deflators of Western Europe and the United States and related price and unit cost variables. The former will determine the market availability of the two areas, the latter the relative potential capacity of the two areas to exploit these markets.

More concretely, the 1968 U.S. balance of payments will depend upon: (1) the imports of goods and services into the United States, (2) the exports of goods and services from the United States, and (3) the net outflow of capital, public and private, short-term and long-term, from the United States.

The U.S. imports of goods and services will be determined primarily by (1) changes in the U.S. GNP and (2) by relative price movements in the United States and Western Europe.

The U.S. exports of goods and services will be determined primarily by (1) changes in the GNP of Western Europe, (2) relative price movements in the United States and Western Europe, and (3) increases in the dividend and interest earnings of U.S. corporations abroad.

The net outflow on private capital and government account from the United States will be determined primarily by (1) relative changes in the GNP of Western Europe and the United States, (2) relative rates of return on capital, and (3) changes in U.S. foreign aid and military expenditures abroad.[2]

THE PROJECTIONS

The projections of the GNP and prices in the United States are simply the projected goals which the government has set for itself, namely, an average increase of 4.8 per cent per year in real GNP between 1960 and 1968 (involving a 1.9 per cent increase in employment per year and a 2.9 per cent increase in output per man-hour), and an average increase in GNP prices of 1.5 per cent per year (permitting a 4.4 per cent increase in hourly earnings per year and a 0.5 per cent increase in export prices). The projected increase in the GNP of Western Europe is simply the arithmetic average of the high and low target figures sub-

[2] It will be recalled that I exclude military expenditures abroad from my services category and include them instead in the category of government transfers.

mitted by the Western European centers to the OECD. The projected growth rate thus derived is 4.2 per cent a year for the period 1960 to 1968. The projected European increase in GNP prices, as calculated by the Brookings study (based on a variety of considerations), is set at 2.75 per cent per year for the period 1960 to 1968, and at 1.5 per cent in export prices.[3]

THE U.S. PAYMENTS BALANCE IN 1968

Based on these projected foundation pillars, and buttressed by all sorts of related variables, the Report comes out with a U.S. international payments balance sheet for 1968 compared with 1961, shown in Table 9-1.

These estimates involve only the basic balance, not the overall payments balance. The basic balance equals the overall balance minus: (1) short-term capital movements, (2) net errors and omissions, which often are a cover for short-term capital movements, and (3) special items such as prepayments of government loans and advance payments on military sales. The items excluded from the basic balance

[3] The initial projections were based on assumptions suggested by the Council of Economic Advisers. In addition, a second set of assumptions was made by the authors themselves. These alternative assumptions provided the basis for alternative projections for the year 1968. Under these alternative assumptions the U.S. growth rate was put at nearly 4.5 per cent from 1961 (compared with 4.8 per cent in the initial assumptions), the GNP price deflator of 1.5 per cent per year was retained, and labor costs per man-hour were put at 3.8 per cent per year. The European boom was assumed to be weaker together with more governmental restraint on inflation. European growth rates were accordingly put at 10 per cent below the OECD targets. GNP price increases of only 11 per cent were assumed in contrast with the 20 per cent under the initial assumptions. Export prices were thus assumed to rise only 7 per cent, contrasted with 11 per cent under the initial assumptions.

Table 9-1. U.S. Balance of Payments, 1961, 1968*
(*in billions of dollars*)

	1961 (actual)	*1968 (initial projection)*	*1968 (alternative projection)*
Imports of goods and services (excluding military expenditures, but including private remittances):			
Merchandise	−14.5	−23.3	−22.4
Services†	− 5.9	− 7.5	− 7.4
Total imports	−20.4	−30.8	−29.8
Exports of goods and services:			
Merchandise	+20.2	+31.4	+27.8
Services	+ 8.1	+11.2	+11.1
Total exports	+28.3	+42.6	+38.9
Net export of goods and services	+ 7.9	+11.8	+ 9.1
Net private long-term capital outflow	− 2.1	− 1.5	− 1.5
Net government transfers, grants, loans, and military expenditures abroad	− 6.6	− 8.4	− 8.2
Net outflow of funds (public and private transfers)	− 8.7	− 9.9	− 9.7
Overall basic balance	− 0.8	+ 1.9	− 0.6

* The data are derived from the Brookings Report, Table VIII-2, p. 216. Attention should be called to the fact that the authors have made an effort (see lower half of Table VIII-2, p. 216) to estimate the feedback effects of changes in military expenditures abroad, government loans and transfers, private long-term capital and investment income, etc.

† Note that military expenditures abroad are excluded in this table in conformity with the statistical materials on balance of payments which I have presented in earlier chapters of this book.

wash out more or less over the long run and are, in any event, completely unpredictable.

GROUNDS FOR IMPROVEMENT

On what grounds does the Brookings study project an improvement in the basic balance of $2.7 billion (from a deficit of $0.8 billion in 1961 to a surplus of $1.9 billion in 1968)? Two factors account for almost the whole gain:

1. An increase in merchandise exports of 11.2 billion, of which $5.5 billion is alleged to be due primarily to the increased buying power of Western Europe incident to the growth in real income, $4.8 billion due to the improved U.S. competitive position incident to the more favorable development of U.S. prices relative to Western European prices, leaving a residue of $0.9 billion due to feedback effects from increased foreign aid and other factors
2. An increase of $1.5 billion in the interest and dividends received on American investments abroad (portfolio and direct)

Offsetting the large increase in merchandise exports, the projection estimates a rise in U.S. merchandise imports of $8.8 billion due, basically, to the large increase in the U.S. GNP of 4.8 per cent per year. This leaves a net increase in the merchandise balance of $2.4 billion. The net gains in merchandise trade, plus the substantial gains in overseas investment income, plus some other minor items amount to $3.9 billion. This is offset in part by an increase in government transfers of grants and loans. All items considered, we obtain a net improvement in the basic balance of $2.7 billion from 1961 to 1968.

The projected growth in investment income is primarily the result of U.S. investment abroad made in the last few years plus further increases from 1961 to 1968. The projections assume a slight decline in the net private long-term capital outflow from $2.1 billion in 1961 to $1.5 billion in 1968. This decline could in part be attributed to the assumed relatively greater growth in the U.S. GNP compared with that of Western Europe. Capital inflows would tend to increase, capital outflows to decline, in response to differential prospective rates of profits.

Since the projections indicate a greater growth in the GNP of the United States relative to Western Europe, one might be led to the conclusion that U.S. imports would increase more than U.S. exports. How to explain the extraordinary rise projected in U.S. exports? The answer is to be found in large part in the improvement in the U.S. competitive position. Europe's unit labor costs are expected to rise relative to U.S. unit costs. Western Europe will experience a decline in the growth of the labor force. This will cause a persistent upward pressure on wages in excess of increases in output per man-hour. European prices will rise relative to U.S. prices. Excess capacity in the United States will tend to keep prices and wages down especially in the metal and machinery industries. U.S. export prices will therefore tend to be kept in line with domestic prices.

UNFAVORABLE FACTORS

In one important respect, however, the export position of the United States will deteriorate. The new average tariff of the European Common Market countries will, in many important products, be higher than the former tariff of the chief supplying countries. Even a 50 per cent cut in the new average tariff will leave a higher rate for twenty-one out of sixty-one selected products than the old tariff of the dominant supplier. Most of the manufactured products which the United States exports to the Common Market countries are concentrated in twenty-two of the sixty-one types selected. Moreover, the Common Market will give preferential treatment to African countries (formerly tied as colonies to Europe), and this discriminates against Latin American countries which are competitors with Africa as exporters of primary products to Europe. Result: Latin American countries will sell less to Europe and can accordingly buy less from the United States. Thus a protectionist Common Market affects U.S. exports unfavorably both directly and indirectly. U.S. agricultural exports will almost certainly be severely injured by the apparent tendency of the Common Market toward agricultural self-sufficiency. All told the authors expect an aggregate export loss of $750 million U.S. exports because of EEC protectionist policies.

Finally, increasing excess industrial capacity in Western Europe will intensify the struggle for markets and challenge our hitherto lead in such products as airplanes, specialized machinery, instruments, and certain chemicals. Yet despite these unfavorable offsets the Report projects the large increase of merchandise exports of $11.2 billion by 1968. The projections, they warn us, are not forecasts; they are informed estimates based on recent trends and current tendencies.

Let us not forget that it was not the purpose of the Brookings study to *forecast* what would happen by 1968. The purpose was to inquire into the probable effect on the U.S. balance of payments of the Administration's objective to achieve a 4.8 per cent growth in GNP per year and to reduce unemployment to 4 per cent of the labor force at least by 1968. The obvious dangers involved in this endeavor, as far as the balance-of-payments problem is concerned, are that a rapidly growing GNP would: (1) sharply increase U.S. imports and (2) raise U.S. prices and unit costs out of line with European prices.

The expected impact of full employment on U.S. imports, as projected in the Brookings study, can be regarded as very solidly based. Merchandise imports, year in and year out, run pretty close to 3 per cent of GNP (a bit above or a bit below). This part of the study's conclusions is not likely to be seriously challenged.

THE U.S. COMPETITIVE POSITION

The projected increase in U.S. exports is far more problematical. The important determinants are: (1) the probable level of West Europe's GNP in 1968, and (2) the probable competitive position of the United States vis-à-vis Europe by 1968 as determined by relative changes in (a) the supply of labor, (b) trade union cost-push pressures, (c) productivity per man-hour, (d) shifts in the distribution of income affecting wages and profits, (e) government wage and price policies, (f) tariff policies, (g) government export aids and subsidies, and (h) monetary and fiscal policies affecting aggregate demand.

In appraising the U.S. competitive position in the next few years, the authors place primary emphasis upon the factors tending to raise European costs and prices. The labor market will be very tight. To achieve the European target growth rate of 4.2 per annum will require a 3.7 per man increase in productivity since very little growth (only 0.5 per cent per year) can be expected in the labor force. Moreover, the workweek in leading European centers is 45 to 46 hours, and some shortening of the workweek is highly probable.

All this suggests a strong upward wage push, all the more so since the share of labor in the distribution of income has until now been kept abnormally low in the Continental European countries—ranging from 55 to 56 per cent in Belgium and Holland to 61 to 62 per cent in France and West Germany, compared with 69 per cent in the United

States. But if these large labor cost increases are to be absorbed from profits sufficiently to keep European prices down to the projected 2.75 increase per annum, where will the savings come from to finance the large investment outlays necessary to achieve a 3.7 per man increase in productivity per year?

This analysis implies not only a strong wage-cost upward pressure on prices but also a strong demand pull. The authors estimate that the required investment will be about 16.9 per cent of 1968 target income, consumer demand 65 per cent, government purchases 16.5 per cent, housing 4.2 per cent, and inventories 1.5 per cent. All this adds up to 104.1 per cent of the target income, indicating an excess demand which, unless severely restrained, would push prices up beyond the projected 2.75 per cent per year increase. The authors of course make no pretense that these precise figures are in any sense forecasts. They are, however, plausible figures and they do suggest that the projected price increase of 2.75 may well prove to be on the low side.

The U.S. competitive position will of course also be affected by developments in the United States. Fuller utilization of industrial capacity will tend to lower unit costs. Europe already has this advantage and indeed is likely to push output beyond lowest unit cost. The American industry can tap a fairly rapidly growing labor force and, for some years, a pool of unemployed workers. International competition is now more keenly felt and trade unions are more aware of the danger of pushing wages so high that foreign imports may make inroads on domestic employment. The pressure on prices is likely to be weaker, relative to Western Europe, both in terms of cost push and demand pull.

In addition, the U.S. competitive position will be affected by what happens in third countries—the primary producing countries. In the decade 1953–1963 the decline in the prices of primary products boosted European profits since the cost of raw materials is an important item in European manufacturing costs. But the severe decline in the export earnings of the primary producing countries in this decade hurt U.S. exports, since these countries are large importers of U.S. manufactured goods. In the years ahead, the authors assume that the export earnings of the primary producing countries will be relatively better than in the last decade. This will weaken the competitive position of Europe and strengthen the position of the United States.

The imponderables involved leave wide scope for differences of opinion about the probable outcome. Moreover, unanticipated new factors will doubtless emerge. And underneath all the market imponderables lie the deeply rooted structures of production which tend to perpetuate underlying trends. If one places strong emphasis on these structural factors one could perhaps conclude that no great change can be expected in the role U.S. exports will play in world trade. And whether one stresses the basic structures or the uncertain and unpredictable imponderables, it is difficult to escape a certain agnosticism with respect to the projected appraisal of U.S. competitiveness in the years immediately ahead.

NET OUTFLOW OF CAPITAL

The third significant variable affected by the U.S. full employment policy is the net outflow of capital funds. This picture, while blurred by a number of imponderables, is, nevertheless, less uncertain. The projected growth of the U.S. GNP is fixed by the full employment and growth goals that underlie the study. We are, however, left to appraise as best we can a variety of European policies, all of which can profoundly affect the European prospective profit rates relative to the U.S. rates. Nevertheless the authors' estimate that net private long-term capital outflows will decline from $2.1 billion in 1961 to $1.5 billion in 1968 will, I suspect, generally be regarded as conservative. It would seem almost certain that the quite exceptionally favorable investment opportunities in Western Europe during the last decade cannot continue at so buoyant a level. Consider the vacuum left by the war destruction, the decimated industrial capacity, and the spectacular increase (from almost nothing) in the demand for consumer durables—automobiles, electrical appliances, etc. These increases in the nature of the case cannot last. The European rate of growth of real GNP will almost certainly slow down. This can be expected to reduce the net capital outflow from the United States. But by the same token it tends to check the flow of U.S. merchandise exports to Europe.

In line with the agnosticism expressed above, it could well be that as good a guess as any is that the basic balance will not change very much in the next four years. This indeed is the conclusion reached in the study's alternative projections which are less optimistic than the initial projections. So long as the massive U.S. governmental transfers continue at somewhere near their present level we shall not likely experience a sufficient feedback upon the trade balance to end the persistent U.S. payments deficit.

INTERNATIONAL LIQUIDITY

And if indeed equilibrium is restored, would there then remain no acute world monetary problem? The study concludes that a solution of the U.S. payments deficit will uncover a very serious difficulty for the free world—"the inadequacy of the existing international monetary arrangements for creating reserves adequate to cope with perspective imbalances in payments."[4]

The authors argue that it is imbalances in world payments that give rise to the need for official international reserves.

[4] The Brookings Report, p. 240.

They suggest that imbalances are likely to grow larger and to become more persistent and intractable. The international transactions in goods and services have been growing in the last decade at 6.2 per cent a year, and the study projects an increase from 1961 to 1968 of 4.4 per cent a year. More important, however, than the mere volume of increased transactions is the fact that payments imbalances, while formerly largely of a cyclical character, are more and more due to structural changes—changes in cost and demand associated with technological developments, differential rates of growth, etc. These structural factors operate over long periods. The resulting imbalances pose painful conflicts between domestic and international goals. Adjustments entail gradual shifts of resources over relatively long periods. Imbalances caused by structural factors are likely to persist over several years. The study fails at this point to include in its structural category the highly important nonmarket intergovernmental transfers—perhaps the major cause of the currently persistent imbalances.

The study conservatively estimates that an increase in official international reserves of $21.4 billion is needed between 1961 and 1968. Aggregate official reserves in 1961 amounted to $61.2 billion, of which $41.5 was gold. The authors assume that of the $21.4 billion increase needed by 1968, $3 billion will come from continued U.S. deficits, $4.7 from net additions to the free world's monetary gold stock, leaving a shortfall of $13.7 billion.

POLICY RECOMMENDATIONS

And finally, we come to policy considerations. The Brookings Report cautions against panicky, short-cut restrictive measures to cure the payments deficits. It argues against yielding to the orthodox conventional deflationary remedy. It urges undaunted pursuit of a full employment high growth rate policy of expansion, confident that a prosperous, growing America will be more strongly competitive than a semi-stagnant America. The Report urges firm support for the policy proclaimed by President Kennedy, namely, to stand ready to sell our entire gold stock to any prospective buyer at $35.125 per oz and to reiterate this policy boldly and fearlessly in every payments crisis. I should also support their suggestion to sell $5 billion gold for foreign exchange except for one thing, namely, there would be no buyers except precisely those central banks which already hold far too much gold. True, while there are other and better ways for the United States to acquire foreign exchange, serious difficulties currently present themselves. If indeed central banks prefer larger and larger stocks of gold to international monetary reform, let them have as much of this unearning asset as they can afford to hold.

The Report issued a challenging statement, namely, that the United States should undertake no policy to ease its payments deficit problem which could not be justified on its own merits. This appears to be a good corrective against hasty action by panicky policy makers, but it perhaps is not sufficiently realistic. A panicky patient may indeed apply palliatives to the point of preventing nature's cures. But when the pressure is on, a palliative may prevent strangling. Many European countries, having had long experience with controls and background histories of sharp bargaining, are typically ready at a moment's notice to introduce restrictive measures. Historically the United States tends to shy away from controls, no doubt mainly because we have not been subjected to severe pressures (and some will say because we are novices in sharp international dealings). But the ready adoption of these short-cut measures is destructive of long-term healthy trade relations. There are, however, times when survival demands surgery. Possibly Secretary Dillon's tax on the issue of foreign securities introduced in the summer of

1963 (and later enacted) is a case in point. One of the Brookings' authors, Emile Despres, admitted in testimony before the Joint Economic Committee that if action was deemed necessary, this measure was probably less obnoxious than many others.

The Report suggests that a serious dilemma confronts the free world. The Continental countries are happy with their payments surpluses, which are the counterpart of the U.S. deficits. Yet they deplore the U.S. deficits and by pulling out gold they tend to force the United States into restrictive measures. These restrictive measures, however, if put into effect, would severely curtail European exports and their lucrative tourist trade and perhaps also U.S. military aid. The balmy days of ever more surpluses and an accumulating store of gold would be over. Sermons about "putting your house in order" sound very good from the pious pulpits of central bankers, but this is the last thing that European businessmen would want. So how do we solve the dilemma?

To this question, monetary experts the world over give different answers. The authors of the Brookings Report urge the United States to seek agreement on an international payments mechanism whereby balance-of-payments disturbances can be adjusted without compromising important goals of national and international policy. They believe that adjustments can be made under a fixed exchange rate system if an adequate international liquidity mechanism can be devised which will make available the time needed for making such adjustments.

A very difficult assignment was expertly and courageously performed, and the free world is indebted to the Brookings Institution for undertaking the study. Following its publication, two official studies were inaugurated, as we have noted, at the 1963 Annual Meeting of the International Monetary Fund. The outcome is discussed in the following chapter. The great danger is that the conventional wisdom will prevail. It is always convenient to urge that nothing be done to rock the boat while the storm is upon us, yet at the same time cautiously agreeing that some action should *eventually* be taken once the free world economies are again sailing a smooth sea.

The problem of world liquidity has two facets as envisaged in the Report: (1) A means must be found (other than key-currency deficits) to create a supplement to gold; and (2) in order to prevent the cumulation of structural payments imbalances, it is necessary to have available a sufficient reservoir of actual or potential international reserves to permit time for structural readjustments.

ADEQUATE LIQUIDITY AND LONG-TERM ADJUSTMENTS

The second item deserves to be stressed, as indeed it is in the Brookings Report. It is often said that those who emphasize the first item fail to get at the real problem, namely, the problem of adjustment. But in the world of persistent structural imbalances in which we live, adjustments take time. Hence the urgent need for adequate liquidity.

The Brookings Report does not hesitate to point out that the payments deficits have already gravely impaired our freedom of action. An expansionary fiscal policy of full employment and full utilization of our productive capacity has in some measure been held in restraint. The payments deficits have made us afraid to rise to the full potential of our human and capital resources. The resulting semistagnation, if it continues, may make us increasingly inefficient. Foreign aid, both economic and military, is attacked not on grounds of its own inherent merit, but because it contributes to our payments deficits.

So, in the final analysis, the Brookings Report comes out in support of an institutional arrangement that will permit the liquid claims of surplus countries "to be denominated in an international unit of account, either with the IMF of with a new international payment union associated with it." The authors are careful to point out (a matter we have stressed in earlier chapters) that the new monetary institution should be erected firmly on the limited membership of advanced industrial countries. The basic problem of the underdeveloped countries must be met by programs of long-term foreign aid.

A FINAL DISMAL NOTE

The Report ends on a dismal note—one not welcomed by the authors. It faces the terrible prospect, which we like to believe can and will be averted, of a divided free world: (1) the Common Market and its former African colonies and (2) the rest of the free world: the United States, the United Kingdom, Canada, Japan, the Scandinavian countries and other members of the European Free Trade Association, Oceania, South Asia, and Latin America—in general, the sterling and dollar areas. Should the Common Market develop into a highly protectionist and autarchic area, this would have serious implications with respect to the monetary mechanism of the free world. In this event, it is indeed possible that the suggestion of the Brookings Report to establish two monetary systems might not be altogether inappropriate—the value of each monetary system relative to the other being determined by a floating exchange rate. This development would wreck the cohesion of the free world, and the monetary implications of such a system emphasize the importance of doing everything possible through tariff negotiations to prevent the Common Market from developing into a closed economic system.

chapter ten

COMMENTS ON THE TOKYO REPORTS

At the 1963 annual meeting of the IMF in Washington, D.C. it was decided to undertake two studies designed to explore possible new developments in international monetary reforms. The aim was to find ways of providing world liquidity ample to meet the needs of a rapidly growing trading world without primary reliance upon the key currencies. One of these studies was to be undertaken by the

International Monetary Fund itself, the other by the so-called Group of Ten.[1]

The conclusion reached in these reports, as decided in the September, 1964, meeting of the IMF in Tokyo, was that no new institutions need to be built into the system. Optimism prevailed. There was broad agreement[2] among the central bankers and finance ministers gathered at Tokyo that the international monetary skies were comfortably bright with no really seriously threatening clouds hovering on the horizon. There was a general consensus that the Western world had come through the first two postwar decades with a record of unprecedented achievement. Witness the phenomenal rebuilding and modernization after a devastating war of great national economies and the development of a prosperous and growing world trade.

A large measure of credit was rightly given to the International Monetary Fund for the progress thus far achieved. No one will dispute that the IMF has played a useful role, and increasingly so in recent years. But this does not, by a wide margin, tell the whole story. The IMF has indeed made available, on a limited and short-run basis, international credit—which has helped countries over their balance-of-payments hurdles. But the IMF has not added anything to the *owned* reserves of the member countries. The owned international reserves consist of gold and liquid holdings of dollar-sterling balances—the two currencies which in addition to gold are generally acceptable in international payments. In

[1] The United States, United Kingdom, Canada, Japan, Sweden, Germany, France, Italy, Belgium, and Holland. Switzerland is a "consulting" member.

[2] Note however the sharp difference with respect to several issues between the French and the Dutch on the one side and the American and British on the other. These differences are fully explored later in this chapter.

the postwar period (1945 to 1964) the owned international reserves have grown, partly through net additions to the monetary gold stock from (1) new gold production, (2) private gold boards, and (3) Russian gold sales, but mostly through increased foreign holdings of U.S. dollars.[3]

The Tokyo meeting disclosed an unresolved contradiction which indeed has bedeviled the confused and confusing statements of central bankers and finance ministers throughout the past several years. On the one hand, general satisfaction was expressed again and again with the current state of the international monetary system and especially with the adequacy of world liquidity.[4] Everyone present at the Tokyo meeting was, however, fully aware (and occasionally open or oblique reference was made thereto) that the major explanation for the satisfactory growth of international monetary reserves is the persistent U.S. payments deficits which have piled up year after year for nearly fifteen years despite pious protestations of central bankers and perennial demands that the United States should "put its house in order."

In monetary and economic matters it is often true that the optimum figure is not the largest possible amount on the one side nor the smallest possible amount on the other. It lies frequently in between. With respect to the dollar payments deficits it may well be that the optimum figure is not zero (as is commonly supposed) but rather a figure not large

[3] During the postwar period, holdings of sterling have changed relatively little.

[4] Liquidity means (1) the stock of liquid international reserves (gold plus holdings of dollar and sterling balances) actually held by central banks, private banks and traders and (2) the quantity of potential reserves that can readily be tapped when needed. The first are owned reserves; the second constitute a line of credit potentially available.

enough to cause genuine concern about the stability of the dollar, and yet not so small as to preclude a substantial increase in world liquidity.

This optimum figure will vary with circumstances. Looking back, the actual average of nearly $1.5 billion from 1950 to 1957 appears to have met the needs of this period reasonably well and under the conditions then prevailing occasioned no concern about the dollar. Then came the years of crisis beginning with 1958. There followed, from 1961 on, years of relative tranquility, and there is reason to believe that now again the optimum figure for U.S. payments deficits is settling down at something like $1.5 to $2.0 billion per year.[5]

From 1958 to 1960 inclusive the actual dollar deficits rose to the abnormal and undigestible figure of $3.5 to $4.0 billion. This shock caused a heavy drain on the U.S. gold holdings. The sudden increase in U.S. payments deficits in 1958 to 1960 was caused by a spectacular rise in U.S. capital outflows incident to the return of leading West European countries to currency convertibility together with the alluring outlook for profitable investment abroad. This unexpected increase in dollar deficits left the U.S. monetary authorities bewildered and frustrated, and engendered fears in Europe of a dollar devaluation. A number of Continental central banks ran for cover and converted their dollar holdings into gold. It was the Continental central bankers themselves who brought the crisis of 1960 to a head.[6]

This situation was met head on by the Kennedy Administration and soon confidence was restored. The Fund,

[5] Attention should once again be called to the fact that the U.S. payments deficits, as defined by the Department of Commerce, grossly exaggerate the true size of the deficits.

[6] Note should be made of the honorable exception of Sweden and Canada (of the Group of Ten countries) both of whom actually reduced their gold holdings from December, 1957 to December, 1960.

under Per Jacobsson's leadership, succeeded (against the background of the 1960—and subsequent—episodes) to muster support for a vigorous program of international monetary cooperation. After much discussion and difficult negotiations, the General Agreements to Borrow was finally adopted by ten leading industrial countries. This promised support in time of need, and ensured, one may hope, an end to massive gold drains. The U.S. monetary authorities under the able leadership of Secretary Dillon and Under Secretary Roosa, also took vigorous action. There was quickly built up a strong defensive mechanism—bilateral arrangements (swap agreements, Roosa bonds, etc.).

Supported by these new stabilizing developments, recent experience indicates that a U.S. deficit of $1.5 to $2.0 billion is no cause for world concern. When the IMF gathers for its annual meeting five years hence, it will be no surprise if the monetary authorities of the Western world once again pat each other on the back, basking in the sunshine of adequate, but not execessive, world liquidity—the needed increase having come from continued U.S. deficits of moderate size.

The unresolved dilemma encountered a blank wall in Tokyo. In terms of ideology the central bankers were still calling for an end to U.S. payments deficits. But as a practical matter nobody really wanted this to happen. A balance contrived by means of U.S. restrictive policies would seriously injure world trade. A balance achieved by somehow making the United States sufficiently competitive in terms of traded goods and services to offset the gigantic imbalance created by U. S. military expenditures and untied foreign aid would constitute a hard blow to Western Europe. A balance achieved by completely closing New York to European borrowers or the institution of vigorous controls designed to stop American direct investments abroad would not be in the interest of the world community. Moreover, as was well recognized at Tokyo, no practical alternative to U.S. payments deficits as a source of needed additional reserves is visible over the horizon or indeed likely to become visible in the foreseeable future.

This unresolved dilemma is not unlike that confronting the medieval church with respect to money lending and taking interest. To charge interest was sinful. Yet the inexorable flow of practical affairs chipped away at the firmly entrenched dogma. Today, even enlightened economists, to say nothing about central bankers, shy away from intergovernmental lending. Economists who otherwise are generally rated as internationally minded are nevertheless often rigidly nationalistic when it comes to the question of intergovernmental compensatory finance. Long-term lending is still suspect.

To be sure, international compensatory finance need not operate exclusively in terms of the key-country currencies. Ideally we could eventually develop an international credit-creating institution. But we will not and cannot do so until nationally oriented political interests are sufficiently calmed down so that international credit creation can be managed in terms of the economic welfare of the world community instead of in terms of clubbing down the expansionist policies of individual countries.

Some mild suggestions were indeed made at the Tokyo meeting—measures looking toward a liberalization of Fund activities and especially toward the promotion of intergovernmental compensatory financing between strong convertible currencies. Mr. Dillon suggested that countries with large and growing resources should explore the feasibility of long-term lending to other advanced countries in need of reserves. Studies should be undertaken to explore the potentialities of Fund investments in strong-currency countries and in strong international institutions.

Viewing the conference as a whole, however, the dilemma remained unsolved. The prospect for any substantial expansion of international reserves, other than through a continued increase in the dollar component of the gold-exchange standard, was just not anywhere to be found. Indeed the Group-of-Ten report stated emphatically that there is no immediate prospect of any other currency assuming the function of an international reserve currency. And the report added the significant statement that such a development, should it somehow emerge, could itself raise difficult problems.

This leaves moderate and digestible U.S. payments deficits as the only prospective, available means of increasing international reserves. And what's wrong with that?—Nothing. Bankers should be the first to see that long-term lending is sound business as long as the borrower is credit worthy. And such debts are legitimately renegotiable when they mature as long as conditions can sustain confidence in the soundness of the loan. And is there really anyone who seriously doubts that the United States is credit worthy? Except for the Common Market countries and Switzerland all the world prefers dollars to gold, as low gold ratios testify. And it will be interesting to see in the years ahead whether the high-gold-ratio countries will not, at long last, begin to question whether they are really following good business principles in investing so large a part of their reserves in an unearning asset. There is of course always the matter of near-term speculation in possible dollar devaluation. But with the currently developed insulating mechanisms this type of speculation appears to be highly unprofitable. Prudent investment, so it now appears, will more and more drive the high-gold-ratio countries away from gold into foreign exchange holdings. All this would strengthen the gold-dollar standard.

To make the gold-dollar standard entirely foolproof, the United States should offer a firm gold-value guarantee to all official holders of dollar balances.

It should be noted here that even without a gold-value guarantee, the U.S. payments deficits have not, except in rare crisis years, yielded unwanted dollars. Governments other than the Common Market countries and Switzerland together with private banks and traders everywhere call for more and more dollars. Moreover, the United States has in large part absorbed unwanted dollars, wherever they have appeared. This has been done by gold sales, bilateral swaps, IMF drawings and the disposal of so-called Roosa bonds.

A sharp debate developed in the Tokyo meeting between France and the Netherlands in one side, and the United Kingdom and United States on the other. The French charged that the gold-dollar standard had not prevented inflationary trends over large areas of the industrialized world. They stated their conviction that creditor countries were subjected to strong inflationary pressures originating in the deficit countries. Mr. Maudling and Mr. Dillon both argued strongly against this thesis. Mr. Maudling stated that he could find no evidence of a general world inflation. The value of money, he said, has remained for many years remarkably stable in the United States—the center of the world monetary system. The managing director of the Fund, Mr. Schweitzer, stated that there is not much evidence to support the idea of "imported inflation." The French and the Dutch argued that they were helpless in a world situation where inflation was continuously being fed from the persistent payments deficits of the United States. It was alleged that the creditor countries are confronted with a world imbalance for which they have no responsibility whatever.

The British and American representatives argued that the Continental European countries could quite well manage their own monetary problems regardless of imbalances in international accounts. They could offset the inflow of gold and dollars by the familiar technique of open market operations. The creditor countries, Mr. Maudling contended, do not need to hold more reserve currencies than they wish. The creditor countries could remove trade restrictions and hold down inflation by encouraging imports. The United States offers a rich variety of competitively priced capital and consumer goods. The creditor countries can, moreover, export capital, as did the United Kingdom in the nineteenth century and as the United States did after World Wars I and II. The European problem of inflation, said Mr. Dillon, is its own problem which can be solved by corrective measures at home and by well-known techniques of monetary management.

The British and American representatives argued that in the interest of world stability, debtor countries should not alone carry the burden of adjustment. The United States said Mr. Dillon could easily achieve a balance anytime by drastic measures of a restrictive character, but this would not be in the interest of the world economy.

The Dutch and the French are not happy about the current functioning of the gold-dollar-sterling standard. Nor are they happy about the novel arrangements that have been implemented to strengthen the system in the years 1961 to 1964, especially the bilateral agreements between the United States and a number of leading industrial countries. That these arrangements have greatly improved the outlook for international monetary stability can scarcely be denied. One feels, therefore, a sense of misgiving about future efforts at monetary cooperation when one reads the Tokyo reports and notes the apparent distrust, notably of the French and the Dutch representatives, of the laboriously built-up network of bilateral arrangements which have so effectively brought stability and strength to the key currencies upon which the present system rests. As long as no satisfactory substitute can be found, this is the system we have to live with. The French and the Dutch do not like the key-currency system. Mr. D'Estaing referred to the serious imperfections in a system which makes it possible for the reserve currency countries to finance payments deficits without other countries being fully aware of this fact and without the implementation of corrective mechanisms. He feared that excessive facilities may in this way be granted. A system which permits the deficits of reserve currency countries to be financed seemingly without limit may impose undue burdens upon the creditor countries.

The French and Dutch representatives therefore felt that these bilateral arrangements should be subjected to "multilateral surveillance." This phrase was chosen in place of the phrase "multilateral discipline" which had originally been employed and which, in fact, would have portrayed more accurately the French and Dutch intent. The American and British representatives did not oppose multilateral surveillance as such, provided it assumed the form of full publicity. But they were not in favor of imposing international restrictions which could weaken the position of the key currencies. Bilateral credit arrangements have proved to be useful to handle volatile movements of funds between leading countries. If multilateral surveillance restricted these arrangements, the whole system would become, they believed, more sensitive to speculation and crisis. Indeed the French view of multilateral surveillance suggests political overtones which run counter to international monetary cooperation.

The U.S. monetary authorities defended the position that full reporting is, indeed, desirable and would help to break down the wall of secrecy which too often surrounds the operation of central banks, notably some of the Continental central banks. The United States has already taken the lead in this matter. Witness the various detailed reports by Mr.

Coombs of the New York Federal Reserve Bank on all forms of bilateral arrangements made by the United States. So far so good.

But multilateral surveillance could be a very bad thing if it should give any one country or group of countries a veto power over actions between two strong-currency countries designed to bolster the functioning of the key currencies. Until something adequate has been designed and adopted to take the place of the present gold-exchange standard, highly restrictive multilateral surveillance could destroy the system.

A similar conflict emerged between the French-Dutch point of view and the U.S.-U.K. viewpoint with respect to a possible substitute for the current gold-dollar-sterling standard. The French have suggested a composite currency in place of the prevailing key-currency system. Since gold may not prove adequate to meet world needs, it may be necessary to find new sources to supply the world with international reserves. The creation of reserve assets should not be linked they argued, to fortuitous changes in the balance of payments of reserve countries. The French pinned their faith on gold which, it was argued, is the only monetary element outside the scope of government activities.[7] If and when fiduciary reserves must be added to gold, they should, in the French view, be issued in the form of a composite unit, by the deliberate and concerted action of strong-currency countries. The amount issued should be determined by strict objective rules which should govern the creation of the fiduciary component of the new monetary standard. We face no danger, it was argued, of shortage of liquidity. The danger is rather of an oversupply. A supplementary composite reserve currency should therefore be issued under the strictest

[7] The matter is, in fact, not quite that simple. One needs only to be reminded that gold would quickly lose most of its value if the United States no longer stood ready to purchase gold at $35 an ounce.

regulations. There is always, said Mr. D'Estaing, a tendency to accumulate an oversupply of world liquidity. Cautious regulations would be necessary in order to assess the true need for additional reserves.

Mr. Dillon, on behalf of the United States stated that he was quite prepared to explore the idea of a composite currency reserve. As a means of creating additional credit facilities, it would be useful. It should not be used, however as the French imply, as a means to restrict what we already have. Our main duty, said Mr. Maudling in support of the American position, is to supply liquidity in such an amount, and distributed in such a manner, as to ensure that no unnecessary brake is placed on the expansion of the world economy.

The French-Dutch restrictionist viewpoint is also disclosed in the position which they maintained with respect to the 25 per cent gold payment on members' additional subscription to the Fund quotas. At the Tokyo meeting there was general agreement that the aggregate Fund quotas should be increased. Previously 25 per cent of the quotas was initially paid in gold. The French and Dutch demanded that the 25 per cent rule be rigorously adhered to. The debate on this matter was important and significant in view of the current developments as they affect the key-currency countries. Payment in gold, at this juncture, could cause a severe drain upon the gold reserves of the two key-currency countries. Countries holding dollars or sterling might cash in their holdings for gold in order to meet their subscription obligations. This could weaken the prevailing system.

In order to avoid any such strain, the United States and United Kingdom suggested the use of gold certificates in lieu of actual gold. Mr. Maudling stated that he attached special importance to finding the best method of minimizing the impact on the key currencies of transfers of gold to the Fund.

The widest disagreement between the American-British view and the French-Dutch view developed with respect to where the ultimate control over the creation of new international reserves should be vested. The French-Dutch view appears to be not only that this responsibility should rest with the strong-currency countries (a position with which I personally agree), presumably, in the first instance, the Group of Ten. Beyond that they took the extreme position that each member should have the right to veto any proposal. Mr. Maudling pointed out that with respect to the General Arrangements to Borrow, for example, no member of the group, or indeed any group as such, enjoys the veto power in the granting of new facilities. Mr. Dillon stated, moreover, that the amount of liquidity should not be determined by the Group of Ten, but should be determined within the IMF.

Here I am personally unable to agree fully with either of the opposing views. The suggestion that one country could veto any action is clearly preposterous and could only lead to perpetual stalemate. On the other hand it must, I believe, be recognized that no international reserve currency could stand up which is not based on the strong convertible currencies of countries enjoying an impeccable credit rating. The Fund has 102 members, most of which could not qualify as members of the "international currency club." The strong-currency countries could not accept dictation from the 102 Fund members with respect to such matters as the quantity of international reserves.

Short-term lending to help member countries over temporary balance-of-payments hurdles is one thing. The issue of international money is quite a different matter. However, the Group of Ten should not be an exclusive club. New members should be added from time to time as developing countries acquire status in terms of credit worthiness, currency convertibility and size, and as they begin to play a significant role in international exchange. The modified Group of Ten should control by majority vote the amount of new reserve units to be created by the international reserve authority. In so doing, however, it should take full cognizance of presentations coming up from the broad membership of the Fund. Moreover, the managing director of the Fund should be the chairman of the governing board of the international reserve authority.

Finally, any individual member of the international reserve authority whose currency is sought after and employed in payments transactions should in no way be restricted in making its currency available to traders and central bankers the world over. In other words the aggregate of international reserves would consist of (1) gold, (2) the foreign holdings of strong convertible currencies widely used in international transactions, and (3) the international reserve units issued by an international reserve agency. Thus, side by side with the new international currency would be dollar and sterling working balances employed by traders, private banks, and central banks. To this would be added from time to time other reserve currencies. The establishment of an international credit-creating institution (in short, a world central bank) need not squash the vitally important role which established reserve currencies will continue to play.

chapter eleven

GROWTH TRENDS AND RELATED VARIABLES

The Brookings Report, as we have seen, singles out the relative growth rates and price movements of the United States and Western Europe as the primary determinants of the U.S. balance of payments. This of course relates to those items in the payments balance sheet which are responsive to the market forces of an exchange economy. They involve both trade and capital movements. External to these market-determined components are the nonmarket or politically determined items—government loans, grants, and military expenditures abroad.

In this chapter we shall attempt to gain a little further insight, if possible, into the behavior of modern economies with respect to GNP growth rates and GNP price movements together with related variables, including investment, industrial production, exports, employment, hourly earnings, consumer prices, wholesale prices, and international reserves. The presumption is that the behavior of the past ten to twelve years can help us in some measure to gain some knowledge about how the economies can be expected to function in the future. This does not mean that the past will repeat itself, but it does suggest that past *relationships* can to a degree throw light on the future. Economics is often spoken of as a behavioristic science. This can only mean that armchair philosophizing can go wild, and we do well to look and see how the "economic animal" actually behaves.

GROWTH RATES AND PRICE INCREASES

For example, statements about the relation of growth and prices have ranged all the way from the assertion that price stability promotes growth to the quite different assertion that price increases promote growth. And in terms of statistics it is not to be wondered at (considering the enormous diversity of economic and political structures in the world today—developed and underdeveloped) that support can be found for almost any conclusion. The problem will at least be more manageable if we limit ourselves to the behavior of the advanced industrial countries. Even so there are sufficient structural differences so that a high degree of uniformity of behavior can scarcely be expected.[1]

[1] See Erik Lundberg's brilliant and stimulating article, "Economic Growth, Inflation and Stability: An International Comparison," *Quarterly Review*, Skandinaviska Banken, vol. 44, no. 4, 1963. Professor Lundberg in a guarded and qualifying statement is skeptical that his scatter diagram shows any correlation between growth and

The first thing that stands out clearly in the behavior of the advanced economies since about 1950 is that all countries, without exception, have experienced growth and all have experienced price increases. There is not a single exception to this rule. This in itself tells us that there is some connection between growth and price increases[2] but it tells us nothing about cause and effect relationship. It does not *ipso facto* mean that price increases *caused* high growth rates, though it could mean that price increases of the magnitude that actually occurred contributed to high growth rates. Nor does it mean that growth inevitably produces price increases, though it could mean that high growth rates tend to produce price increases. It could also mean that underlying conditions operated to produce both growth rates and price increases simultaneously. The behavior of modern leading economies during the last dozen or so years does not, however, permit the conclusion that one can just as well expect price decreases as price increases in a rapidly growing society. The behavior of these economies also does not permit one to say that, associated with a given growth rate, we can predict a certain increase in prices.

Let us classify a dozen or so leading countries into groups averaging different rates of growth as follows: (I) high growth rate, (II) high medium growth rate, (III) medium growth rate, and (IV) low growth rate.

---

prices. Clearly there is no proportional relation that would justify any simple conclusion. Professor Lundberg seems, however, to disavow any relationship and this, I believe, carries his skepticism a little too far.

[2] Whether or not growth tends to promote price increases may depend more or less upon whether the growth is demand-led or supply-led. Demand-led growth is likely to bring price increases, while supply-led growth (cost reducing techniques, increased supply of productive factors) may tend to promote price decreases, or at least price stability. See the Brookings Report, pp. 18–23.

Table 11-1. *Growth Rates and Price Increases,* 1950–1960*

	Per cent growth† per year	*Price increase‡ per year*	*Average for group*
I. High growth rates (real GNP per person employed):			
Japan	7.6	4.6	Growth = 6.1
Austria	5.5	5.1	Price increase
West Germany	5.2	3.3	= 4.3
II. High medium growth rates:			
Italy	4.2	2.5	Growth = 4.1
Switzerland	4.2	1.2	Price increase
France	4.0	6.5	= 3.4
III. Medium growth rates:			
Netherlands	3.5	3.3	Growth = 3.0
Norway	3.3	4.2	Price increase
Sweden	3.1	4.8	= 3.6
Denmark	2.7	3.2	
Belgium	2.6	2.3	
IV. Low growth rates:			
United States	2.3	2.5	Growth = 2.1
United Kingdom	2.1	4.0	Price increase
Canada	2.0	3.2	= 3.2

* Data from OECD and UN publications. I am indebted to Mr. Franz Ettlin for the statistical calculations for Tables 11-1 and 11-3.

† Percentage increase, compounded, in GNP (constant prices) from 1950 to 1960.

‡ Percentage increase, compounded, in the GNP price deflators from 1950 to 1960.

If we omit Japan from the first group we obtain the following comparison between the four groupings.

	Growth	*Price increase*
Group I	5.3	4.2
Group II	4.1	3.4
Group III	3.0	3.6
Group IV	2.1	3.2

There are indeed significant variations for individual countries, but for the most part these variations reinforce the conclusion that high growth rates and large price increases are associated, but not proportionally. We might indeed have expected such high-growth-rate countries as West Germany, Italy, and Switzerland to have experienced larger price increases than the relatively moderate ones actually registered. That this did not occur can largely be explained by the fact that in the decade 1960 to 1960 these countries were able to tap an enormous labor reservoir while all the other European countries were confronted with a narrowly restricted labor market. From 1950 to 1960 employment in West Germany increased by 46 per cent, and in Switzerland 35 per cent, while Italy absorbed a 50 per cent increase from 1954 to 1962. Using the *base* 1953, the average *index* of employment in these three countries rose to 141 by 1960, while for France, the United Kingdom, the Netherlands, Sweden, and Belgium it rose to only 107. West Germany absorbed 12 million refugees and besides reduced her pool of unemployment from 10.3 per cent in 1950 to 1.2 per cent in 1960. Switzerland was able to draw a large labor force from surrounding countries and to cut her own unemployment pool from 9.6 per cent in 1950 to 1.2 per cent in 1960. Italy could draw upon her vast unemployed labor resources in Naples and the poor southern rural districts. The extraordinary growth rates of Japan, West Germany, Italy, and Switzerland could probably not have been achieved at the relatively moderate price increases experienced, had it not been for the availability of large pools of labor.

GROWTH RATES AND INCREASES IN RESERVES

West Germany, Italy, and Switzerland averaged growth rates of 4.5 per cent with average price increases of only 2.5 per cent per year. This combination would appear to be very

Table 11-2. *Gold and Foreign Exchange Holdings*, 1960 (*index numbers; base*, 1950 = 100)

West Germany	824
Italy	494
Netherlands	352
France	253
Norway	222
Sweden	211
Belgium	167
Denmark	139
Switzerland	131
United Kingdom	91

favorable for their balance of payments, and so it was. West Germany's gold and foreign exchange holdings increased from $190 million to $5,823 million from 1950 to 1960, Italy's from $602 million to $2,973 million, and Switzerland's from $1,570 million to $2,053 million.[3]

The West German holdings in 1950 were so abnormally low that this figure should clearly be ruled out. For the

[3] *OECD General Statistics*, 1963, pp. 68–69.

index number given in Table 11-2, therefore, I have used 1952 as the base year for West Germany, while for all the other countries the base year is 1950.

West Germany and Italy stand out far above the rest with an average index of gold and foreign exchange holdings of 659 against an average of 205 for France, Belgium, the Netherlands, Denmark, Norway, Sweden, and the United Kingdom. Switzerland, already overstocked in 1950 with $1,570 million of gold and foreign exchange (mostly gold), still added another half billion to her resources in the course of the decade.

GROWTH RATES AND INVESTMENT

Growth rates affect capital flows in the balance of payments primarily through their impact upon the prospective rates of profit. The effectiveness of these rates can be judged in part by the volume of investment. Table 11-3 compares growth rates with the ratio of investment to GNP.

Japan and Norway are special cases. Japan is experiencing an explosive growth starting from the relatively low capital stock and low output characteristic of underdeveloped countries and suddenly bursting forth as a leading industrial power. Such a country is confronted with a vast vacuum into which investment can flow. It is this vacuum that explains both the high growth rate and the high investment ratio—each is the cause of the other, and both spring from the embryonic stage of industrial evolution in which Japan has found herself. Could the United Kingdom experience the same rate of growth if she undertook an equivalent per cent of investment in plant and equipment? The imperious law of diminishing marginal productivity of capital gives an emphatic negative answer. It could well be, of course, that the United Kingdom might wisely raise her

Table 11-3. *Growth Rates and Investment*, 1950–1960

	Per cent growth per year	*Investment* (per cent of GNP)*	*Average for group*
I. High growth rates (real GNP per person employed):			
Japan	7.6	23.2	Growth = 6.1
Austria	5.5	17.5	Investment = 19.1
West Germany	5.2	16.7	
II. High medium growth rates:†			
Italy	4.2	15.1	Growth = 4.1
France	4.0	13.3	Investment = 14.2
III. Medium growth rates:			
Netherlands	3.5	17.9	Growth = 3.0
Norway	3.3	24.2	Investment = 16.5
Sweden	3.1	15.3	Investment
Denmark	2.7	13.7	excluding
Belgium	2.6	11.6	Norway = 14.6
IV. Low growth rates:			
United States	2.3	12.2	Growth = 2.1
United Kingdom	2.1	11.2	Investment = 13.8
Canada	2.0	18.1	

* Investment ratio, excluding housing construction.
† Data missing for Switzerland.

investment ratio more or less in line with that of Continental Europe. But even this may be doubtful. To compare her investment position with that of Japan would be quite meaningless.

Norway represents a different case. Her very large postwar program of investment relates to the peculiar structure of the Norwegian economy. Her huge merchant marine and the hydroelectric projects require vast investment outlays.

Let us omit Japan and Norway and combine the high and high medium growth countries. We then get the following summary results:

	Growth	*Investment ratio*
Group I (high)	4.9	16.2
Group II (medium)	3.6	15.5
Group III (low)	2.2	13.5

There appears to be a fair degree of correlation between growth and investment. But the relation is not a simple one, and there are individual irregularities. It is reasonable to suppose that a high investment ratio is induced by favorable underlying growth factors, and on the other side, investment is clearly a necessary, but not a sufficient, condition for growth. The statistical relation of investment to growth could be substantially strengthened if we included expenditures on education as a part of domestic investment outlays. But for the balance-of-payments problem it is the impact of the traditional capital investment on the capital account that matters, and here the conventional measurements of investment are perhaps quite adequate.

INDUSTRIAL PRODUCTION AND PRICES

From the *OECD General Statistics* and the *International Financial Statistics* I have assembled some additional data that throw further light on the movements of the leading market determinants of the balance of payments—growth and price movements. The variables involved are industrial production, wholesale prices, consumer prices, hourly earnings, and the physical volume of exports and imports covering the period 1953 to 1962. Again we classify the countries into groups ranked according to their place in the industrial production scale.

For consumer prices in the low and medium groups the average index is 120 while for the high and upper medium groups the average index is 129; for wholesale prices the

Table 11-4. Industrial Production and Prices, 1962
(*index numbers; base,* 1953 = 100)

	Growth	*Wholesale prices*	*Consumer prices*	*Average for group*		
I. High growth rates (industrial production):						
Italy	222	102	123	Growth	= 202	
West Germany	199	106	118	Wholesale prices	= 115	122
France	185	136	155	Consumer prices	= 128	
II. High medium growth rates:						
Norway	168	115	130	Growth	= 167	
Denmark	168	106	133	Wholesale prices	= 108	120
Holland	166	103	127	Consumer prices	= 130	
III. Medium growth rates:						
Canada	144	109	113	Growth	= 141	
Sweden	142	115	133	Wholesale prices	= 108	113
Switzerland	141	104	115	Consumer prices	= 118	
Belgium	137	103	112			
IV. Low growth rates:						
United Kingdom	133	119	131	Growth	= 132	
United States	130	109	113	Wholesale prices	= 114	118
				Consumer prices	= 122	

indices are 111 and 112 respectively. The conclusion is practically the same as that found in the GNP deflators, namely, that price increases have been substantial for all groups and that these increases do not differ greatly from group to group. The behavior pattern for modern economies is, however, clear: along with growth go price increases. To this there is no single exception.

INDUSTRIAL PRODUCTION AND EFFICIENCY WAGES

Consider next the relation of growth as measured by increases in industrial production per worker employed in industry to (1) hourly earnings, (2) efficiency wages (i.e.,

Table 11-5. *Average Growth, Hourly Earnings, Efficiency Wages, and Consumer Prices,* 1962 (*index numbers; base,* 1953 = 100)

	Growth (industrial production per worker employed in industry)	*Hourly earnings*	*Efficiency wages (hourly earnings output per worker, or labor cost per unit of output)*	*Consumer prices*
I. High growth rates: Italy, West Germany, France	153	188	123	128
II. High medium growth rates: Norway, Denmark, Holland	150	187	125	130
III. Medium growth rates: Canada, Sweden, Switzerland, Belgium	127	147	116	118
IV. Low growth rates: United Kingdom, United States*	127	143	113	122

* For the United States I use hourly earnings in manufacturing divided by output per man-hour.

hourly earnings divided by output per worker), and (3) consumer prices. Unless there is a marked redistribution between profits and wages, we should expect a fairly close relation between the movements of efficiency wages and consumer prices. This proves in fact to be the case except for the low-growth countries, notably the United Kingdom.

The figures for high and high medium growth rate countries are almost indentical. In round numbers these countries experienced a 50 per cent increase in output per worker, a 25 per cent increase in labor cost per unit of output (i.e., efficiency wages), and a 30 per cent increase in consumer prices. For the medium group the increases in each case are roughly one-half those of the higher growth group: output per worker 26 per cent, efficiency wages, 16 per cent, and consumer prices, 18 per cent.

GROWTH RATES, EXPORTS, AND IMPORTS

Finally we come to the relation of growth to exports and imports. One is tempted, upon examining Table 11-6, to say that while countries which pushed exports hard experienced large growth rates, it took an ever-increasing push to get a given increment of growth. Turning the causal relationship around the other way, we could say that the higher the growth rates, the more effective their impact upon exports.

Growth, as we have seen, is somehow associated with price increases. This, however, has apparently not acted as a brake on exports because, as we have noted, price increases have been remarkably uniform, broadly speaking, in high, medium, or low growth rate countries. This is true whether prices are measured in terms of GNP price deflators, consumer prices, or wholesale prices. But in the final analysis it is export and import prices that carry weight in world trade. One must, however, not lose sight of the general structure of the price system and the interrelationship of the various price components and their impact on overall efficiency wages. And as indicated earlier, there are other factors such as product differentiation and selling techniques which play an

Table 11-6. *Growth, Exports and Imports*, 1962
(*index numbers; base*, 1953 = 100)

	Growth (industrial production)	*Exports (volume)*	*Imports (volume)*	*Average for group*
I. High growth rates:				
Italy	222	377	304	Growth = 202
West Germany	199	281	348	Exports = 288
France	185	205	216	Imports = 289
II. High medium growth rates:				
Norway	168	180	190	Growth = 167
Denmark	168	182	223	Exports = 190
Holland	166	207	224	Imports = 212
III. Medium growth rates:				
Canada	144	139	129	Growth = 141
Sweden	142	222	202	Exports = 184
Switzerland	141	180	254	Imports = 196
Belgium	137	194	200	
IV. Low growth rates:				
United Kingdom	133	134	141	Growth = 132
United States	130	124	156	Exports = 129
				Imports = 148

important role within the viable range of price competition.

For the United Kingdom exports and industrial production have increased at the same rate, imports slightly more. In the case of the United States, exports lagged slightly behind the growth rate of industrial production but imports rose somewhat more. This may possibly be related in part to military stock piling. For all the more rapidly growing countries, exports and imports both increased more rapidly than industrial production. World trade has clearly, for the Continental countries of Western Europe, played a big role in growth.

SUMMARY VIEW: THE IMPACT ON THE BALANCE OF PAYMENTS

Where does this leave us with respect to the all-important problem of the impact of growth and full employment on the balance of payments? Growth is clearly associated with high exports and high imports. If we are interested in enlarging the U.S. *share* in world trade, growth is imperative. But if we are interested simply in the balance of payments, the picture is blurred. Growth clearly means larger imports—an adverse effect. But it also stimulates exports in various and diverse ways. Growth promotes technology and fuller capacity utilization and, therefore, lower unit costs than can be achieved in periods of sluggish growth. Strong growth rates produce (or at least have produced) substantial price increases. These produce action and reaction between countries, and so the net effect of price increases is largely neutralized. There remains the impact of growth upon capital flows. Here it appears that any country which increases its rate of growth relative to its competitors will improve its overall payments balance.

All this relates to the market exchange economy operating under the play of market forces. It involves private transactions whether in merchandise trade or services, or private capital movements across international borders. It leaves out of account the transfer problems—government loans and grants and military expenditures abroad. These are not determined by market forces operating through income and price changes. They are exogenous factors, external to the exchange economy. They do indeed disturb the normal market-equilibrating forces. They have indeed, as we have noted, feedback effects which to a degree serve to transform the money transfers into a real transfer. But this takes time. And as long as the U.S. money transfers continue on as large scale as in recent years, it may well turn out, as the more moderate and more plausible alternative projections of the Brookings Report indicate, that the basic balance deficits may not soon be eliminated. The transfer problem is the heart of the whole matter. The solution cannot quickly be found in the trade balance without seriously disturbing the structure of world trade. The long-run solution lies in the internationalization of the world capital markets.

chapter twelve

WILL HISTORY REPEAT ITSELF?

THE TWENTIES

With the benefit of hindsight, it is not difficult to see that the decade of the twenties was rife with serious distortions that afflicted both domestic economies and international economic relations. In the United States two profoundly disturbing factors loomed above everything else. One was the fantastic stock market inflation that culminated in the 1929 crash; the other was the drastic increase in the American tariff culminating in the Smoot-Hawley Tariff Act of 1930.

The former distorted the domestic economy; the latter seriously disturbed international equilibrium.

Viewing the twenties from the vantage point of the present against the background of the devastating depression of the thirties, one can easily see that drastic measures would have had to be taken to avert the disaster. At the time this was not evident to anyone. Knowledgeable people in the buoyant twenties believed that depressions were a thing of the past, that high prosperity could continue indefinitely. God was in his Heaven and, if all was not right with the world, at least it was with the American economy! After the event, one realizes that no ordinary measures could have prevented the collapse. The things that needed to be done were, by a wide margin, not in the political cards.

SINS OF OMISSION

Even now that our horizon has been pushed back far beyond the limited vision of the twenties and thirties, there are plenty of people, perhaps a majority, who shiver at the mere recital of the measures we should have taken. Different "economic doctors" would no doubt even today offer quite different remedies. A major cause of economic disaster is the great difficulty of achieving a consensus. For myself I offer the following. And since some of the problems of the twenties are still with us, or at least lurk in the wings, the measures here suggested for the twenties may well have some relevance for the future. The remedies suggested apply, it will be noted, in no inconsiderable measure to countries with surpluses in their balance of payments.

Among other things (I am by no means exhausting the list) the United States should have introduced in the twenties the following reforms:

1. Raise the stock market margin requirements to 100 per cent
2. Drastically reduce the U.S. tariff by unilateral action
3. Undertake a vigorous program of fiscal and monetary expansion
4. Appreciate the dollar or cooperate with the United Kingdom in devaluation of sterling

These measures tie in together. No one of them can stand on its own feet. A program of monetary and fiscal expansion would have driven the stock market still higher unless accompanied by the strong measures of restraint suggested by tariff reduction and the 100 per cent margin requirement. A drastic reduction of the tariff would have caused deflation and unemployment unless accompanied by a program of expansion. And a strong program of expansion would have produced price inflation without a realignment of the dollar and sterling.

Not only would these measures have promoted stability, growth, and expansion in the American economy, they would also have lifted the international economy and eased the way to balanced world trade and international monetary stability.

The United Kingdom was suffering from a cost structure too high in terms of world prices. This, to be sure, was in no small measure due to the fatal mistake of reestablishing the old gold parity in 1925. British industry found it difficult to carry on with this load on its back. Unemployment ranged from 10 to 17 per cent throughout the twenties. The British complained that the United States was not playing the gold standard game fairly. On the basis of the huge inflow of gold into the United States in the first part of the twenties and again in 1928–1929, the United States should, according to gold standard theory, have experienced a great expansion in income and prices. This would have increased American imports, lifted aggregate incomes all over the world, and so greatly stimulated British exports. Indeed in the late twenties Governor Strong of the New York Federal Reserve Bank was instrumental in instituting, under British pressure, a program of monetary ease. But the booming stock market defeated his program. Monetary restraint was reinstated.

In the twenties, world equilibrium demanded an expansion of the American market. This required tariff reduction and income expansion. Up to 1928 the disequilibrating effect of the American tariff was in part disguised by the large outflow of capital from the United States. The foreign securities publicly placed in the United States mounted steadily higher from the beginning of 1925 to the middle of 1928, ranging from $1 billion in 1925 to $1.8 billion in the twelve-month period from July 1, 1927, to July 1, 1928. In addition there was a large volume of direct investment. Beginning with the middle of 1928, however, foreign loans began to decline. By 1929 the figure had fallen to less than half the 1927 level.[1]

The cost and availability of loans tightened up in 1928. Moreover foreign countries were being "loaned up." Overcapacity was developing. Interest and dividends owed to the United States on past investments were rising. Imports into the United States were restricted by the prohibitive tariff. Gold poured into the United States in large volume after the middle of 1928.

THE GOLD PROBLEM

So today's problems of international liquidity are not new. They plagued the world in the twenties and thirties in much the same manner as now, though we are now, I believe, very much better prepared to meet them. In the twenties the problem of gold scarcity loomed large. The high point in

[1] See my *Economic Stabilization in an Unbalanced World*, Harcourt, Brace & World, New York, 1932, pp. 80, 81, 90, 102–108.

gold production was reached in 1915 at $470 million. From then on it declined steadily to $319 million in 1922. Thereafter the production increased a little to $408 million in 1928. The League of Nations' Gold Delegation reported a probable production of $410 million in 1932 and then a progressive decline to $370 million by 1940.

To meet this situation three radical changes had been made by 1928. First, in many countries gold was no longer employed as a circulating medium. The result was a substantial increase in the gold reserves of the central banks. Prof. Gustav Cassel (employing a somewhat naive quantity theory) estimated that this change alone permitted an increase in the price level of about 24 per cent (above 1913) calculated in terms of gold. Second, many of the central banks of Europe were permitted by law to hold foreign exchange as part of their reserves. This effected a further gold saving which according to Cassel's estimates permitted a further increase in the price level of about 18 per cent. Finally, a considerable portion of the gold which before the war had been utilized in the form of jewelry and plate had, under the stimulus of war patriotism, been turned over to the government and added to its monetary gold stock. These three changes combined were sufficient to justify, Cassel believed, a world price level 40 to 45 per cent above 1913, measured in terms of gold. This (perhaps by accident) was approximately the U.S. price level in the decade of the twenties.

Today, payments surplus countries tend to hoard, as we have seen, high gold ratios. Similarly in the twenties the gold problem had to do in large part with an abnormal distribution of gold. France and the United States were the heavy gold absorbers. This imposed credit restrictions on England, Germany, and other countries. World prices sagged, while U.S. prices rose 4 per cent from May, 1927, to September, 1929, and French prices rose 9 per cent from October, 1927, to March, 1929. Still, in neither country was credit expansion allowed to reach the level implicit in the massive importation of gold. In France the gold was largely sterilized in the Central Bank and in the United States credit expansion was restrained by the Federal Reserve maintenance of a level of gold reserves approximately twice the legal limit.

SHORT-TERM LIABILITIES

The U.S. balance-of-payments crisis revolves today around the growth of short-term liabilities relative to the U.S. gold reserves. The immediate problem is how to get rid of the overhang of short-term indebtedness. Some efforts have been made, as we have seen, by the U.S. Treasury to convert a part of these short-term obligations into longer-term bonds. And in previous chapters of this book we have examined a wide variety of proposals which come to much the same thing, namely, ways and means of getting out from under the overlay of short-term debt.

In the critical early thirties, European central banks were holding, as today, large balances of foreign exchange which had accumulated over a considerable period. The total of short-term international indebtedness had reached about $10 billion by the end of 1930. These accumulations had come to be regarded as more or less normal. But under the impact of the Depression, sweeping withdrawals of short-term credits put a terrific pressure upon the central banks. There was no IMF upon which central banks could fall back for help, but even here the difference is not as great as might be imagined.

In the thirties the Bank for International Settlements,[2] which began operations on May 17, 1930, was, to a degree,

[2] For large parts of this chapter I have relied heavily on the excellent Annual Reports of the Bank for International Settlements, the first of which appeared on May 19, 1931.

a central bank for central banks. As the holder of central banks' reserves, the BIS was called upon to come to their aid. Large holders of foreign exchange were converting their balances into gold. The central banks that were losing gold were compelled to draw out their deposits with the BIS. In consequence central bank deposits with the BIS fell by December, 1931, to about half the level of the preceding August. Central banks, operating under severe pressure, demanded the granting of emergency credits by the BIS. The BIS made strenuous efforts to facilitate the conversion of the superabundant accumulation of short-term assets into longer-term assets and more permanent investment. But the resources of the BIS were severely limited. The urgency of such conversion was clearly recognized, and studies were undertaken to set up an international organization outside the BIS whose function it would be to grant long-term loans. This suggests that many of the proposals which we surveyed in Chapter 6 are not altogether new.

The BIS did participate in a subscription to long-term bonds issued by two international mortgage banks organized by private international banking groups. The BIS organized a syndicate of central banks which contributed funds to grant emergency aid to the National Bank of Hungary. Three central banks joined the BIS to extend a credit of $100 million to the German Reichsbank. In this manner the BIS was being forced, under the impact of the deepening depression, to shift over from merely helping to stabilize balance-of-payments fluctuations of a seasonal or transitory character to the granting of credits that in the nature of the case could not quickly be repaid.

GOLD-EXCHANGE GUARANTEE

Nor is the gold-exchange guarantee which we discussed in Chapter 3 a novelty. The second Annual Report of the

BIS covering the fiscal year April, 1931, to March, 1932, reported that the central banks, in which the BIS had accumulated claims in consequence of the granting of credits, agreed that the investments of the BIS would retain the same gold value as that which the investments had when they were originally made. This agreement between central bankers made thirty years ago is of particular interest now in view of the opposition of many central bankers today to a gold-exchange guarantee.

1931: A FATEFUL YEAR

In May, 1931, came the collapse of the Austrian Credit-Anstalt followed in June, 1931, by the Hoover moratorium which called for a one-year moratorium on intergovernmental debt payments. In July, 1931, an international conference was called which met in London, but the acute financial crisis could not be stayed. In September, 1931, came the fall of sterling and this led almost immediately to the suspension of gold or the gold-exchange standard by six other countries. By the end of the year sixteen countries had either abandoned gold or introduced rigorous exchange control. Standstill agreements on debt payments and exchange restrictions became the standard order of the day.

Exchange restrictions in England were aimed at capital movements but in most countries they were aimed primarily at the control of imports. Foreign exchange was allocated for the necessary imports of raw materials. Importers were allotted a certain per cent of their "normal" requirements as determined by their import volume for some earlier period. Import quotas were imposed on specific goods. Countries made bilateral clearing arrangements to help balance the trade between two countries.

At the time of the British crisis (September, 1931) several countries, especially England, Germany, Japan, Hungary, and Sweden suffered heavy losses of gold. The central banks of France, Switzerland, Holland, and Belgium quickly converted their foreign exchange into gold and by the end of October had added about $650 million of gold to their holdings. Private hoarding of gold developed extensively. But soon confidence in sterling was restored and gold began to come out of hiding, induced by the gold profit incident to the appreciation of sterling.

INTERNATIONAL CONFERENCES

The London International Conference of July, 1931, (referred to above) deserves special notice. It engineered a $100 million credit to the German Reichsbank. It set up a study group to inquire how to convert short-term debt into long-term. This suggests comparison with the resolution in the 1963 annual meeting of the IMF to set up two study groups to inquire how to ease the problem confronting the key-currency countries. The London conference study group reported on August 8, 1931, but the conclusions were vague and inconclusive and nothing came of them. It remains to be seen what may come out of the 1963 effort.

Later in December, 1931, a Committee of Eleven reported on the general problem of intergovernmental debts and concluded that the only step capable of reestablishing confidence was a complete reshuffling of the debt problem. And so another government conference was scheduled to meet in Lausanne in June, 1932. There were studies and conferences, but little action except that precipitated by the flow of events. At the end of 1932 some $6 billion of short-term indebtedness was still outstanding, of which one-half was blocked by standstills, moratoria, and exchange restrictions.

THE GLASS-STEAGALL ACT AND EASY MONEY

Another point of comparison with current problems was the Glass-Steagall Act of February 27, 1932. Under this act government securities were made eligible as backing for Federal Reserve notes and deposits, thereby freeing the gold (over and above the legally required 40 per cent) which had been tied up owing to the shortage of eligible paper. This freed an enormous amount of the U.S. gold stock for international payments. We were bolder then than now. Every time it is now proposed to eliminate the 25 per cent gold cover, monetary conservatists oppose or at least argue that nothing must be done until the dollar problem is already solved. The "confidence" argument is invariably the conservatists' final bulwark of defense against any reform.

Freed by the Glass-Steagall Act from the severe gold restraints previously imposed, the Federal Reserve Banks purchased $1.1 billion of government securities in the open market and thereby created substantial excess reserves and an easy money policy. Similarly in June, 1962, Great Britain undertook a massive conversion of $2 billion of the public debt from a 5 per cent interest rate to 3½ per cent. Finally the U.S. Banking Act of 1933 prohibited payment of interest on demand deposits.

GOLD HOARDING

Hoarding of gold was intensified in the first half of 1932. During this period European central banks converted $700 million of their dollar holdings into gold. In the first quarter of 1933 there was a further loss of U.S. gold to the central banks of France, the Netherlands, Switzerland, and England.

The Preparatory Commission for the Monetary and Economic Conference stated that "present day legislation in many countries renders much gold unavailable for international use." The third Annual Report of the BIS said: "Central banks should combat any conception that gold is properly employable as a store of wealth, or that its primary object is to assure internal convertibility of notes so that all who will may hoard gold coin on demand, to the detriment of the public good and the general economic welfare" (p. 11).

THE BRITISH EXCHANGE EQUALIZATION ACCOUNT

Another point of comparison with current developments can be found in the activities of the British Exchange Equalization Account of 1931 and the U.S. Exchange Stabilization Fund of 1934. These operated in the exchange markets to stabilize the rate of exchange. As we have seen, the U.S. Treasury and the Federal Reserve System have recently begun operations in the foreign exchange markets to support the dollar.

The British Exchange Equalization Account when set up was supplied with Treasury notes which it could sell in the open market against sterling balances. And with these balances it could buy foreign exchange, especially French francs, and convert this into gold. If foreign funds flowed into England, unduly increasing the monetary base upon which bank loans to business could be extended, the Equalization Account could counteract this inflow by selling securities in the open market, thereby tightening up on bank credit. Conversely if funds flowed out of England, it could buy securities, thereby placing new funds at the disposal of the commercial banks.

THE U.S. EXCHANGE STABILIZATION FUND

The U.S. Exchange Stabilization Fund was set up at the time of the gold revaluation of January, 1934. Two billion dollars of the gold profit of $2.8 billion resulting from the devaluation of the dollar was placed at the disposal of the Stabilization Fund. This gold supplied the means by which the Fund could buy foreign exchange and operate in the foreign exchange markets. The Fund was not empowered to make open market purchases and sales in the domestic market, so that operations designed to offset inflows and outflows of funds abroad had to be undertaken by the Treasury itself. This was done for a limited period in 1936–1937.

THE DECLINE OF FOREIGN EXCHANGE

In general after the fall of sterling in September, 1931, the value of official holdings of foreign exchange by all countries drastically declined. In 1929–1930 aggregate official foreign exchange holdings amounted to about $11 billion. By the end of 1932 foreign exchange holdings had dwindled to about $1 billion (mostly held by Scandinavian countries and sterling area), while the aggregate monetary gold stock was nearly $12 billion. Foreign holdings of dollar balances had fallen by the end of 1933 to one-sixth of the 1930 holdings.

THE ROLE OF GOLD

By the end of 1931 only eight countries were still on the gold standard, ten countries were operating on a controlled flexible exchange rate basis, and the rest had introduced exchange control.

The United States abandoned gold in April, 1933, but under the Gold Reserve Act of January, 1934, the dollar was again linked to gold.

In July, 1933, the "gold bloc" was formed with six countries—France, Belgium, Holland, Italy, Poland, and Switzerland—declaring firm adherence to the gold standard. Shortly thereafter the British Commonwealth countries issued a declaration calling for international action: (1) to raise wholesale prices, (2) to institute a program of easy money and low, long-term interest rates, and (3) to undertake public capital expenditure. The declaration urged no prior international commitments on the sterling exchange rate.

THE FAMOUS LONDON CONFERENCE

In July 27, 1933, the famous London Monetary and Economic Conference with sixty-four countries represented was held. The Conference report contained five resolutions calling for: (1) currency stabilization, (2) gold to be reestablished as the means of exchange value, (3) economy of gold by keeping gold out of internal circulation and reducing gold minimum ratios to 25 per cent, (4) central bank collaboration, and (5) international cooperation to stabilize cyclical fluctuations.

President Roosevelt sent two messages to the London Conference in which he declared that a sound internal economy is more important than the price of its currency. This calls to mind the current controversies in the United States about the extent to which we should allow the deficit position in our balance of payments to restrain domestic policies designed to promote full employment and higher rates of growth. Roosevelt further declared that the United States stood squarely for a stable purchasing power dollar. This he said was more important than a fixed exchange rate. Gold, he said, may well serve as the metallic reserve. And once better world equilibrium is restored, there should be international consultation in the matter of optimum distribution between countries of the world's monetary gold stock. Roosevelt declared that the United States was committed to a revaluation of the dollar in terms of commodities and that this was an end from which the United States could not be diverted. We are interested, he said, in American commodity prices. What is to be the exchange value of the dollar in terms of other currencies is not and cannot be said to be an immediate concern. The exchange value of the dollar will ultimately depend upon the success of other nations in raising the prices of their own commodities in terms of their national moneys; it cannot be determined in advance of our knowledge of such fact. As noted above, however, by January, 1934, the dollar was again linked to gold, but with the proviso that the President could alter the rate within stated limits.

WORLD PRICES IN THE TWENTIES AND THIRTIES

The BIS in its sixth Annual Report of May, 1936, voiced the opinion that several currencies were out of line with world prices in 1924 to 1930, but suggested that these overvalued currencies might well have made the necessary adjustments had the decline in world prices not occurred. The Report might well have added that a moderate rise in world prices would have eased still more the position of the overvalued currencies and facilitated a process of adjustment. What the world needed in 1930 was a moderate "inflation" of say 3 to 4 per cent per year. Had the banker mentality, always cautioning restraint, been supplanted by the spirit of enterprise, which welcomes buoyant expansion, the history of the thirties could have been different.

PUBLIC SPENDING AND RECOVERY

The BIS reports in the late thirties straddled the issue of public spending on borrowed funds. The reports mistakenly argued that such spending tends to retard the natural fall in interest rates. Neither theory nor the experience of the thirties justifies this view. Spending from funds borrowed from the banking system tends to lower the rate of interest, as World War II demonstrated. And, moreover, in the thirties the volume of "voluntary" saving that was seeking investment outlets was so great that increased government borrowing would have had no striking effect on interest rates. The United States at any rate was immersed in the "liquidity trap."

Already by 1936, the BIS was worrying about an economic boom. Increased government spending was coming at the wrong time, so it was said. The Report overlooked the continuing vast unemployment and the excess capacity. The Report itself stated that world production had just reached the 1929 level by 1936. In the intervening years the labor force had grown and per worker productivity had increased. There was no shortage of capacity to produce. Demand was still greatly inadequate. It took World War II to make this crystal clear to all.

THE GOLD BLOC DEVALUATIONS

The big event of 1936 was the devaluation, on September 25, by the gold bloc countries led by France. These countries had suffered gold losses intermittently since 1933. These losses had become very large in September when speculation about approaching devaluation was rife. After holding out for five years, devaluation at last proved to be inescapable in view of the increasing disparity which separated the price levels of the gold bloc from the depreciated currency group. Economists have often argued that the proof of overvalued currency is the persistence of payments deficits. This test is, however, demonstrably invalid because an overvalued currency country can protect its payments balance by deflation of its costs and prices and by highly restrictive measures, such as exchange control and import quotas. The report of the Economic Committee of the League of Nations to the Financial Committee in 1936 suggested, quite rightly, that the restrictive measures applied by the gold bloc countries strongly suggested that these currencies were overvalued.

The devaluation of the French franc in 1936 is notable in the respect that this is one of the rare occasions when a devaluation was engineered in a climate of international co-operation. The French devaluation was welcomed by the United States and the United Kingdom and both countries agreed beforehand that they would take no countermeasures. Moreover, both countries in the famous tripartite agreement declared their intention to support the exchanges so as to forestall any speculative short-term capital flows.

Other countries were invited to cooperate in the hope that competitive devaluations could be avoided. The tripartite agreement made clear the distinction between a currency *adjustment* and competitive exchange depreciation.

All persons or corporate bodies domiciled in France were required to surrender any gold ingots, bars, or coins held on September 26, 1936, at the previous par rate. Importation or exportation of gold was prohibited. France thus followed the example set by the United States in 1934. Later the French law was changed to permit full market value to be paid to French holders of gold. In the United States gold holders received only the old par value. Some 5 to 6 billion French francs of gold had been hoarded in the period 1931 to 1934. Under the de-hoarding law it was estimated that perhaps 40 per cent of the hoarded gold came out of hiding. In the interest of solving the evil of private gold hoarding it is a pity that France later restored the right to hoard gold.

While the currency depreciations in 1931 generally led to fluctuating exchange rates (more or less stabilized by the operations of exchange equilization accounts or stabilization funds), the 1936 devaluations were made at specific rates and supported at these new fixed rates by stabilization funds.

Belgium, Holland, and Switzerland quickly joined in the declaration of the Tripartite Monetary Agreement. In all then, six countries (France, United States, United Kingdom, and these three) cooperated to support the new rate structure, and technical facilities were provided to facilitate the exchange of these six currencies into gold. Other countries could obtain gold against sterling in the London gold market at current market prices. Gold continued to be extensively used in view of the small holdings, as noted above, of foreign exchange.

The tripartite agreement represents a highly significant development. It brought sharply to the fore a recognition of the fact that the revaluation of any leading currency is a legitimate concern of other countries. The tripartite agreement pointed the way toward close international collaboration in monetary policy. In a way it could be regarded as a forerunner of Bretton Woods.

In contrast to the tripartite agreement and its efforts to achieve a freer system of international exchange, Germany declined to devalue and chose to stick to a rigid system of exchange control. While French prices quickly responded to devaluation, reaching, by 1937, levels in line with the price levels of the United States and United Kingdom, Germany's prices remained at a lower level.

GERMANY AND BILATERAL TRADE

Thus Germany became the leading proponent of bilateral bargaining and clearing agreements. Under these agreements exporters had to wait their turn in receiving payment. The exporter thus had to tie up working capital in involuntary trade credits.

To remedy this situation a new device was invented, namely, the "payments agreement." Under these agreements the trader was made directly responsible to see to it that prior arrangements to ensure payment had been made. The matter was not left to the general exchange market. Instead the importer was required to obtain beforehand a permit of payment which would assure the seller that foreign exchange would be available when the payment date arrived. Being equipped with this permit, obtained from the exchange authorities, the traders were able to gain access to ordinary banking credit facilities.

Proposals similar to the later European Clearing Union were made to arrange credits to pay off accumulated balances between countries. But nothing effective came out of these proposals.

PRICE RELATIONSHIPS REESTABLISHED

Following the Tripartite Monetary Agreement, the old price level relationship between the United States, the United Kingdom, and France was pretty much restored. Only Germany of the leading countries remained out of line. And the old exchange rates were largely reestablished. From January 1, 1936, to September, 1936, the dollar-sterling rate fluctuated around $5.00. From the date of the tripartite agreement to April, 1937, the rate was fairly stable around $4.90. From then on to February, 1938, it rose slowly again to around $5.00.

THE EFFECT OF THE DEPRECIATIONS

What benefit could then have come from the depreciations? Each country strove to regain its old competitive position. In monetary terms countries seemed to be back very much where they were before.

Some very important things had, however, happened. As soon as England went off gold in September, 1931, her commodity price level ceased to fall, while the price levels in the countries still tied to gold continued to decline. The U.S. wholesale price level rose sharply immediately after gold was abandoned. Both British and American prices continued to rise with some temporary interruptions until the recession of 1937 set in. French prices rose rapidly after the 1936 devaluation.

These developments point to the conclusion that the restraints imposed by the gold-exchange standard played a role in the deflationary process. Had it been possible for all these countries simultaneously to pursue expansionary fiscal policies, the deflation need not have occurred. The limited gold supply need not have restricted the quantity of available bank credit. The development of central banks everywhere made credit expansion possible even on a limited gold base though this in many cases required further banking and monetary reform. The gold-exchange standard per se was not the primary cause of the Depression. The deflationary forces were let loose when the extravagant investment boom, especially in the United States, had exhausted itself. The political climate of the time was quite unprepared to offset this decline by expansionary fiscal policy. Once these deflationary developments got under way the gold-exchange standard proved to be a well-greased slide down which all the leading economies raced, each in competition with the other, each exporting its deflationary impact upon its neighbors.

The limited gold supply was for the time being cured by the depreciations and devaluations. Raising the price of gold in terms of all the leading currencies amounted to a vast increase in the monetary gold stock. How much human labor would it have taken to produce the increased monetary gold stock which depreciation created overnight—all around about a 70 per cent increase?

Already by 1938 the gold problem was shifting from one of scarcity to one of excess. Monetary experts began to argue that there was too much gold! New production was up. De-hoarding was adding to the supply. What to do? Proposals were made to put gold coins again into circulation. And some thought the price of gold should be reduced. So rapidly can the wheel of fortune turn.

LESSONS FROM THE THIRTIES

When one surveys the developments in the early thirties, certain conclusions stand out.

Countries were trying desperately:

1. To engage in price and wage cutting
2. To balance their budgets
3. To get out from under their short-term liabilities
4. To convert their foreign exchange into gold
5. To protect their gold holdings by all manners of restrictive devices

Everywhere economic forces were in retreat. All efforts were directed at salvaging something out of the wreckage.

What was needed everywhere was a clarion call to advance.

Yet, in the then prevailing climate of opinion, the frantic efforts at survival are perfectly understandable. The only policies that could have saved the day were utterly unthinkable. Even today, expansionist policies are regarded as "dangerous" and "reckless." But could anything be more dangerous than the timid, restrictive policies actually pursued in the desperate days of the thirties? Hoover's Secretary of the Treasury cautioned us not to rock the boat. Two-thirds of the American labor force was still employed! Even the mild New Deal measures instilled fears of inflation. In late 1933, with 15 million unemployed, I attended a meeting of the New York Statistical Association, and what was the topic under discussion—"The Danger of Inflation"!

Let us suppose that truly expansionist policies had produced some inflation, possibly even of a dimension similar to that experienced in the United States during and immediately after World War II. Would anyone wish to trade the U.S. prosperity and inflation of 1942 to 1947 for the terrible U.S. depression of the thirties? One is reminded of the half-serious suggestion, born of a sense of desperation, by Prof. Irving Fisher—that bold and courageous monetary inventor—to scatter dollars all over the country from airplanes! What were we afraid of? To create adequate monetary demand is not difficult. We were afraid to trust ourselves with the powerful instruments of central bank credit and government fiscal policy.

WILL HISTORY REPEAT ITSELF?

Will the current inadequate gold-exchange standard inevitably produce another terrible collapse? Will the thirties sooner or later be repeated? There are, indeed, those who profess to think so. But it is safe to say that the overwhelming majority of economists all over the free world believe that modern advanced countries would not again tolerate a cumulative depression and deflation. And, moreover, they know how to prevent such a disaster. This is not the danger that needs to be feared. The current gold-exchange standard, backed by the IMF and the supplementary arrangements engineered in large part by the United States, does not face the threat of collapse.[3] But it does act as a persistent restraint on domestic freedom of action. The danger is not that of collapse. The danger for the United States is a semistagnation rate of growth and continued high unemployment.

These are solid grounds for improving the current international monetary mechanism. But we are not justified, I believe, in taking an alarmist view of the problem. There is much that we can learn from history. But it is an oversimplification to conclude that history must repeat itself.

[3] Let me here quote Professor Triffin who has sometimes used phrases which have seemed to some of his critics as unduly alarmist with respect to the danger that the history of the thirties will repeat itself. In Harris's *The Dollar in Crisis*, Triffin says (p. 278): "May I take objection, in passing, to Mr. Altiman's suggestion that I might regard the extension of the gold exchange standard of the 1920's as having possibly been 'a primary factor in the deflation that began in 1929.' All I said is that it 'led . . . to the devaluation of the pound sterling, to the collapse of the international gold exchange standard, and to the consequent *aggravation* of the world depression' (*Gold and the Dollar Crisis*, p. 9). That is enough, to my mind, to condemn the system without blaming it in addition for other cyclical developments, the world agricultural crisis and other sins of commission or omission in the economic policies of the 1920's."

appendix

THE FINANCIAL PROBLEM OF UNDERDEVELOPED COUNTRIES

As noted in several of the preceding chapters, the monetary and financial problems of the underdeveloped countries are very different from those of the developed countries. Yet all are linked in a trading world which requires an international medium of exchange and international institutions designed to promote worldwide trade and finance. But there are special problems that primarily concern the countries that are still in the early stages of industrial development.

THE IMPACT OF FOREIGN AID ON INTERNATIONAL MONETARY PROBLEMS

Against the background of the Marshall Aid grants and subsequent American aid programs, one encounters foreign nationalistic reactions that are far removed from the goal of sharing the burden of international monetary collaboration. Mr. Roosa, for example, has asserted: "Many countries today object to our balance-of-payments deficit on the grounds that we are financing an aid and military effort which they could not afford, or would not willingly undertake, by foisting on them dollar deposits which they have no need to hold."[1] That these dollar holdings, far from being worthless, can be invested in interest-bearing and highly valuable securities is not even mentioned. Also overlooked abroad is the excessive use of the New York capital market as a source of funds for the rich countries of Western Europe. If the appraisal quoted above is even remotely correct, we are indeed a long way from any general acceptance of international responsibility for the development of the primary producing countries.

The problems confronting the underdeveloped countries make up a formidable list. The more serious of these are as follows:

1. Cyclical or episodic *fluctuations* in the prices of export commodities.
2. The downward *trend* in the decade 1953 to 1963 of their export prices, while their import prices have, if anything, risen.
3. Restrictions placed upon the exports of the primary producing countries by the advanced countries as a means of protecting themselves against the so-called "ruinous competition" of low-wage products.

[1] Robert V. Roosa, "Assuring the Free World's Liquidity," Federal Reserve Bank of Philadelphia, September, 1962.

4. The capital flight from underdeveloped countries seeking safety and security abroad.
5. Inflation. In moderate form this may help to supply capital; in extreme form, it destroys growth, causes inequities, and incites revolutions.
6. The low level of education, lack of skill, technical know-how, and research in the underdeveloped countries.
7. The lack of the "underpinnings" of industrial development—railroads, roads, public utilities, electric power, etc.
8. The shortage of capital.

The first five points affect the balance of payments both in terms of short-run fluctuations and longer-run trends. And the last items reflect the shortage of human skills and physical capital.

THE UNITED NATIONS DEVELOPMENT DECADE

Considered in terms of the median or average standard of living, we are confronted with two worlds—rich countries and poor countries. Unless one has visited Asia, Africa, or Latin America, one can have no conception of what poverty can mean. The recent report of the United Nations entitled *The United Nations Development Decade* contains well-attested statements which are almost beyond belief. The document asserts that there are more people suffering from hunger and want than ever before in human history. And while the advanced countries have been reaching year by year, and often with an accelerated pace, higher and higher living standards, the underdeveloped countries continue to live just at the narrow margin of bare subsistence.

A SUBSISTENCE LEVEL

Subsistence, it is true, is a flexible term. A person's life may be cut short by starvation at a rapid pace or at a slow pace. The pace is slower now than formerly, as is attested by the rising length of life. People in the underdeveloped countries live longer than formerly (but in a state of semi-starvation) owing primarily to the progressive eradication of malaria, cholera, etc. The per capita food supply, according to the United Nations report, is just about holding its own. "In Asia and the Far East, calorie and animal protein supplies per capita are just back to pre-war levels. In other under-developed regions calorie supplies per person are above pre-war levels, but animal protein supplies per person are still below pre-war levels." Thus all around the record registers little if any gain. The *per capita* standard has not risen. And in absolute terms the *number* of human beings living in the condition of malnutrition and near starvation is now in the second half of the twentieth century larger than ever before.

"One of the basic problems facing the world, in particular the greater part of Asia, Africa and Latin America, over the next decade will still be hunger. According to a recent authoritative estimate, about one-sixth of the world's population—roughly 500 million people—today suffer from a lack of sufficient calories, and twice that number suffer from malnutrition or diet deficiencies in terms of vitamins, minerals and proteins."[2]

In some respects other than food the statistical measurements of progress indicate some improvement. Yet the number of people unaffected by progress has increased. Thus in most underdeveloped countries the *average* level of education is rising, yet the *number* of illiterates may also be rising. In India the number of people who could read and write increased by 40 million from 1951 to 1961. Yet the absolute number of illiterates had by 1961 risen by 11 million.

Many observers are impressed with the record of the

[2] United Nations, *The United Nations Development Decade,* New York, 1962, p. 41.

absolute number of people whose condition has improved, forgetting that the number of these remaining behind in abject destitution is also on the increase. Certainly the number of people who have in some sense reached the status of lower middle or even middle class has increased in perhaps all underdeveloped countries. The industrial population is growing. Yet the well-nigh hopeless rural masses have increased in absolute numbers. Industrialization is indeed proceeding, but not fast enough to prevent growing unemployment. Some progress in yield per acre, some increase in arable land (through irrigation etc.) does indeed produce more food. But population growth may have fully offset these gains. Agricultural progress, racing to keep up with medical progress, has so far failed to provide the growing masses with higher nutritional standards. More and more are indeed escaping the bondage of poverty. But more and more people remain at the bare subsistence level.

CAPITAL SHORTAGE

Thus the distribution of income and wealth the world over is becoming more and more concentrated in the advanced countries. One reason for the growing disparity of income is the increasing gulf with respect to scientific knowledge, technical know-how, skills, and the general level of education. Moreover, capital formation, though less important relative to knowledge than formerly thought to be the case, nonetheless remains a necessary condition for modern development. And saving is a far more difficult process for poor countries today than it was in the early days of capitalism when the working masses could easily, without fear of any effective retaliation, be exploited. Today communication is instantaneous throughout the world. The poor countries live in a rich world and they know it. The governments in the underdeveloped countries are compelled to take cognizance of pressing wants. To squeeze savings in any volume out of the backward economies today is not only inhuman, it is also, in terms of politics, impractical. And so the two basic conditions for rapid growth and progress—education and capital—are lacking.

Capital is lacking because the vast multitudes live at a bare subsistence level with no surplus for saving. There are, indeed, rich families, often very rich, at the top. But too often they have little confidence in the future of their own country and prefer to seek safe havens for their wealth in the advanced countries. Programs of reform, which should help to instill faith in progress, often tend to drive capital abroad. Capital flight is a serious matter in many of the underdeveloped countries.

CAPITAL FLIGHT

Historically, in the advanced countries, social reform and the welfare state came slowly and gradually under the pressure of rising labor movements and social democratic political parties. The privileged classes resisted these movements but finally accommodated themselves to the new order because there was no other place to go. This is not so today in the underdeveloped countries. The privileged classes can shift their financial assets to rich and secure countries. It does little good to point out that the welfare state, as it has developed, far from having destroyed the prospects of private enterprise, has by and large enhanced its opportunities. For it must be recognized that the case of the underdeveloped countries presents far greater risks. There is the risk of Communist revolutions or, at any rate, the prospect of a long period of political turmoil. Land reform and tax reform are less likely to take the evolutionary route now than formerly.

In 1963 the aggregate contribution of all donor countries to foreign aid amounted to around $7 billion.[3] In addition to these governmental contributions, some $2 billion of private capital was invested in the poorer areas. Against this inflow of private capital must be set an outflow of "flight" capital of an undisclosed amount but estimated at possibly approaching $2 billion. The seepage of capital flight is one of many serious roadblocks to development.

THE GROWING GAP BETWEEN RICH AND POOR COUNTRIES

It is generally said that per capita real incomes in the underdeveloped countries taken as a whole has increased in recent years at about 1 to 1½ per cent per annum.[4] Yet the standard of living, especially in the basic necessities, appears, as we have noted, not to have increased at all. There is no inconsistency between these two statements. The per capita output (i.e., real income) includes such things as steel mills, electric power, irrigation projects, railroads, etc. They may still be in process of being built and so can add nothing to the standard of living of the masses, yet they are counted in the year's gross national product. And even when completed, they mean far more in terms of anticipated future living standards than in terms of the current flow of utilities. Thus the current standard of living always lags behind the process of growth and capital formation.

But whether calculated in terms of current living standards or in terms of per capita output including the output of

[3] See *Economic Report of the President*, January, 1964, pp. 157–159.

[4] "Taken as a group, the rate of progress of the underdeveloped countries measured by income *per capita* has been painfully slow, more of the order of 1 per cent per annum than 2 per cent." *The United Nations Development Decade*, p. 6.

capital goods in the process of completion, it is unmistakably clear that the gap between the poor countries and the rich countries is rapidly growing wider and wider. The annual growth in per capita production in the advanced countries in recent years is several times greater (see Chapter 11) than the estimated growth of 1 to 1½ per cent per capita in the underdeveloped countries. Only in terms of life expectancy is the gap between the rich and the poor countries narrowing. In terms of population the poor countries are growing rapidly. In terms of per capita output of goods and services they are lagging farther and farther behind the advanced countries.

BALANCE OF PAYMENTS

Everything centers, as we have noted, upon two basic problems: (1) the perennial balance-of-payments difficulties and (2) the insatiable need for capital. The first could perhaps be likened to cases of pneumonia. The patient may have to be put into an oxygen tent to keep him alive. The crisis is a deadly one, but it is short-lived. So too is the crisis phase of the underdeveloped country's payments problem. Once over the acute crisis, however, there remains the problem of sustenance and nourishment. The underdeveloped countries desperately need capital in which to grow. They lack foreign exchange to pay for their imports. But the basic problem is that of capital shortage.

The IMF has played a significant, though scarcely adequate, role, in helping the primary producing countries over their balance-of-payments difficulties. It could do more. It could make drawing rights automatic, as urged by Bernstein. It could take greater risks. It has accumulated large reserves which permit greater boldness. In addition there is reason to believe that the advanced countries have learned that the very survival of the free world requires a degree of international cooperation that transcends a strictly business calculus. They can be expected, we have a right to hope, to underwrite a bolder lending program than the IMF has thus far practiced.

TECHNICAL KNOW-HOW LACKING

The deeper problem, however, (without which there can be no growth, only precarious survival) is how to obtain the capital needed for development—investment both in human resources and in physical plant and equipment. We have learned in recent years that important as physical investment is, technical know-how, skills, research, and general education are even more important. Said the chairman of the Board of Governors, Mr. Saad, in his opening address at the annual meeting of the World Bank and Fund in 1962: "Much attention has been given to the need for natural resources—capital and industrial materials—but of basic importance are the people and their qualities. Uneducated, unhealthy and apathetic people are great drawbacks to energetic development programs. General education and public health programs are essential to overcome these handicaps."[5]

Historically, the laggards in industrial development, once they got going, moved forward at a faster rate than the leaders. This of course was due to the fact that the revolutionary developments—the steam engine, the railroad, electricity, mechanization, and repetitive processes—these accumulations of technological knowledge were not acquired in a day. The leader had arrived by slow and tedious processes. But the followers could quickly install the completed innovations. This sequence apparently is now broken. The advanced countries are experiencing rapid rates of

[5] *Summary Proceedings*, Annual Meeting, 1962, p. 15.

growth based on costly research, wider markets, new products, and automation. The backward countries do not have enough scientists and technically trained people to absorb the new technology. And the capital requirements for modern, large-scale industry are enormous. Thus it becomes increasingly difficult for the underdeveloped countries to obtain a foothold on the escalator of a rapidly ascending technology. Progress is spotty and uneven—more rapid in certain sectors of the economy and in certain favored geographical areas. But taken as a whole, herculean efforts are needed to overcome the peculiar (and perhaps unprecedented) conditions that hold the underdeveloped countries back in their struggle to industrialize and to take their place in the general march of progress of worldwide trade.

THE TESTIMONY OF LEADING DELEGATES

Responsible leaders of the underdeveloped countries, while concerned about foreign aid, are even more concerned about the decline in their export earnings and the restrictions imposed by the industrial countries to choke off the so-called "disruptive competition" of low cost manufactures from the low-wage underdeveloped countries. One obtains an impressive insight into these problems from the speeches made in the annual conferences of the IMF and the World Bank. I propose, in order to help clothe a verbal skeleton with flesh and blood, to quote and in part to paraphrase a number of these testimonials.

With the "prices of primary commodities persistently weak," said Mr. Saad, the 1962 chairman of the Board of Governors of the IMF and the World Bank, "the inflow of development capital little more than offsets the weak trend of export earnings." Mr. Eugene Black, then head of the World Bank, noting the gains made by the industrialized countries from the fall in the prices of primary products, stated that a reasonably typical European country had found its total import bill in 1961 about 8 per cent less than it would have been had 1956 prices still prevailed. The Australian representative, Mr. Holt, cited the case of his country's exports having suffered a decline in price terms of 33 per cent in 1961–1962 compared with 1953. The Colombian delegate pointed out that in 1954 (a peak year) it cost nineteen bags of coffee to buy an automobile; in 1962 it cost thirty-two bags. A medium tractor cost 131 bags in 1950 and 295 bags in 1962. The Pakistanian delegate emphasized the insufficient access to the markets of industrial countries in the case of new products. The Ceylon representative noted that the trade between the developed countries was increasing much faster than between the developed countries and the primary producing countries. The Fund has indeed been giving assistance on an expanding scale in recent years, but this, he said, is "only a trickle compared with the drop in commodity prices of 14 per cent between 1959 and 1961." The Tunisian delegate observed that the protective agricultural policies of the advanced countries together with the continued introduction of substitute products seriously affect the demand for the products of primary producing countries. Again and again the delegates referred to the serious impact of the drop in export prices and the difficulty of marketing exportable products because of tariff restrictions, quotas, and consumption taxes in the advanced countries.

One could summarize the dominant concern, as one delegate put it, by saying that, for the underdeveloped countries, the persistent decline of export prices represents a threat to the stability of the world economy comparable to the concern felt by the industrial countries about international liquidity.

TRADE NOT AID

Some delegates expressed concern about the impact of protectionist blocs, especially the Common Market, on the future export prospects of the underdeveloped countries. More important than aid for the backward countries is trade. "While long-term loans at low rates or even outright grants are necessary and welcome, it is essential," said the delegate from Ghana, "that the developing countries continue to have access on a non-discriminating basis to the markets of the industrial countries."

It is often said that the solution for the underdeveloped countries is to industrialize as rapidly as possible. But this, to be successful, requires opportunity to export to the industrialized countries. Yet as soon as inroads are made, trade barriers are put up, or euphemistically termed "voluntary" limitations are imposed on the exports of underdeveloped countries.

"Trade not aid" is an appealing slogan since it seems to suggest that the whole job of development can be achieved through enlightened self-interest without any sacrifice on the part of the advanced countries. As we have seen, however, to enable the underdeveloped countries to participate fully in the growth of world trade will require sacrifices from the advanced countries quite apart from the matter of financial aid. The "fall in commodity prices in recent years has nullified much of the net increase in the assistance given to the developing countries."[6] "Progress could certainly be made if the main industrial countries were to devote as much attention to promoting trade as to dispensing aid."[7]

The president of the Ministerial Council of the OECD at the Paris meeting, November 20, 1963, is reported as saying that unless some agreement is reached on how to give the

[6] *The United Nations Development Decade,* p. 5.
[7] *Ibid.,* p. vii.

underdeveloped countries a fair share of the world market "our efforts in direct aid may be frustrated over and over again."[8]

More important than aid is a program to promote larger export earnings. The foreign exchange earnings of underdeveloped countries run currently at around $20 billion per year. These earnings could be increased if the rich countries would collaborate in an international commitment to give favorable treatment to the export products of the poor countries. In this connection I wish to quote a few highly relevant paragraphs from Gunnar Myrdal's *The Challenge to Affluence*.

> [The] rational thing would indeed be to afford the underdeveloped countries not only an equal but a preferential treatment in the markets of the rich countries. Such a policy would help them in their development efforts much more than any "aid," and it would steer higher export earnings right into the economies of the underdeveloped countries and not, as "aid" usually does, through government offices. [p. 145]
>
> [The] rich countries will have to accept the responsibility of their advanced states and be prepared to move on their own towards freer trade, as Britain did a century ago when it was the only rich country, while at the same time accepting the right of the poor countries to protect their development and, even more, affording them a preferential treatment by the rich countries in their own markets. [p. 155]
>
> The rapidity by which the development towards universal free trade for the rich countries with the right to protection for the underdeveloped countries, and even preferential treatment for their products in the markets of the former, will proceed, will depend very much on whether the United States is strong enough to supply a determined lead. [p. 156]
>
> The Trade Expansion Act is aimed mainly at freeing trade among the rich countries. No similarly dramatic challenge has been presented by the United States to stabilize the markets for traditional exports from the underdeveloped countries and still less to give them preferential treatment for exports of industrial products. [p. 157]

[8] *The New York Herald Tribune,* November 21, 1963.

At the world conference on trade in Geneva, April, 1964, the United Kingdom presented the following program of trade promotion in behalf of the underdeveloped countries, subject to the approval of the British Commonwealth countries. The ten-point plan calls for:

1. A freeze on new barriers to the trade of less developed countries in products of particular interest to them
2. An end to quotas adversely affecting developing countries
3. Removal of duties on tropical products
4. Removal of duties on primary products from developing countries
5. Reduction of tariffs on semiprocessed and processed products from developing countries
6. Ending of internal taxes and revenue duties applying specifically to products wholly or mainly produced in developing countries
7. Granting of preferences by the developed countries to the poorer nations
8. Exchange of preferences among developing countries
9. Stabilization of commodity prices
10. Supplementary financial assistance to developing countries with balance-of-payments problems

DECLINE OF EXPORT EARNINGS

Altogether apart from the matter of artificial restriction of markets is the twofold cause of unsatisfactory export earnings, namely, a declining demand for primary products relative to world trade and the violent short-run fluctuations of primary product prices.

Efforts have been made to meet this situation by means of international commodity agreements designed to stabilize and support commodity prices. Unfortunately, their history is a dismal one. Yet continued effort along these lines are being made.

Edward M. Bernstein has proposed a plan[9] which was presented to the Organization of American States and to the Alliance for Progress at its meeting in Punta del Este in 1961.

Under this plan an Export Stabilization Fund would be established either as an independent institution or as a subsidiary of the IMF. The plan provided that whenever the export receipts of an underdeveloped country fell below the average of the preceding three years, such a country would be eligible to borrow from the new institution two-thirds of the amount of the shortfall in its export receipts. On the other hand, in the event that its export receipts rose above the average of the preceding three years, the country in question would be obligated to repay two-thirds of the excess to the Export Receipts Stabilization Fund.

The plan has been studied by the UN Committee on Commodity Trade and has been referred back to the United Nations for further study. It is not clear what would happen if, as is likely, the credits and repayments would fail to balance out over time. Presumably it could turn out to be, in effect, a grant, insofar as the repayments failed to match the borrowings. It would amount to a subsidy from the leading industrial countries whose resources would be behind the plan.

This leads me to suggest that a better plan might be to build up an insurance fund for losses incurred by underdeveloped countries due to declines in export prices below an agreed upon level. The insurance fund would be established by the leading industrial countries which would agree to contribute to the fund each year any windfall gains accruing to them from imported raw materials purchased at prices below the norm. The ideal way would be to load the

[9] Edward M. Bernstein, *Hearings before the Subcommittee on International Exchange and Payments*, 87th Cong., 2d Sess.

cost on the importing industries who would pay the insurance premiums. If this was agreed upon between all leading industrial countries, the competitive situation would not be disturbed. And industries would have the advantage of being able to plan ahead on the basis of a floor price for its raw materials, knowing that all its competitors would be paying the same price.

Raw materials and labor are the primary costs of industrial products. Industry has enjoyed a windfall in the decline of raw material prices since 1954. This decline eased the profit margin as trade unions pressed for higher wages. Business and labor were the gainers; the underdeveloped countries were the losers.

A group of UN experts made a proposal in 1949 which could be implemented to support the export earnings of primary producing countries. It was suggested that each government accept the responsibility of offsetting any depletion of the international monetary reserves of foreign countries caused by a fall in its demand for imported goods and services due to a decline in its internal effective demand.[10] This could be amended to read: "due to a fall in the export price of primary products." Each country would make a deposit of its own currency with the IMP of an amount equal to the decline of its imports.

COMPENSATORY FINANCING

In 1963, the IMF undertook a new program of "compensatory financing of export fluctuations." The Fund decided to create a new additional drawing right, not to exceed in the normal case 25 per cent of the member's quota, for

[10] United Nations *National and International Measure for Full Employment,* New York, December, 1949.

the purpose of providing assistance to countries experiencing balance-of-payments difficulties arising from export shortfalls. This extra tranche will become available in cases where the shortfall is temporary and largely caused by circumstances beyond the member's control.

A CUSTOMS UNION

In view of the unfavorable foreign trade record of the underdeveloped countries and the import restrictions which they face in the industrial countries, it could well be that one helpful approach might be to seek a broadening of their markets for manufactured products within a customs union of their own. Admittedly the economies are largely competitive rather than complementary. This presents serious difficulties. The area of Latin America comprises considerable diversity of natural resources with a population of 220 million. The per capita income is very low, partly because of small, restricted national markets. A customs union could presumably in some measure promote large-scale enterprise based on a continent-wide market. This would, of course, need to be implemented in terms of step-by-step reductions in internal tariffs across the board until eventually the whole area would be set up with a common external tariff.

It would require more than mere tariff reductions to achieve large-scale industrial expansion.[11] Development agencies would have to be set up to promote expansion. This would involve the cooperation of business firms both from the underdeveloped countries of the area in question and from advanced countries. What needs to be gained is the

[11] Harvey S. Perloff and Romula Almeida, "Regional Economic Integration in the Development of Latin America," 1963. (Mimeographed.)

economics of scale, the advantages of specialization, and the external economies that flow from the location of diversified industries operating in the same area.[12]

Local, national markets are sufficient to permit, at least up to a point, the development of the simpler consumers goods like textiles. But there are severe limits to this development as all underdeveloped countries have learned. To achieve even an intermediate degree of industrialization requires the development of industries producing capital goods, iron and steel products, machinery, electrical equipment, automatic products, railroad and highway equipment, chemical products, etc. These require much larger markets than local, national markets can provide. Hence the need for a customs union covering a large region or even a whole continent.

The development of a customs union would also serve to promote the joint development of international river basins. Interregional programs, involving irrigation projects, electric power, and the full development of the basin's agricultural, mining, and forestry resources would broaden and deepen the economic base upon which a large market for manufactured products could be built within the general framework of a customs union.

Indeed, whenever the idea of a common market for the underdeveloped countries is broached, fear is expressed, not that it would not succeed, but that it would succeed too well. It is feared that foreign enterprise with its superior knowledge, access to new technology, command of capital resources, and international connections would capitalize on

[12] The gains from integration relate less to reallocation of *existing* resources, but rather to a "more rational allocation of resources coming into existence from increments of growth of the region as a whole over a long period of time." See A. A. Farag, "Economic Integration in Latin America," *Economia Internazionale,* November, 1963.

the vast opportunities of a free trade integrated market to the disadvantage of the smaller national firms.

INTERNATIONAL FINANCIAL ASSISTANCE

Having canvassed various approaches to the problems confronting the underdeveloped countries (other than aid) and recognizing that some of these approaches may prove useful, it remains nevertheless true that aid must play an indispensable role if significant progress is to be made. More and more countries are contributing to foreign aid, and international institutions are playing an important role. Financial assistance is currently being provided by various agencies among which the most important are: (1) the IMF, (2) the World Bank and related institutions, and (3) governmental programs such as the Development Assistance Committee of the OECD countries, the U.S. Agency for International Development, thc Alliance for Progress, etc.

As noted in an earlier chapter the aid given to underdeveloped countries to help them cover their balance-of-payments difficulties has expanded considerably over recent years. The aggregate distribution by the IMF of financial assistance (under which is included not only actual drawings but also new standby arrangements) to underdeveloped countries amounted in the six-year period 1948 to 1953 to $334.5 million, in the five-year period 1954 to 1958 to $1,041.6 million, and in the four-year period 1959 to 1962 to $2,794.7 million. These are aggregate figures for each period, not annual averages.

Also with respect to long-term capital investment, the volume of aid rendered by the International Bank for Reconstruction and Development (commonly called the World Bank) has substantially increased. Moreover, a new institution, the International Development Association, has been established, affiliated with the World Bank and designed to provide easier credit terms. Another new institution, also associated with the World Bank, is the International Finance Corporation, designed to assist in the borrowing by private enterprises in cases where sufficient private capital is not available on reasonable terms and without the help of government guarantee of repayment.

The aggregate capital of the World Bank, subscribed by its seventy-five member countries, amounts to $20.5 billion, of which only one-tenth is paid in, the rest being subject to call. The Bank had paid out around $6.5 billion by June 30, 1962, in loans. The funds so loaned came partly from subscriptions but mainly from the sale of bonds. These bonds are usually denominated in U.S. dollars and about half of the outstanding bonds have been purchased by American investors.

The geographical distribution of loans made up to June 30, 1962, was as follows:[13]

	Billions
Asia	$2.2
Latin America	1.5
Africa	0.9
Europe	1.5
Australia	0.4
Total	$6.5

Of this total about one-third was invested in electric firms, one-third in railroads, highways, airports, and waterways, and one-third irrigation, steel plants, and other industries.

The World Bank is run on strictly business terms. The long-term lending rate has ranged from 5 to 6½ per cent with an average maturity of fifteen years. Strict banking

[13] See "World Bank-IDA," International Bank for Reconstruction and Development, Washington, D.C.

principles are applied. Loans will not be made to prospective borrowers who are likely to be unable to service the debt either because of a weak domestic fiscal position or because of foreign exchange difficulties. The latter is important since the loans are made in dollars or other convertible currencies.

World Bank loans are designed to provide the foreign exchange needed to cover the cost of imported equipment and services needed for the project. Local material and labor costs are paid for by the borrowers out of their own funds.

The Bank supervises the projects while in construction and continues to keep in touch after operation begins throughout the life of the loan. The net earnings of the Bank have been substantial and by now amount to around $70 million per year, excluding the 1 per cent commission charge. Reserves of $700 million have been accumulated. Aggregate loans made in 1962—the banner year—amounted to nearly $900 million. Some critics have argued that even on prudent banking principles the Bank could play a more expansionist role.[14]

Indeed it became increasingly evident that something needed to be done to put international lending on a more liberal basis. The "mounting pressure of commitments for repayment of principal and interest or profit on previous investments, combined with the uncertainty and lack of dynamism of export earnings in many underdeveloped countries, underscored the importance of increasing the proportion of assistance in forms that would bear less heavily on the balance of payments than conventional loans.[15]

Accordingly a new institution was set up in September, 1960, affiliated with the World Bank—the International Development Association. It is designed to offer very generous

[14] Note should also be made of the operations of the International Finance Corporation.

[15] *The United Nations Development Decade*, p. 5.

credit terms. The loans may run for fifty years and bear no interest whatever. Amortization begins after ten years at the rate of 1 per cent per year for ten years and thereafter for the remaining thirty years at a 3 per cent rate. There is a service charge of three-fourths of 1 per cent, payable on the amount of the loan outstanding. Sixty-two countries have joined the association. Advanced countries pay their subscription in convertible currencies, the underdeveloped countries, one-tenth in convertible currencies, the rest in their own currency. Total subscriptions by June 30, 1962, amounted to $917 million, of which $757 million consisted of convertible currencies.

The first IDA loan was made in May, 1960, and by June 30, 1962, loans amounting to $235 million had been made to eleven countries. In 1963 the executive directors recommended a new round of contributions to IDA of $750 million of convertible funds.[16]

Another new development, but operating on strict banking principles, is the International Finance Corporation organized as an affiliate of the World Bank in July, 1956. Membership consists of seventy-two countries, which together have subscribed the capital of about $100 million.

The IFC was established to make investment in private industry in the underdeveloped countries. The World Bank restricts its loans to government undertakings and does not make loans to private industry unless they are guaranteed by the foreign government. The IFC, however, may invest directly in the stock of private companies or make con-

[16] In July, 1964, the World Bank decided to take two steps to increase loan funds in easy terms. The Bank will transfer half of the past years' earnings to the IDA which makes soft-currency loans on easy terms. The Bank will also stop placing its 1 per cent interest commission in each loan in a special fund and will instead put it into the general earnings pool where it will be available for future distribution to the IDA.

ventional loans which may be combined with equity features. There is no government guarantee. By September, 1962, it had made fifty-two investment commitments totaling some $70 million dollars. In 1963 the IFC was able to offer its support to industrial projects both by direct investment in capital shares and by a combination of loan and equity investment.

U.S. FOREIGN AID PROGRAMS

The foreign aid extended by the U.S. government has a long history going back to World War I. Immediately after World War II it became evident that extensive aid would be necessary. At first this was implemented by increasing the capital of the Export-Import Bank by $3 billion to make loans for reconstruction. In autumn of 1945 the United Kingdom found it necessary to seek assistance either in the form of a loan or grant. The amount urgently needed, as they saw it, was $5 billion. After prolonged negotiation the United States agreed to a loan of $3,750 million. The United States made the fatal mistake of demanding that sterling should be made convertible within twelve months after receipt of the loan. Within six weeks after convertibility had been restored, the bulk of the loan was exhausted, as should have been expected in view of the accumulated sterling balances that had been built up during the war and which could not readily be funded into long-term obligations. So the American loan helped British creditors without affording much aid to the United Kingdom.

In February, 1947, President Truman inaugurated a program of military and economic assistance to Greece and Turkey. In June, 1947, Secretary of State Marshall proposed a general aid program for European reconstruction. Marshall aid began in April, 1948, and under this program

Western European countries received altogether over $25 billion in economic aid.

Aid was next directed to the underdeveloped countries. In his inaugural address in 1949, President Truman proposed a program of technical assistance, mainly in the fields of agriculture, public health, and education, to underdeveloped countries. One highly important piece of aid legislation was the passage of Public Law No. 480 under which large quantities of U.S. food surpluses have been made available to underdeveloped countries. Payment for these supplies is made in the local currency of the receiving country, and these currencies are in turn loaned back to the country in question at low rates of interest.

In 1961 the Peace Corps was authorized with an initial appropriation of about $65 million, which was substantially increased in subsequent years. The volunteer members of the Peace Corps reached about 10,000 by the end of 1963.

Finally, in 1961 the United States undertook at the Punta del Este Conference an extensive new program of aid to Latin America under the aegis of the Alliance for Progress.

During World War II lend-lease grants amounted to about $47 billion. And for the postwar period 1945 to 1963 the aggregate grants and loans came to around $88 billion, allocated as follows:

	Billions
Net military grants	$33
Net economic aid grants	40
Net economic aid loans	15
Total	$88

Economic aid (loans and grants) for the year 1962 ran to about $3.5 billion. Of this about $2.0 billion went to Asia, $0.5 billion to Africa, and $1.0 billion to Latin America.

About one-half was in grants and half in loans. In the case of Latin America about 80 per cent was in loans.

The U.S. long-term development loans charge interest rates of only three-fourths of 1 per cent with a maturity of forty years and an added grace period of ten years. This must be regarded as extremely generous. Yet I have never been able to see why we made outright gifts to the highly endowed advanced countries of Western Europe in the Marshall Aid program, while we now resort in large measure to making loans to the underdeveloped countries.

A PROGRAM FOR THE UNITED NATIONS

The United Nations prospectus on the development decade (published in 1962) makes far-reaching proposals for action. It sets forth what could be achieved if such and such things were done. And, indeed, in any rational view of future world developments, the proposals must be regarded as extremely moderate. They call for a capital assistance development program which involves a levy of only 1 per cent of the national incomes of the advanced countries—the figure suggested by the General Assembly. This, at present rates of growth of GNP in most of the leading countries, would represent only from one-sixth to one-third of the *annual increase* in the GNP of the advanced countries. That even this contribution is being cold-shouldered indicates how complacent the rich countries are. Yet it is surely no exaggeration to say that the problem of lifting the underdeveloped countries (which include two-thirds of the world's population) to a tolerable level of existence is of the same dimensions as war itself. In wartime we unhesitatingly devote one-third to one-half of our productive energy to the prosecution of war, and *mirabile dictu* we achieve this without suffering any serious decline in consumption standards.

In a crisis the productive capacity of modern societies is colossal. By and large it is perhaps true that world leaders do see that this crisis is truly upon us but they fail to communicate to their fellow citizens any sense of urgency. Yet we are here dealing with basically the same forces of world chaos and world destruction that we face in war.

INDEX